Critical Issues in HRD

*New Perspectives in Organizational
Learning, Performance, and Change*
JERRY W. GILLEY, SERIES EDITOR

Critical Issues in HRD

A New Agenda for the Twenty-first Century

New Perspectives in Organizational Learning,
Performance, and Change

Ann Maycunich Gilley,
Jamie L. Callahan,
and
Laura L. Bierema
EDITORS

**PERSEUS
PUBLISHING**

A Member of the Perseus Books Group

Many of the designations used by manufacturers and sellers to distinguish their products are claimed as trademarks. Where those designations appear in this book and Perseus Publishing was aware of a trademark claim, the designations have been printed in initial capital letters.

Cataloging-in-publication-data is available from the Library of Congress.
ISBN 0-7382-0763-2

Perseus Publishing is a member of the Perseus Books Group.

Find us on the World Wide Web at http://www.perseuspublishing.com

Perseus Publishing books are available at special discounts for bulk purchases in the United States by corporations, institutions, and other organizations. For more information, please contact the Special Markets Department at the Perseus Books Group, 11 Cambridge Center, Cambridge, MA 02142, or call (617) 252–5298, (800) 255–1514, or e-mail j.mccrary@perseusbooks.com.

Text design by Tonya Hahn
Set in 10.5-point Minion by the Perseus Books Group

First printing, December, 2002
3 4 5 6 7 8 9 10—05 04 03

Publisher's Note

Organizations are living systems, in a constant state of dynamic evolution. The series *New Perspectives in Organizational Learning, Performance, and Change* is designed to showcase the most current theory and practice in human resource and organizational development, exploring all aspects of the field—from performance management to adult learning to corporate culture. Integrating cutting-edge research and innovative management practice, this library of titles will serve as an essential resource for human resource professionals, educators, students, and managers in all types of organizations.

The series editorial board includes leading academics and practitioners whose insights are shaping the theory and application of human resource development and organizational design.

Contents

7 ■ Performance Coaching   123
Jerry W. Gilley, Nathaniel W. Boughton, and Erik Hoekstra

8 ■ Performance-Focused HRD   147
L. Michael Wykes

9 ■ Organizational Learning: A Reflective and Representative Critical Issue for HRD   161
Jamie L. Callahan

Figures and Tables

Figures

Tables

Introduction

The complexity of society today permeates all personal and professional aspects of our lives. Challenges arise daily—the routine, novel, foreseen, and unexpected. Those responsible for human resource development (such as managers, supervisors, executives, leaders, HRD professionals) are certainly not exempt from these challenges. In fact, many of the key issues facing organizations and their employees manifest themselves in HRD concerns such as productivity or motivation.

What are the critical issues facing HRD? To answer this question, a survey was sent to practitioners and academics responsible for human resource development. Their responses frame the context of this book and are addressed by experts in the various content areas. Chapters one through four encompass the large-scale issues of leadership, HRD transformation, change, and globalization. Chapters five through eight discuss individual issues, including human capital metrics, performance management, coaching, and performance-focused HRD. Chapters nine through twelve entail organizational learning, training transfer, HRD evaluation, and social consciousness.

Why are these issues critical? To address this question, the first step is to identify what constitutes a "critical issue." *The American Heritage College Dictionary* defines *critical* as "pertaining to, or the nature of, a *crisis*; of decisive importance with respect to the outcome; crucial." In turn, *crisis* is defined as "a decisive or vitally important stage in the course of anything; a turning point." The term *issue* can truly have multiple meanings, several of which could be quite relevant in addressing what constitutes a "critical issue" for HRD. The definition that seems most appropriate is "a point or matter the decision of which is of special or public importance." Thus, a critical issue for HRD is a matter of research or practice that has special significance to HRD because it marks a vitally important stage or turning point. A simpler way to think of a critical issue is that it is an area of research or practice that contributes not only to the survival of HRD, but also to its growth and future development. Thus, this book explores some of the critical issues facing those responsible for HRD.

The Editors

A Return to Leadership

Chris Petty

The question, "Who ought to be boss?" is like asking,
"Who ought to sing tenor in the quartet?"
Obviously, the man who can sing tenor.
—Henry Ford

Is American business experiencing a growing leadership problem? With several recent high-visibility failures, combined with the faltering of many large firms, it would appear so. At the heart of the matter is a significant issue fracturing organizations—a growing rift between employees and their leaders.

What's Going On?

At the end of 2001, thousands of loyal and unsuspecting employees in one, now infamous, company watched their jobs and, in some cases, their life savings evaporate within days. Hard-working employees who had trusted their leaders were betrayed. Because of Enron's sheer size and the dramatic pace at which it declined, it has become the poster child of corporate abuse and fiscal mismanagement. Enron represents the tip of a very disturbing iceberg—a symptom of a larger problem.

Warren Buffet, one of the nation's most respected investors, recently remarked, "Though Enron has become the symbol for shareholder abuse, there is no shortage of egregious conduct elsewhere in corporate America" (2002, 3). Suspicion and mistrust are brewing across much of the workforce.

Some corporate leaders are simply losing touch. Those they lead are, understandably, losing confidence and trust in their leaders. Employees are seeing organizational leaders who appear to have only their personal interests in sight. Workers are feeling less and less connected with top management. They

1

are feeling increasingly expendable and disposable, all for the purpose of enriching CEOs and top leaders. All the while, these same leaders appear to be walking away from their failures with multimillion-dollar exit bonuses or millions in forgiven "loans." Is it any wonder that workers increasingly do not trust their leaders? This has drastic and undesirable effects on organizations and their bottom lines.

What can be done? Do HRD professionals have the tools to conduct a "leadership checkup" in their own organizations? If they find something out of kilter, can they advise senior management of the problem and help steer them back on the course of transformational leadership? Let's hope so. For the future of HRD and the firms they serve, it's time for a return to leadership.

The Importance of Leadership

Everyone has ideas on what it is to be a leader, yet perspectives differ significantly. In its most basic form, the *American Heritage College Dictionary* describes a leader as "one who has influence or power." Unfortunately, simple definitions offer no practical value for the user. Even graduate-level textbooks describe leadership with simple platitudes and phrases, such as "the ability to inspire confidence and support among the people who are needed to achieve organizational goals" (Dubrin 2000, 264).

Even the army, an institution centered on leadership, has a fairly simplistic definition of leadership, "the process of accomplishing the mission by providing purpose, direction, and motivation" (Field Manual 22–100, 1–4). This, at least, implies that in order to be effective, a leader must apply some specific ingredients to his or her organization. Definitions do not make usable theories—they fail to address the "how."

How does one inspire support, create a team, and gain confidence? How does one know if he has this "ability," and what is meant by "inspire"? How does the would-be leader provide purpose and direction? How do leaders create trust? Eventually, HRD practitioners need the ability to answer these questions as leadership becomes more and more central to organizational success.

Leadership, that powerful yet elusive concept, has escaped proper understanding for centuries. Ask ten different people to explain leadership, and one will almost certainly get ten different answers. Leadership, like love, has always been considered an abstract term with different meanings for different people. Because of this, it has always been difficult to coalesce into a single universal theory or road map for practical application. Yet leadership is arguably the most decisive element for any organizational achievement, and has continued to show its powerful effect throughout history. As a result, practitioners and scholars have tried to understand and catalogue this phenomenon with varying degrees of success.

Obviously, leadership is much more than running a business to produce results. Yet, even with all the conflicting theories, leadership is about guiding organizations through change. If there is one organizational theme that will continue to be required in larger and larger doses, it is organizational change. Tom Peters (2001b) predicts that leadership will be the most important element in business. As such, leadership becomes the most decisive element in organizational change.

Although this important concept can, at times, become lost in the day-to-day practice of Human Resource Development (HRD), this is a grave mistake. It is time for HRD practitioners to make a return to leadership and "plant the flag" in this key terrain.

"Planting the flag" means owning the domain of leadership within organizations. Manufacturing had a central role in organizational success at the turn of the last century. This was replaced with marketing and finance over the past several decades. As we advance into the twenty-first century, change is in the wind. As organizations increasingly compete with advantages in information and culture, leadership itself will begin to occupy the center stage of organizational success. This should not be lost on those in HRD. Manufacturing knows the product. Marketing knows the customer. Finance knows the money. Most important, HRD knows employees, their leaders, and how the latter create a winning culture with the former in order to sustain a lasting competitive advantage. After all, according to Burke (1992), leadership is a transformational factor in organizational development and change.

Seeing this future, HRD practitioners should understand all aspects of leadership in order to have lasting impact and organizational leverage. This understanding of leadership will flow into recruiting, selecting, nurturing, growing, and intervening on behalf of leaders everywhere in the organization.

Even though a firm scientific grasp of leadership has proven elusive, it is gradually coming into better focus with recent behavioral-science discoveries. As science sharpens our view, the connection between leadership and organizational change is becoming more fundamental than ever. After all, leaders find the future. Then they work with people and processes to bring their organizations to that future. Sounds simple enough.

In theory, it is actually a straightforward proposition. Because change is a constant, organizations can only survive if they continually renew themselves (Gilley and Maycunich 2000). Strategic HRD focuses on this renewal process, which is all about change—a change that comes primarily through people.

Changing people requires leadership to create the force required to move from the present organizational state of being to the desired future state. Therefore, HRD is largely about leadership and its relationship to organizational learning, performance, and change. What could be more directly embedded, or central, to the field of HRD than leadership?

Creating a Leadership Framework: The Leadership Continuum

Anyone who deals with leadership or management issues, organizational change, or human resources needs a firm grasp of leadership. These are the *leadership stakeholders*. This portion of the chapter attempts to capture key leadership ideas and recent discoveries while putting them into a consolidated framework. In this way, this chapter hopes to be a great synthesizer of leadership thought.

According to Kotter (2002, 3), "leadership isn't mystical and mysterious. It has nothing to do with having charisma or other exotic personality traits." And "it is not the province of a chosen few." Yet, it certainly can be confusing. The myriad of ideas on leadership, while insightful, need some form of unifying framework to create synthesis and simplicity and, therefore, relevance for leadership stakeholders.

Leadership is more science than art. To use Bowers and Franklin's (2000, 222) definition of science, it is "discernable in replicatable terms—objective, understandable (rather than mystique), verifiable, and predictive." To advance the field of leadership to this level requires an effective model that captures the components and processes of this concept called leadership. Only then will leadership be "objective, understandable, and predictive."

To begin, one needs to acknowledge the various levels of the leadership continuum (figure 1.1). This continuum defines the maturity, effectiveness, and, in some cases, the type of leader the organization has or needs. The purpose is to create a mental picture that conveys the important idea that leadership covers the spectrum from weak to strong. At the left side is leadership in its weakest form—*tyrannical*. At the extreme right of the continuum is leadership in its best form—*transformational*. This theory of leadership asserts that these levels of leadership, and all those in between, are similarly created. *Transformational* leadership is enabled by a certain set of *talents and skills*, and produced by certain leadership *methods*. As one moves away from this ideal level of leadership, it is precisely because the leader either does not possess the required sets of *talents* and *skills*, or is not deploying them in accordance with good leadership *methods*.

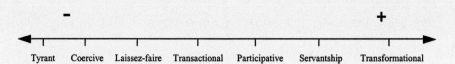

FIGURE 1.1   The Leadership Continuum

Anyone responsible for, or placed in charge of, people is a leader, whether one likes it or not. An individual falls somewhere on this continuum according to the level of leadership brought to the organization. As we will later explore, the level of leadership is determined by one's *talents, skills*, and *methods*.

The lowest form of leadership, *tyrannical*, lies on the left end of the continuum. This negative form of leadership oppresses, as tyrants care only about themselves and use people for personal gain. This is normally not a big area of concern for most organizations.

The next level is *coercive* leadership, which is still negative but not quite as ineffective as the tyrant. As the name implies, this leader moves the organization through the power of coercion, employing the "do-it-because-I-told-you-to" model based on the leader's formal position of power. These leaders use formal threats, such as punishment, and informal threats, such as public humiliation, to get things done.

Next, *laissez-faire*, a neutral type of leadership, is essentially the absence of leadership. This person merely occupies the position but has no material effect on the group. This leader succumbs totally to organizational inertia. Over time, the organization obeys the Second Law of Thermodynamics—the law of entropy—and wears down to a more disorganized, ineffective, and inefficient state.

Transactional leaders subscribe to a behaviorist worldview as they enter into relationships as negotiations. The transactional leader's mantra is "If you do this, then I will do that."

Moving up from the transactional leader one finds a cluster of leader capabilities called the *participative* leader. Dubrin (2000) defines *participative* leaders as those who share decision making with the group. He includes subgroupings of consultative, consensus, and democratic within this category of leadership. At this level, leaders are able to tap into the power of the group's ideas and motivations more than the other leadership domains.

A further progression is *servant* leadership. According to Gilley and Maycunich (2000, 55), a servant leader is "willing to put the needs, expectations, interests, and success of employees above his or her own." These leaders do more than listen to their employees or incorporate their ideas—they actually serve the group. The servant-leader domain incorporates the best of coaching and mentoring with an eye toward truly growing and nurturing employees.

At the far right of the continuum resides the most capable and appealing of all leaders, the *transformational* leader. Transformational leadership represents the highest form of organizational leadership. According to Dubrin (2000, 282), transformational leaders "develop new visions for the organization and mobilize employees to accept and work toward attaining these visions." He goes on to say that research does indeed prove that transformational leadership actually results in better business-unit performance than more traditional leadership styles.

According to Gilley and Maycunich (2000), transformational leaders have the extraordinary effect that they do because they create meaning for employees. They create conditions where employees "develop, transform, grow and flourish" (Gilley and Maycunich 2000, 53). As market conditions and the competitive landscape continue to change, transformational leadership will become even more critical for sustaining competitive advantage in the future. It is fitting that all leaders should aspire to this level of leadership. Therefore, this is the level on which the organizational-leadership model is based.

The leadership continuum prompts an accompanying set of questions. What leader ingredients or processes determine where someone rests on this continuum? What can leaders do to move to a higher level? For example, what can the transactional leader do to become a transformational leader? This demonstrates the need for a comprehensive leadership model that more clearly shows leadership not as some mysterious "art" but as a process with inputs (talents and skills), methods, and outcomes.

The New Organizational-Leadership Model

Some HRD experts believe no model or system can adequately capture the circumstances, conditions, and situations in which leaders influence others (Roberts 1987). Yet, intuitively, most people understand that leadership is no accident. Those who are led certainly know when they have effective leadership, and when they do not. Furthermore, great leaders are able to repeat this process, whether as team leaders in multiple cross-functional teams or as midlevel managers moving up to CEO.

Effective leadership is more than just a random act or grouping of behaviors and attributes. Leadership follows some rules—some ordered formula or process that can be discovered and explored. This exploration allows leadership stakeholders to unlock the components and processes of leadership that are central to understanding leadership itself.

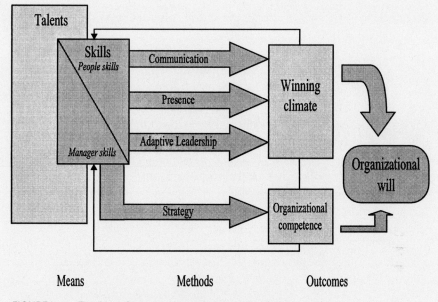

Means   Methods   Outcomes

FIGURE 1.2   The New Organizational-Leadership Model

Some common threads enable effective leaders to succeed time and again. The fact that most great leaders succeed intuitively does not change the fact that they are following a pattern or system that others may learn and apply. The "organizational-leadership model" (figure 1.2) captures this fact and presents it in a business setting. In addition, this theory integrates new discoveries such as climate and emotional intelligence that represent important findings in the underlying "physics" of the trade. Last, the new model creates an ordered framework that enables leaders to understand the components and processes of leadership in more detail.

This new model is built on an organizational foundation. It is composed of three major parts: the *means*, the *methods*, and the *outcomes* of leadership. The *means* of leadership are the ingredients. They enable the *methods* of leadership, which can be thought of, in a cooking analogy, as the recipe. These methods, in turn, produce leadership *outcomes*. *Outcomes* represent the finished cake coming from the oven. All the while, the leader operates within the context of a human system, providing the need for contingent, dynamic inputs.

Something as dynamic as a leadership process must have the flexibility to adapt and adjust to changes in the environment. The organizational-leadership model allows for this reality, while acknowledging the systematic process of leadership. This new model illustrates the ingredients and the recipe for the highest form—transformational leadership. Lesser levels of leadership will have, by definition, one or more of the components within this model undeveloped or not sufficiently deployed.

This new organizational-leadership model begins with the idea that the most effective leaders, in our case transformational leaders, possess certain talents that predispose them to be better leaders than others. These talents are discovered and refined. On top of leaders' talents are the skills they bring to the leadership process. These skills can be learned and practiced, and generally fall into two separate categories: people skills and manager skills. "People skills" deal with interpersonal issues, while "manager skills" are the more technical, or "things-oriented" skills that leaders must successfully apply at all levels in different degrees for success.

The *means* of leadership enable the *methods* of leadership, which fall into three general categories. *Methods* answer the question of how leaders do what they do. These leadership methods are *communication*, *presence*, *adaptive leadership*, and *strategy/planning*. Through these *methods*, leaders transfer their talents and skills into leadership *outcomes*.

Leadership outcomes are a *winning climate* and *organizational competence*, which are directly produced by leaders. When these two outcomes are combined they produce a powerful result known as *organizational will*. These three outcomes represent a leader's output in the organization, which separates a transformational leader from the rest of the pack.

In addition to leadership outcomes, one of the most fundamental issues acknowledged by this new model is the organizational system in which leaders apply their trade. This view of leadership acknowledges a leadership process of *means* and *methods* operating within an environment to produce leadership *outcomes*. With the right leadership outcomes, the organization can then produce extraordinary results. Failure to produce positive-leadership outcomes results in poor organizational outputs.

Additionally, this leadership system is embedded in an environment that demands consideration of certain situational and contextual factors. These situational factors change with time as societal norms or special circumstances change.

The final important piece of the model is the feedback loop between leadership outcomes and leadership skills, and between organizational outcomes and management skills. These vital connections enable leaders to adjust *means*, *methods*, and resources accordingly.

The Means of Leadership

Leaders begin with a set of *talents* and *skills* that largely determine whether someone can go the distance to transformational leadership. *Talents* are the innate, genetically coded predispositions that create natural strengths and abilities within any individual. *Skills*, on the other hand, are learned through instruction, practice, and experience. The *means* of leadership are simply the aggregation of these *talents* and *skills* that the leader brings to an organization. Central to this model is the idea that talents and skills are distinctly different concepts.

Talents.   Buckingham (2001) describes talents as "special natural abilities or aptitudes," recurring patterns of thoughts, feelings, or behaviors that can be productively applied. Talents are literally created by the unique combinations of synapse connections in the brain, and therefore cannot significantly change after the midteen years. He further asserts, through empirical analysis, that without underlying talent in a certain area, one can never create a true strength in that area (Buckingham 2001). Therefore, *talents* are central to transformational leadership.

Natural talent plays into the science of leadership. Underlying any leader is a set of talents that were genetically determined at the outset. Organizations are recognizing that the underlying talents of those they hire are crucial for success. The Gallup organization is one firm pioneering this field. Through an extensive historical database, Gallup has found successful ways to match positions with underlying talents. This includes senior leadership jobs at many large firms. In effect, they have developed *success profiles* that help organizations screen for leaders with the talents that have proven to be correlated to organizational success. Two underlying leadership talents are common to effective leaders. These talents are the innate qualities of *intelligence* and *selfless will*.

Intelligence, or mental capacity, is an obvious start for effective leadership. Drucker (1992) believes that the "foundation of effective leadership is thinking through the organization's mission, defining it, and establishing it, clearly and visibly." Leadership begins with thought, therefore intelligence is crucial for effective leaders.

Goleman (1998) found a direct link between the intelligence of leaders and organizational performance; intellect was a driver of outstanding performance, especially cognitive skills such as big-picture thinking and long-term vision. Numerous additional studies have also identified leaders with higher intellectual ability as achieving higher productivity and morale (Dubrin, 2000). *Intelligence* is no accident. It is an innate talent that enables some leaders to excel, while others remain marginally effective.

The other critical talent for transformational leaders is *selfless will*. This term embodies the components of will, conviction, confidence, courage, passion, and selflessness. This innate talent enables leaders to manage uncertainty and keep the organization moving in the right direction under all conditions and through all challenges. *Selfless will* gives leaders an infectious determination, while at the same time enabling their vision. This willpower becomes a wellspring of strength. It creates a tenacity of purpose that transcends the world's everyday obstacles.

Servant leadership and selflessness are inexorably tied to this important talent called *selfless will*. It is the selflessness that prevents the great leader from becoming a megalomaniac, concerned only with himself. It is this quality of selflessness that enables great leaders to put the needs of the organization and the mission before their own. With selflessness and competence come trust. With trust and confidence come cohesion—a key aspect of the leadership outcome of a *winning climate*. Therefore, *selfless will* becomes a crucial leader talent that flows directly into a leadership outcome.

Selfless will also includes courage, which has both a physical and moral component. The leader of true conviction is courageous to the point of putting himself in physical danger to accomplish his ends. Great generals do not calculate any concern for themselves when they make tough decisions (Meigs 2001). They are not afraid of personal risk on the battlefield or moral risk to their authority in the halls of power; their decisions are guided at all times by that internal compass of conviction.

In simple terms, transformational leaders communicate their *selfless will* to the group in terms of a vision. Vision then becomes an enabler of *organizational will*—a leadership outcome. Transactional leaders have no need for vision, but for transformational leaders, it is essential.

Collins (2001) reinforces this idea—he found that the leaders of the best companies possessed a talent he called "Level 5" leadership. Level-5 leaders build organizations of enduring greatness through a strange mixture of personal humility and will. These leaders were "self-effacing individuals who displayed the fierce resolve to do whatever needed to be done to make the company great" (21). Collins noted that this finding was exceptionally difficult to grasp in that it flies in the face of current logic of larger-than-life leaders who ride in to save the day. Level-5 leadership is closely aligned with this model's concept of *selfless will*. Both concepts are indeed similar, innate, and quite decisive in the effectiveness of leaders.

Skills. Skills are tools, techniques, and procedures that can be learned through instruction or experience. *Skills* can be acquired and developed, while *talents* can only be discovered and honed. Although there is, undoubtedly, some level of overlap between them, this is a vital acknowledgment that should be developed fully into the current school of leadership thought.

Skills build on the leader's natural base of *talents*. Overall, skills are those attributes and behaviors that can be learned through education, training, or experience. They cover a wide variety of areas but can generally be broken down into two distinct categories, *people skills* and *manager skills*—both of which are essential to transformational leadership. Effective leaders are effective precisely because they exercise *people skills* and *manager skills* appropriate to their situation. Mutually exclusive definitions of leadership and management ignore the reality of the two being inexorably tied together.

It is appropriate to look at all leaders as developing and exhibiting both *people skills* and *manager skills* on a continuum appropriate to their responsibilities. As the name implies, *people skills* deal with people issues—perceptions, emotions, values, and beliefs. *Manager skills*, on the other hand, deal with things—systems, processes, information, controls, and numbers. Effective people skills enable effective leadership methods—good *communication*, appropriate leader *presence*, and *adaptive leadership*. Effective management skills enable sound *strategies and plans*. All four of these *methods* combine to create positive leadership outcomes.

People Skills.   The model identifies three sets of people skills—*character*, *emotional intelligence*, and *communication skills*. Leaders must acquire and refine these skill sets to excel in leadership. These people skills are the key that enables leaders to understand and tap into the powerful reservoir of human emotions, values, and motivations. These form the levers for transformational leadership.

The first people skill is *character*. Although some may find it odd to categorize character as a people skill, it meets the criteria. It is clearly a skill that can be learned, and it deals with the perceptions, values, and beliefs of people. It is no accident, then, that character represents a strong foundational people skill for great leaders. It is character that forms the most basic connections and relationships between an organization and its leader.

Character represents the inner person—the complete moral and ethical base of the individual. All other attributes are built on this foundation. Character shapes the way leaders view the world and their role in it. Character is the filter through which all decisions and perceptions must pass. In our current society, good character sees virtuous purpose, respect for individuals, and higher values and goals rather than self-comfort and self-advancement. Conversely, in the context of today, flawed character sees personal gain, self-indulgence, and few, if any, noble goals. The result on the organization is predictable.

The leader of good character has the inner strength that guides him in his everyday life. Thus, a sound moral and ethical base is driving the organization. Character and integrity, springing from humanity, are fundamental to the exercise of transformational leadership.

Emotional intelligence, sometimes referred to as *EQ*, is the leader's ability to read, understand, and relate to those around him. This relatively new discovery continues to shed more light into the practice of leadership. This people skill is closely tied to character, yet remains a distinct concept. According to recent work by Goleman (1998, 93), emotional intelligence is the "sine qua non of leadership."

Goleman (1998) found that emotional intelligence is created by the neurotransmitters of the brain's limbic system, which govern feelings, drives, and impulses. The four components of emotional intelligence are self-awareness, self-management, social awareness, and social skill. To be effective one does not need display them all. For example, some of history's greatest transformational leaders, such as Churchill and de Gaulle, did not display empathy, a key component of social awareness, yet did display high levels of other EQ components at crucial moments in history (Maccoby 2000).

The next crucial *people skill* is communication. Leaders spend the majority of their time communicating (Malone 1983). As such, skill in communication is an obvious enabler of leader effectiveness. Transformational leaders are adept at communicating in a variety of ways, including speaking, listening, and writing.

Effective leaders understand the power of language. They use language to sell ideas, shape climate, and transfer important information and feedback on a daily basis. One of the secrets of effective transformational leadership centers on language and communication, according to Dubrin (2000). Transformational leaders inspire us by using colorful language, metaphors, and analogies. It's about communicating ideas, purpose, a worthy end-state, in other words, a *vision*.

Consequently, poor communication hinders leaders' effectiveness. Leaders who fail to listen or let others communicate miss important opportunities to gain insights and understanding. Lee Iacocca was described as too powerful at meetings, causing him to miss important inputs (Greenwald and Madigan 2001). According to Maccoby (2000), some of the key flaws that make leaders narcissistic, rather than transformational, stem from poor communication skills. These include poor listening skills and leaders being overly defensive.

Skill in communication is an obvious tool for the leader. This set of *people skills* forms a powerful medium for connections, ideas, and for leveraging the leader's own internal *selfless will* and *professional competence* into organizational vision and, ultimately, *organizational will.*

Manager Skills. Transformational leaders must not rely solely on *people skills.* In order to succeed in producing leadership outcomes, all effective leaders require certain *manager skills.* These represent the task-based competencies that leaders apply to organizational systems, processes, and resources to help ensure success. *Manager skills* enable leaders to understand issues, make plans, solve problems, organize and control resources, and make decisions. *Manager skills* can best be grouped into two categories: *professional competence* and *strategy/planning.*

Professional competence represents the leader's ability to understand and apply the knowledge and tools of his chosen trade. This encompasses the "technical skills" that include an understanding and proficiency in specific activities that involve methods, processes, procedures, and techniques that contribute directly to expert power. Dubrin (2000) uses the example of Bill Gates having technical competence in programming as the basis for his success in launching Microsoft.

This skill area is largely responsible for exploding the myth that great leaders can lead in any organization as long as they pick up some fundamentals. When Jack Welch took over at GE, he changed the way leaders were rising up through the ranks for this very reason. Instead of cycling people through different divisions to learn a little about a lot, he left managers in divisions longer to immerse them and enable them to truly learn the business. Welch determined that it takes, on average, a full decade to truly learn a business. Welch's results in training future leaders speak for themselves (Peters 2001a).

Effective leaders bring the appropriate level of professional knowledge to a firm and add value to the collective body of organizational knowledge. In so doing, the leader adds relevant judgment and decision-making skills to successfully guide the organization to its future state.

Transformational leaders are usually associated with *vision,* but what about *plans*? A vision without a plan is merely a dream. Transformational leaders understand this and consequently "close the loop" between a vision and a plan via the *strategy/planning skill.*

Leading, in its most basic form, means moving a group from one place to another, or from a current state to a future state. This implies problem solving. A leader, whether planning a route on a map or setting out to change the culture of an organization, is solving a problem. By extension, virtually all organizations exist to solve problems. Most often this is a market-related problem expressed as a consumer demand. Naturally, leaders play the key role in this endeavor by helping their organizations successfully solve these problems. Transformational leaders require a strong dose of the *manager skill* set known as *strategy/planning* to be successful and make the dream a reality.

The Methods of Leadership

Transformational leaders produce *organizational will*. This represents the crucial outcome that separates truly outstanding leaders from those who fall short. With *organizational will* any organization can produce extraordinary results. Yet a gap remains. How do leaders transfer their talents and skills into leadership outcomes, and most importantly, *organizational will*? In other words, how do leaders do what they do? What are their methods?

In this model, leaders utilize four methods in order to create a *winning climate* and *organizational competence*, which then combine to produce *organizational will*. These methods of transformational leadership are *communication, presence, adaptive leadership*, and *planning*. Through these four routes, effective leaders leverage their talents and skills into leadership *outcomes* that help ensure organizational success.

Communication. "A man does not have himself killed for a few halfpence a day, or for a petty distinction. You must speak to the soul in order to electrify the man" (Field Manual 22–100 1999, 3–16). Napoleon spoke these words nearly two centuries ago about the power of leader communication. Communication is probably the most obvious *method* of leadership; after all, it is easily observed. Most people readily think of great leaders as being effective communicators.

"Communication is the backbone of leadership," says Don Duffy, a Chicago-based executive producer with Willias/Gerard, a leading communications firm. "People need direction and leadership, and without constant communication you have no leadership" (Baldoni 2002). The national tragedy on September 11, 2001, provided a forum for then New York City mayor Rudolph Giuliani. Jack Welch, a leadership icon himself, complimented the former mayor, saying, as a leader "Giuliani has set the tone. . . . he's communicated to every constituency" (Leadership is back 2002). Both Welch and Giuliani understand the importance of this *leadership method*.

Great leaders jump off the pages of history largely because of their highly effective communications. John F. Kennedy, Franklin D. Roosevelt, and Abraham Lincoln solidified our nation with their keen insight into communication.

Communication stirs the soul, and effective leaders understand and use this tool wisely. After all, leaders transfer ideas, vision, purpose, and direction through all types of communication. Effective communication applies in all leadership situations.

In many ways communication represents the actual connections between individuals and ideas, bonds of purpose that create a group. This even leads to organization-specific words, phrases, and shared stories that serve to build these connections into a common culture.

People need communication to feel this connection. In a survey of employees, 65 percent said open communications was "very important" in their decision on whether to take their current job (Simonsen 1997). Most people have a feel for this leadership method in that they have, at some point, experienced the impact of leader communication, or the lack thereof.

Great leaders tell a compelling story about where their organizations are going; they create compelling vision statements or strategic intents that keep their employees moving in the same direction. Wal-Mart's leaders have done this with the slogan "low prices, every day." With this mantra behind them, employees know what to do every day for their business to stay out front, without the need for a thick book of instructions to guide them (Useem 2001).

According to Keegan (1987, 321), one of the first imperatives of command has always been the ability to speak "with all the arts of the actor and orator to the soldiers under his orders." This is not acting. This is sharing purpose and meaning with soldiers whose lives are at stake and, therefore, need it most.

Presence.   Great leaders know when and how to position themselves for maximum effect. This is not to be confused with leaders who drop in for the photo opportunities designed solely to enhance their own images. This leadership method, referred to as *presence*, is designed for maximum positive effect on the organization, not the leader.

Presence refers to the leader's ability to act in a manner appropriate to the situation. It is a leader being in the right place at the right time to make important decisions. It involves setting the example, living the vision, and sharing in the triumphs as well as the pain and suffering. It is a leader at the right place gathering the right information for his or her assessments and decisions. Presence entails building the common bond by being there, listening, and telling the organization's compelling story. *Presence* is setting the example of the culture the leader wants to create by "walking the talk." Combining these important subcomponents of presence comes down to this—*presence is a leader consistently being and acting at the point of maximum effect to improve the organization.*

This point of maximum effect changes weekly, daily, even hourly. One moment it might occur in the boardroom, while the next it might be in the employee cafeteria as one talks and listens to the people of the organization.

Leader presence is about setting the example and inspiring others, yet it has a very practical side, as well. Effective leaders throughout history have understood and applied this leadership method with great effect. On a hot summer afternoon in Asia, Alexander the Great's weary army was in desperate need of water. His men found a small amount of water in a spring and gathered it in a helmet for their commander. Alexander "took it and thanked them, but then poured it out in sight of everyone; and at this action the army was so much heartened that you would have guessed that all had drunk what Alexander had poured away" (Kolenda 2001, 106). This powerful act had great effect on his men. Alexander's presence was theatrical, to be sure, but in this time of heroic leadership it was highly effective in moving his organization where he wanted it to go. It was done for maximum organizational effect.

Presence is also about gathering the right information for the leader to have influence. In the words of legendary Miami Dolphins coach Don Shula, "You can't coach from the press box" (Blanchard 2001, 216). A leader must be at the "point of action" in order to truly understand morale and develop a genuine feel for the realities on the ground. General Matthew Ridgway put this idea in practice upon his assumption of command in the Korean theater of war. Within forty-eight hours of taking over, he moved his headquarters farther north, closer to the fighting, and personally visited every division and corps commander (Meigs 2001).

Effective leaders understand and apply this leadership method with acumen. They understand the human element of their organizations because they are building on the *people skills* of emotional intelligence and *character*. This fact enables them to leverage the leadership method called *presence* for maximum effect. Whether the leader sprinkles it with the theatrical or sticks to the practical, *presence* is designed for positive effect on the organization, not the leader. This method can only be well deployed by the leader who possesses the talent of *selfless will*.

Adaptive Leadership.   *Adaptive leadership* is closely related to the well-known concept called *leadership style*. *Leadership style* is the "typical pattern of behavior that a leader uses to influence his or her employees to achieve organizational goals" (Dubrin 2000, 275). *Leadership style* is a component of *adaptive leadership*. In other words, if leaders are effectively practicing *adaptive leadership* they are producing the right *leadership style* for the given situation.

Adaptive leadership has three primary components—deducing follower readiness, understanding situational context, then applying the appropriate leadership style in light of the first two. This component of leadership, while a more recent discovery, is beginning to find its way into the leadership framework.

Style is a key driver of organizational climate, which in turn drives organizational performance (Goleman 2000). Emotional intelligence, a key *means* of leadership previously explored, is at the root of this vital leadership skill. Most people have some familiarity with the idea of leadership style as a particular way in which a leader deals with people—almost like a personality. This view only scratches the surface.

A leader's style is largely determined by emotional intelligence and situational context. *Adaptive leadership*, then, is the leader's ability to apply the right leadership style, appropriate for the people and the situation, in order to maximize organizational productivity and climate. *Adaptive leadership* is directly related to controlling organizational climate, and is therefore, a key *method* of leadership.

In the past, *adaptive leadership* and its accompanying leadership styles have been thought of as innate talents. This prevented leaders from thinking they could influence this area. This view is changing. A recent study conducted by the consulting firm Hay/Mcber, found that people use six distinct leadership styles in different organizational situations (Goleman 2000). According to this study, leaders with the best results do not simply rely on one leadership style. Rather, they apply the right leadership style for the right situation, similar to a golfer choosing the right club for each particular shot during his game. Great leaders learn to use the right styles for the right situations and can seamlessly transition between styles by accurately reading their organizations. This skill defines the adaptive leadership that is so crucial to the transformational leader.

Adaptive leadership starts with leaders recognizing the situational context in which they act. In a time-constrained or emergency environment, leaders need to act quickly. This naturally pushes them into autocratic and authoritative modes, both of which offer quick-decision-cycle times as advantages. In other environments, however, the leader has much greater flexibility to choose the style that is best suited for the group. Once the leader has assessed the environmental time constraints, the next concern is determining follower readiness.

According to the original work done by Hersey, Blanchard, and Johnson, readiness is determined by the ability and willingness of the follower to accomplish a given task (Yeakey 2002). Groups with both high ability and willingness require guidance and coaching, while groups with low willingness

Leadership Style	Characteristics	When appropriate
Coercive	demands immediate compliance	in a crisis, or to kick start a turnaround
Authoritative	mobilizes people toward a vision	when change requires a new vision
Affiliative	creates harmony, builds emotional bonds	to heal rifts, overcome distrust
Democratic	creates consensus through participation	to build buy-in and get input
Pacesetting	sets high standards for performance	to get quick results from motivated teams
Coaching	develops people for the future	to help employees improve performance

FIGURE 1.3   Leadership Styles

and low ability may require a more authoritarian approach. The point is, leaders apply the right style only after they have assessed their followers.

As leaders complete their follower assessment, they then choose among six styles to maximize performance from the group. The six leadership styles are coercive, authoritative, affiliative, democratic, pacesetting, and coaching (*see* figure 1.3). Most people will recognize these distinct styles from their experiences. What is new is the idea that great leaders can move with relative ease between these styles. These styles are based on the leader's level of *emotional intelligence*, a leadership skill previously explained. This again reinforces the concept that leadership *means* (talents and skills) enable *methods*, which produce leadership *outcomes*.

The late David McClelland, a noted Harvard University psychologist, found that leaders with strengths in multiple emotional-intelligence competencies were far more effective then their peers who lacked such strengths (Goleman 2000). (The leadership styles that these competencies produce are explained in figure 1.3.)

Leaders who demand immediate compliance to their wishes characterize the *coercive* leadership style. They actively manage the details and demand immediate performance. By most people's standards, this style is considered bullying and oppressive, and although it has a negative overall effect on climate, there are situations, such as during a crisis, in which this style is most fitting.

Leaders who urge their people to "follow them" toward a compelling vision are exhibiting the *authoritative* style. They are self-confident and enthusiastic; they tend to be visionary and motivate people by ensuring that everyone knows how their work fits in with the organization's goals (Goleman 2000). By focusing their attention on the vision and the future, they ensure that all parts of the organization understand how they will get there in the end. This is a highly effective leadership style in most situations. If there were to be a default mode of effective leadership, the authoritarian style would fit the bill precisely because it capitalizes on the power of vision, and creates a strong sense of purpose throughout the organization.

Leaders who focus on creating harmony and trust within the organization are displaying the *affiliative* leadership style. To these leaders, people and relationships come first, before tasks and goals. These leaders build the emotional bonds that help organizations succeed. This style lacks the power of vision and purpose of the authoritative leadership style, but, according to Goleman (2000), it is particularly effective when leaders need to build team harmony, create trust, or repair human-relationship damage.

Leaders finding consensus before action are displaying the *democratic* leadership style. As the name implies, this democratic style is used to get people's buy-in and support for organizational policies and decisions. This style is highly effective in building trust and support within the organization. Its weakness, though, is that it can greatly limit flexibility and is unresponsive to time pressures. According to Goleman (2000), this style works best when leaders are uncertain about the best direction to take and the group decision-making process can legitimately help steer the right course.

Leaders who set the example and expect everyone in the organization to meet their standards characterize the *pacesetting* style. This style is very demanding. Even though these leaders are out front leading by example, they are very intolerant of someone who does not possess their very demanding standards. This style is quick to produce burnout and attitude problems within organizations. The pacesetting style, like the coercive style, has a place in the repertoire of leaders, but it must be used sparingly for maximum effect. It is no surprise that the pacesetting style has an overall negative effect on organizational climate (Goleman 2001).

Leaders who focus their efforts on developing individuals within the organization are deploying the final leadership style—*coaching*. Leaders use this style to develop people with an eye on long-term individual improvement. This places leaders in the role of counselor and mentor, rather than traditional boss. In this role leaders help their people identify and assess talents, strengths, and weaknesses, and create meaningful performance-improvement plans to help along the way. Their focus is doing what is right for the organization by emphasizing the development needs of its individuals. The coaching leadership style has been shown to improve overall business results. This requires intense dialogue, which drives the organization's climate (Goleman 2000).

These leadership styles all have effects on climate—some positive, some negative—yet there is a time and place for each of them. According to the work of Goleman (2000), a leader's style drives organizational climate. Something of a surprise, though, was the fact that the *authoritative* style had the most consistently positive effect on climate. Following the *authoritative* style in producing positive climate effects were the *affiliative, democratic,* and *coaching* styles, all fairly close to each other in terms of effects. Not as surprising was the fact that the pacesetting and coercive styles had a negative effect on organizational climate.

Strategies and Plans.   This method of leadership combines leaders' *intellectual talents* and *manager skills* to, essentially, plan backwards from the vision, or end-state. Transformational leaders see the big picture—the future state—and are able to develop realistic plans to move the organization there. They allocate resources, set priorities, set intermediate objectives and milestones, monitor progress, and adjust, as necessary, all in order to keep the organization moving forward.

This *strategy and planning* method normally follows two lines—effectiveness and efficiency. Plans dealing with effectiveness are normally more strategic in nature. These plans deal with the question of whether or not the organization is headed in the right direction and producing the right outputs to get there. Efficiency planning, on the other hand, deals with processes and operational excellence. Once the organization knows what business it wants to be in and the outputs required to take it there, it can then focus on how to best get there. These questions center around ideas of cost, cycle-times, and best practices. These all help create competitive advantages for the organization that distinguish it from peers.

Successful leaders operate by effectively integrating all four of these *leadership methods.* They *communicate* effectively, apply their *presence* with precision, exhibit *adaptive leadership* to the situational context confronting them, and create solid *strategy/plans* from which to act. Transformational leaders operate with the four methods previously described and use them intuitively. Most leaders, unfortunately, operate with one of more of these *methods* undeveloped.

Outcomes of Leadership

Simply put, transformational leaders produce *organizational will.* This is the *end,* or ultimate output, of leadership. *Organizational will* is the state of being where members of an organization share the ability and desire to move toward a common vision. They are aligned with the same values, goals, attitudes, and expectations (*a winning climate*), combined with the competence to get the job done (*organizational competence*). Producing true *organizational will* is the highest form of leadership success. *Organizational will* flows from two intermediate leader outcomes: *organizational competence* and *winning climate* .

Organizational Competence.   *Organizational competence* is a precondition for *organizational will*, and, as such, great leaders understand this leadership outcome. Through their *professional competence*, effective leaders understand the components that make up their organizations. These components are people, equipment, processes, money, and information. They understand what these components need to do and how the various components must work together to be successful. By using the leadership method of *strategy/planning*, transformational leaders develop plans to ensure their organization's components are working together in order to produce the right outputs. In other words, leaders ensure *organizational competence*.

Winning Climate.   A *winning climate* combines with *organizational competence* to produce *organizational will*. Climate entails the atmosphere and attitudes that permeate the organization. According to Burke (1992, 131), climate is "the collective current impressions, expectations, and feelings of members of local work units. These in turn affect member's relations with supervisors, one another, and with other units."

No two organizations share the same climate because no two organizations share the same leader and the same people. Yet climate is directly affected by the leader (Goleman 1998).

Climate and culture are closely related concepts. Culture is generally longer term and more deeply embedded in the organization. Burke (1992, 130) defined culture as "the way we do things around here . . . the collection of overt and covert rules, values, and principles that guide organizational behavior."

Effective leaders focus on climate, which over the long term successfully shapes culture. Therefore, leader-controlled climate is decisive, and makes organizations unique in positive or negative ways. For this reason a *winning climate* is a leadership outcome required for transformational leadership.

The Leadership End-State: Organizational Will

Ultimately, effective leaders create *organizational will*. This is achieved when leaders have created both *organizational competence* and a *winning climate*. *Organizational will* represents a total organizational-level alignment of vision, *climate,* and *competence*. In other words, the members of an organization share the motivation to achieve the vision, trust in their leaders, and know that they have the skills to achieve the goal. It represents a truly collective purpose embodied in an organization—a unique form of synergy that is the final and highest-order leadership outcome.

Transformational leaders create the "single spirit of passion and belief." Through *climate* and *competence*—both direct leader outcomes—leaders produce *organizational will,* which is characterized by organizations that have the capability to produce, believe in what they are doing, and trust their leaders. With *organizational will* in place, the leader is, by definition, transformational, and has done the best a leader can do.

Conclusion

HRD professionals spend their careers helping organizations learn and grow—increasing the renewal capacity for the firms they serve. Yet how many professionals truly understand leadership, the most significant driver of change and culture? This chapter begins a change—a change as important to HRD as transistors were to the technology advances of the past quarter century. HRD is no longer about reviewing résumés and lining up the occasional training program. HRD is about organizational renewal, learning, and change—all of which are dominated by leadership.

The strength of this new organizational-leadership theory is that it presents leadership in a simplified and unified whole, while including some important new concepts in behavioral science theory. Just as scientists continually probe the depths of matter to refine the underlying physics, so too must HRD professionals continually probe, explore, and update leadership theory to unlock the basic "physics" contained therein. HRD's view of leadership must evolve. This is the only way HRD professionals can be sure they know what makes leadership work.

Leadership—how it works and how it doesn't—needs to occupy a central position in the field of HRD. It is, therefore, time to embrace a framework that decodes this complex subject. Utilizing a clear model of how leadership actually works at the highest (transformational) level allows us to guide leaders at work in our organizations. HRD practitioners can then "plant the flag" in this emerging critical organizational terrain.

With a better understanding of the *means, methods,* and *outcomes* of leadership, HRD practitioners can demystify leadership and better understand its complex nature. If leadership is viewed as a system, with leadership inputs (*talents* and *skills*), methods (*communication, presence, adaptive leadership,* and *sound planning*), and outcomes (*a competent organization* with a *winning climate,* which combined create *organizational will*), the practical application for HRD professionals is immense.

Strategic HRD and Its Transformation

Jerry W. Gilley
Scott A. Quatro
Susan A. Lynham

It is virtually impossible to open any book, magazine, or newspaper and not be struck by the evidence of big, transformational change going on all around us. Whether in the form of merging companies or industries, shifting national or international boundaries, or evolving ecosystems, we are continually confronted with shape-shifting change. And in light of this change, we have two choices: to be indiscriminately shaped by it, or to step up to it and influence its outcome and effect on us. History has shown us that those organizations that have chosen to step up to change, to take it by the proverbial horns and act as an interdependent part of this fast transforming environment, have done better at long-term survival and performance than those that have not (Schwartz 1991; Senge 1990).

As a result of this changing world, organizations and organizational life as we know them are changing significantly before our eyes. No longer can organizations act in isolation of their external and international environments. Fast disappearing are the days of the semiopen system, hierarchically structured, singularly bottom-lined or internally focused organizations. Instead, organizations are learning to think and act in an intricately connected global economy where markets have gone from being supply-based to demand-based; where previously there was power in withholding information to a reality in which power now lies in information sharing and strategic information partnering, where communities that once were stable and easy to define have become increasingly mobile and ever changing; where the internal and external environments of organizations were largely known they are predominantly unknown; where mass consciousness characterized our societies to a societal character punctuated by individual realities and the emergence of situational lifestyles; and where brain-powered industries that were inextricably linked to the industrial worker are being replaced by brainpower industries driven by the knowledge-reliant worker (Snyder 1996).

On face value these changes may not seem significant; however, they are having a massive, shape-shifting effect on organizations of today. These effects are bringing about significant changes to the nature and character of organizations and the workforce. The implications of some of these changes for organizations and workers are highlighted in Table 2.1.

This environment of chaos and continuous transformational change in today's organizations requires all players in the organizational arena to fundamentally reinvent themselves and the ways in which they interact with and contribute to the enduring performance and future agility of the organization (Eichinger and Ulrich 1995). Such changes require a reframing of how organizations and their components think about and conduct strategy, and how they respond to leadership and the management of change. A brief overview of the shift in the strategic equation facing organizations is presented in Table 2.2.

The demands of today's global business environment require that organizations be nimble and flexible on all fronts and at all times (Drucker 1994). Competitive advantage is driven by the ability to continually outlearn and outperform the competition, and the competition is more elusive and unknown than ever before (Kotter 1996; Tichy 1983). In this information age, people and the abilities they offer, in new and not-yet-imagined arenas, have become an integral part of the equation of long-term survival and high performance of our organizations. People who can imagine the unimagined, who can continuously learn and unlearn in the face of the unknown, who can act strategically, through joint vision, learning, and information-sharing, and, in the long-term interests and survival of the organization, have become the undeniable source of sustainable performance and economic survival (Horwitz 1999; Pfeffer 1995). Developing this human competence and unleashing this human expertise is of greater strategic value to organizations, and, indeed, to society, than ever before (Torraco and Swanson 1995; Swanson and Holton 2001).

It is this development and unleashing of human expertise that is the business of the field of Human Resource Development (HRD). That HRD should be employed and act strategically within the external and internal context of

TABLE 2.1   Implications of Our Changing World for Organizations and Workers

FROM ⟶	TO
Implications for Organizations	
Age of organized organizations	Ability to understand, facilitate, encourage processes of self-organization has become key competence
Existence for benefit of shareholders	Concerned with stakeholders of all kinds: employees, communities, customers, suppliers, and shareholders
Focus on bottom line	Balanced-scorecard measures
Share of market	Share of customer; reflects ever-increasing focus on customer
Economies of scale: what you know about all of your customers	Economies of scope: what you know about each customer
Internal focus on operations and efficiency. Cutting debris to achieve success (downsizing, reengineering, and so on)	Revenue growth to achieve success
Competitive advantage from traditional business models (for example, cost, technology, distribution, manufacturing, products)	Workers as primary competitive advantage (for example: competence, ideas, innovation, speed, and responsiveness)
Company owns tools of production	Individuals/employees own tools of production
Reason-based logic	Chaos-based logic
Implications for Workers	
Extraneous part of the organization	Central resource
Organizations "know all"	Personal knowledge and individual learning
Receivers of information	"Owners" of information, producers and conduits.
"Busy-ness" valued	Outputs are valued
Identity based on job/position	Identity based on contributions
Complete education in early-adult life	Continual development
Knowledge is forever	Half-life of knowledge
Single-looped learning	Double-looped learning
Valued for degrees and social position	Valued for output
Lifelong employment	Short-term and multiple jobs/careers
Work for pay	Work for fulfillment
Procedural tasks	Knowledge and systems tasks
Precedent for how things are done was clear	Not one way—create the best way for given situations
Blue-collar skills are valued	Reorienting of skills is necessary to succeed
Generalized	Specialized; focus on application and relevance to business
One way to team	Multiple ways to team; focus is networks, flexible, virtual

© Ruona and Lynham 1999

the organization has become critical, not only to the organizations who seek their products and services, but to the very discipline itself (Dare 1996; Gilley and Maycunich 1998; Horwitz 1999; Torraco and Swanson 1995; Walton 1999). But what does it mean for HRD to be strategic? To answer this question first we have to consider the meaning of *strategic*.

TABLE 2.2 An Overview of the Age-Shift Implications for Strategy Making and Strategic Engagement in Organizations

FROM ⟶	TO
Implications for Strategic Thought and Action	
A single worldview	Integrated, multiple worldviews
Reduce complexity to some simple few rules	Need for imagination and scanning
Driven by a threat of short-term impact	Driven by a threat of long-term impact
Belief that it is possible and useful to predict the future	Belief that the future cannot be predicted, and, therefore, irreducible uncertainty cannot be ignored; anticipation and response to multiple, plausible futures
Assuming future will be like the past, with a few embellishments	Assuming the future is unknown and can't be known; expect the rules to change every 5-7 years
Plans are a mechanism for reducing risk	Plans are a mechanism for balancing acceptable, calculated risk with unwarranted levels of risk
Few "golden" rules to achieve strategic success Get high market value share and soon	Competitive advantage from insights into marketplace's future and turbulent markets
Relying on performing similar activities better than rivals do	Choosing to perform different activities than rivals, or doing the same activities differently
Belief that seeing further is seeing better	Belief in balanced looking ahead while paying attention to what's happening now
Grounded in analysis	Evolves organically through constant give-and-take
Forecasting done by experts	Involving decision-makers in seeing past outcomes to driving forces that could move the business in various directions
Deciding what is to be forecasted	Allowing multiple plausible futures to emerge from both the natural agenda of the environment and decision-makers
One-time development of "best" strategy, calendar-driven	An ongoing strategy process. Continuous and emergent, dynamic learning process on a real-time basis. • Wall (1997) "Strategy is what the organization decides to do and then what you learn out of doing it ... a series of kind of hypotheses that a company tests against the needs of customers and realities of marketplace."
Emphasizing the plan	Emphasizing action
Realizing goals and tactics	"Stretch" goals that drive out-of-the-box thinking; targets that require a shift from business as usual
Drawing from brainpower at the "top"	Strategizing openly to many people, especially those that are younger and older than the guardians of the status quo
"Telling the future" to organizational members	Inclusive strategic conversations about the future

© Ruona and Lynham 1999

The word *strategy* (*American Heritage Dictionary*) can be traced back to the Greek words *stratos*, meaning *army*, and *agein*, meaning *to lead*. Undeniably military in origin and flavor, the word *strategic* was derived from *stratagem*, meaning "a military maneuver designed to deceive or surprise an enemy ... a clever, often underhand scheme for achieving an objective," and first emerged in the early 1800s, coming to mean "the art of planning military operations" (Barnhart 1995, 765). In later years the meaning of the word was expanded to include business and other arenas of competitive action: "1. of or relating to strategy; 2. important or essential in relation to a plan of action; 3. essential to the effective conduct of war; 4. highly important to an intended objective; 5. intended to destroy the military potential of an enemy."

Synonymous with the act of planning and the outcome of goal achievement, the act of strategic action demands skillful artistic and scientific ability and intent (Kemper and Kemper 1996; Walton 1999). In the context of today's organizations and the discipline of HRD, "to be strategic" requires HRD to be an integral and essential part of organizational strategy making and execution (McCracken and Wallace 1999, 2000). This means that through the development and unleashing of human expertise, HRD is required to play both a strategy-shaping and strategy-supporting role in organizations (Torraco and Swanson 1995), that it should act in proactive and transformational ways within organizations, and that it should be essentially results-driven and results-aligned.

Just like their environmental and organizational counterparts, these shifts in the role and expertise of HRD are most significant. These shifts demand that HRD move away from merely acting to helping implement strategy already formed and handed down by the brainpower at the top of the organization, to being a fundamental player in both the shaping and supporting of strategy (Horwitz 1999; Provo et al. 1998; Swanson, Lynham, Ruona, and Provo 1998; Torraco and Swanson 1995); they require that HRD stop being activity-driven and start being results-driven (Broad and Newstrom 1992; Gilley and Coffern 1994); and they require that HRD engage less in a transactional manner and more in a transformational manner within the organization (Gilley, Maycunich, and Quatro 2002). The discipline's inherently strategic nature is captured aptly in a definition of strategic HRD (SHRD) offered by McCracken and Wallace (1999, 288):

> . . . the creation of a learning culture, within which a range of training, development and learning strategies both respond to corporate strategy and also help to shape and influence it. It is about meeting the organization's existing needs, but it is also about helping the organization to change and develop, to thrive and grow. It is the reciprocal, mutually enhancing, nature of the relationship between HRD and corporate strategy.

This role- and expertise-shifting requirement of HRD is not only of strategic and critical importance to the future of organizations, but also to the future of HRD itself.

Activity-Based Versus Results-Driven HRD

To remain competitive in a global economy, many organizations are developing a more integrated HRD approach. Unfortunately, many HRD programs are perceived to be merely internal training houses for employees, and thus are viewed as "outside" the mainstream of the firm. Under this condition, little attention is given to the outcomes of training or its impact on employee performance. Further, some HRD professionals are not taken seriously because they are considered to be noncritical to the success of the organization (Brinkerhoff and Apking 2002). Occasionally, some HRD professionals are viewed as having no credibility because "they don't live in the real world, facing the problems other organizational members face" (Gilley and Maycunich 1998, 25). This occurs when HRD professionals spend their time designing classroom-based training events, facilitating workshops, seminars, or meetings, and scheduling conferences. In essence, they view training as an end unto itself. Management reinforces this belief by not allowing HRD initiatives to be used as a strategic tool in improving organizational performance and effectiveness.

HRD professionals weaken their organizational image by behaving as though they are in the business of delivering training; their energy is directed toward the number of training courses they deliver and the number of employees they train. This "training for training's sake" philosophy, where activity is the basis for justifying one's organizational contribution, typically relies on employees' responses to training as a means to justify their existence rather than on learning transfer or the impact of training.

Brinkerhoff and Gill (1994) and Gill (1995) identified five deeply held beliefs that contribute to the training-for-training's-sake philosophy of HRD. These beliefs, which appear to anchor HRD professionals in this philosophy, affect one's behavior, actions, and decisions. The anchors are:

1. Training makes a difference, which is evident because so many HRD professionals honestly think that training by itself can change an organization and improve its performance and effectiveness.
2. Training is only a job for HRD practitioners, which leads them to develop an attitude that training is exclusively their responsibility.
3. The trainer's purpose is to manage training programs causing HRD professionals to behave as if their department is tangential to other operational units.
4. Training's purpose is to achieve learning objectives; thus, many HRD professionals believe accomplishing learning objectives is the primary purpose of training.

5. Training events must be enjoyable activities rather than challenging learning opportunities, which is evident by use of reaction evaluations.

Clifton and Nelson (1992) identified a sixth belief, which is *training is designed "to fix" employees' weaknesses*. When HRD professionals believe they are in the business of "fixing" employees, training becomes remedial in nature, giving employees the impression that something is wrong with them.

These beliefs cause senior management to seriously question the value of HRD. As a result, HRD professionals are often treated with a lack of respect and, often, are the first to be eliminated during periods of financial difficulty (Gilley and Maycunich 1998). Robinson and Robinson (1989) referred to programs that exhibit these six characteristics as activity-based HRD.

Activity-Based HRD

Activity-based HRD programs are characterized by HRD practitioners whose primary responsibility is identifying, selecting, and evaluating training programs from a myriad of outside *training houses* or vendors. These HRD practitioners, who also redesign programs to fit within their organizational culture, are referred to as *brokers of training programs*. This "clearinghouse approach is primarily what is wrong with the HRD profession because it allows training activity to become the focus of HRD, which produces long-term damage to the image and credibility of HRD" (Gilley and Coffern 1994, 31).

When providing formal training activities is the primary objective of activity-based HRD programs, it becomes the principal focus of HRD practice. Accordingly, organizations begin to hire more and more trainers in an effort to "keep up" with ever-increasing training demand. Broad and Newstrom (1992) point out that activity-based practitioners make little if any effort to ensure that training is being transferred to the job by employees. In fact, managers and executives often refer to training as "something that those trainers do" and fail to see employee development as their responsibility (Gilley and Maycunich 1998). Such an attitude becomes the Achilles' heel of activity-based HRD programs. It is common for these practitioners to conduct a greater number of needs-assessment activities to identify the next series of training sessions and use reaction evaluations to identify employees' perceptions of training.

Fortunately, a more sophisticated type of intervention known as *isolated performance* emerges in activity-based HRD programs. This intervention requires minor environmental redesign, incentive/motivation-system changes, and job aids to fix isolated performance problems (Silber 1992). The outcomes of most isolated performance interventions are short-lived, however, because the "system" has not really changed enough for real performance improvement to occur (Dean 1999). Examples of isolated performance interventions include training in supervisory skills, time management, meeting management, and interpersonal skills.

In activity-based programs, HRD practitioners' organizational effectiveness strategy is simplistic in that they focus on improving individual employee performance. As a result, little attention is given to how learning interventions affect overall organizational performance, competitiveness, or efficiency. In other words, activity-based practitioners answer the question, "What skills, knowledge, attitudes, and abilities are required to enhance individual performance?" It could be argued that they lack a comprehensive organizational effectiveness strategy.

HRD practitioners who provide numerous training activities commonly develop partnerships with department and division managers. These HRD practitioners are able to establish better customer relationships and enhance their understanding of organizational operations. However, these relationships are a natural by-product of increasing training activity and are not an HRD practitioner's primary objective.

To complicate the situation further, senior management considers activity-based HRD programs as a cost because their budgets are used to support nonrevenue-producing activities such as training services (Gilley and Maycunich 1998). Erroneously, executives hold HRD managers accountable for producing service activity rather than tangible organizational results. By definition, the funds made available to activity-based HRD programs do not produce organizational results. Consequently, HRD is viewed as a cost to the organization (to provide activity) rather than as an investment (to produce results).

Gilley, Maycunich, and Quatro (2002) refer to activity-based HRD practitioners as *transactional* because they engage primarily in exchanges that result in services (for example, training programs) consumed by internal clients. These often relatively short-term engagements have little strategic value and are based on nonempirical inquiry typically based on immediate and short-term needs. Gilley et al. (2002) suggest that this resembles a retail approach in which HRD exchanges its training programs for internal monetary value without the benefit of serious dialogue or evidence of integration or application. As this process becomes common, the HRD program falls prey to the *services-for-hire approach*. Unless corrected, this approach locks out HRD practitioners from serious strategic discussions and engagements. The final outcome often is an HRD program that is either outsourced or eliminated during difficult economic periods.

Results-Driven HRD

Activity-based HRD practitioners have not yet addressed the most important question confronting them, which is, "How can HRD help the organization accomplish its strategic business goals and objectives?" This question serves as the focus of another type of HRD program known as *results-driven HRD*.

In results-driven programs, HRD professionals work collaboratively with management at all levels to improve organizational performance. Results-driven programs are not mere training houses within organizations; instead they help organizational leaders implement and manage change to improve organizational effectiveness. Several core strategies are commonly used in results-driven HRD programs, including:

- Setting Strategic Direction: Helping business units set long-range strategic goals and develop tactical plans in support of those goals.
- Linking Learning and Change Initiatives to Business Strategy: Assuring that learning interventions and change initiatives are in concert with business goals and objectives (Brinkerhoff and Apking 2002).
- Enhancing Leadership Development: Helping ensure that current leaders have appropriate leadership and management skills to produce organizational results.
- Implementing Performance-Management Systems: Helping improve performance through the use of appropriate development and feedback strategies linked to the compensation-and-rewards system, which includes identifying competency maps for all job classifications, performance standards, and evaluation methods used to enhance employee and organizational performance (Dean 1999b).
- Implementing Transfer of Learning Processes: Helping managers install effective strategies that improve learning transfer.
- Assessing Organizational Effectiveness: Helping leaders determine what their needs are and which services will have the highest organizational impact.
- Facilitating and Managing Change: Helping leaders develop effective plans for implementing change and understanding the human implications of change (Gilley and Maycunich 1998, 44).

For today's senior management who believe that HRD programs should be used to improve organizational performance and effectiveness rather than simply provide training activities, results-driven HRD programs are viewed as an investment rather than a cost (Gilley and Maycunich 1998). Therefore, results-driven HRD programs must provide services that help the organization achieve its strategic business goals. Of course, this requires professionals to change their HRD philosophy from that of the deliverers of training events to one dedicated to improving organizational effectiveness.

Another characteristic of results-driven HRD is the movement from improving employee performance to enhancing organizational performance and effectiveness. Although this shift proves subtle, HRD interventions and initiatives are now targeted at improving overall performance problems rather than fixing isolated ones. Silber (1992) characterizes results-driven programs as ones that utilize *total cultural interventions* by professionals who examine problems and provide solutions in a context that addresses the organization's values and corporate culture. This type of intervention can have the most positive impact on organizational performance and effectiveness, because HRD professionals use techniques that help them determine the influence of organizational policies, procedures, and culture that can impede performance and prevent the implementation of organizational change. Implementing total cultural interventions also requires a collaborative relationship between HRD professionals and senior management (Gilley and Maycunich 1998).

Successful progression to results-driven HRD requires professionals to develop a complete understanding of the organization, its politics, culture, business, and industry. Professionals must have excellent organizational development skills in order to analyze and evaluate all aspects of the firm, design and implement performance-management systems, and facilitate and manage change initiatives.

Results-driven HRD programs operate like those of consulting firms, where professionals are assigned to a variety of projects and initiatives. Under this operational approach, Gilley and Maycunich (1998) believe that HRD professionals have three development responsibilities. First, they are responsible for building strategic business partnerships throughout the organization as a means of facilitating organizational change, thus enhancing the image of HRD and its professionals. Second, they are responsible for establishing management development partnerships as a way of improving the professional nature of managers and supervisors. Third, they are responsible for serving as agents of change responsible for organizational development partnerships, which improve the organization's performance capacity and effectiveness.

Gilley and Maycunich (2002) refer to results-driven HRD professionals as *transformational professionals* used as strategic instruments to improve organizational effectiveness, competitive readiness, and renewal capacity. As such, results-driven HRD professionals help employees develop diagnostic skills used in performance analysis and problem-solving activities. These skills also address *what is achieved* (performance outputs) rather than *what tasks* (performance activities) are performed (Rummler and Brache 1995). Accordingly, transformational professionals examine the organizational structure, job design, workflow, performance appraisal and review processes, employee attitudes, performance criteria and standards, and quality improvement processes for the purpose of identifying ways of improving performance.

Barriers to Results-Driven HRD.   Why do HRD professionals have such a difficult time embracing the obvious advantages of a results-driven approach? Two primary reasons drive HRD professionals' resistance to adopting a results-driven approach: (1) fear and (2) lack of skills. HRD professionals' fears include:

- losing their "safe and secure" training positions;
- giving up their current positions for a new role, regardless of the benefit;
- telling management NO when they request a training solution;
- taking chances; a results-driven program places them on unfamiliar turf;
- initiating personal change;
- being convinced that training events by themselves add value to the organization.

Lack of skills is evident in HRD professionals who are:

- convinced that training is the answer to all performance problems; therefore, they have difficulty embracing other approaches;
- unable to identify the causes of poor performance;
- convinced that performance will improve if learning takes place;
- unable to make the transition from trainer to organizational development change agent.

Redesigning and Repositioning HRD: The Domains of Strategic HRD

As the United States and other leading nations continually evolve toward service-based economies, the need for business practitioners to be "HRD-minded" becomes more critical. In a service-based industry, an organization's people are ultimately the product, and such a reality poses very significant challenges for the firms competing in that industry. Most of these challenges have to do with the people employed by the organization and the quality of the services that they provide to the organization's customers (Parasuraman et al. 1985). Hence, the critical need for HRD to become more results-based and less activity-based, and to move from "activity-based" to "results-driven," becomes apparent (Robinson and Robinson 1999). No longer can organizations afford to develop and administer generic "training programs" for their employees. Rather, such organizations must recognize the potential results-based impact of such learning interventions.

The mandates for the redesign of HRD into a key driver of organizational strategy via the three practice domains of organizational learning, performance, and change are clear (Greer et al., 1999). Prioritization of these three domains of HRD practice enables organizations to develop and leverage their overall mix of HRD activities as a true source of competitive advantage (Brockbank 1999).

The proposed redesign of HRD around the three core practice domains of organizational learning, performance, and change has profound implications for today's HRD professionals, and for all business practitioners regardless of their specific functional responsibility (Gilley and Maycunich 2000) (*see* figure 2.1). This is especially true given the changing complexion of the world economy.

Organizational Learning

When confronted with organizational problems, organizational learning-oriented HRD professionals typically rely on learning solutions to address the issues. They believe that learning is a precondition to performance improvement and change; therefore, learning is essential when dealing with most organizational problems (Knowles 1990). These practitioners place great value on group learning as a way of bringing about organizational change (Marquardt 1999; Watkins and Marsick 1993).

HRD professionals who embrace organizational learning believe as Bierema recently wrote, "HRD is about *development*, not profit, and HRD practitioners

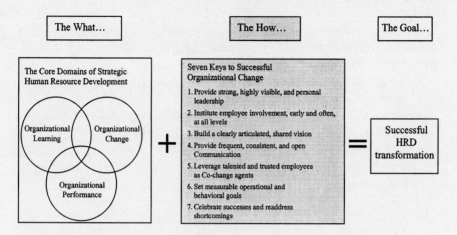

FIGURE 2.1   A Model for Redesigning and Repositioning HRD as a Key Driver of Corporate Strategy

need to carefully consider how their work impacts human growth, not just the corporate wallet. It has also been argued that focusing on individual development has long-term benefits for the individual, organization, and society." She continues by pointing out that "there are long-term costs associated with failure to provide the resources and infrastructure to support whole person learning such as turnover, mistakes, and employees leaving to work for the competition. There are also social costs of such neglect that will impact lives, communities, and the environment" (2000, 292). These comments nicely frame the philosophical bias of an organizational learning practitioner.

Senge (1990) reported that, from an organizational learning perspective, HRD professionals are motivated to create learning cultures that foster continuous employee learning. Redding (1994) suggests that this belief is based on a conviction that learning is the key to organizational effectiveness. Learning-oriented professionals embrace the principles and practices of the learning organization (Senge 1990), action learning (Marquardt 1999), critical reflection (Argyris and Schon 1996), transformative learning (Mezirow 1991) and their application within organizations.

Organizational Performance

Organizational performance–oriented HRD professionals believe they are responsible for analyzing performance problems, isolating the cause of performance breakdowns, and recommending or designing interventions used to address them (Gilbert 1978; Harless 1970; Mager 1975). They strongly protest the *training-for-training's-sake philosophy* and suggest that training is seldom the intervention of choice in most performance-improvement situations (Silber 1992). Rather, they maintain that:

- management action is most appropriate to improve organizational performance (Stolovitch and Keeps 1999);
- systems theory, behavioral psychology, and knowledge management are essential tools to examine performance shortfalls (Brethower 1999);
- the human-performance system is an excellent guide to improve organizational effectiveness (Fuller and Farrington, 1999; Rosenberg 1996);
- compensation and reward systems, organizational structure and culture, job design, and motivational factors should be designed to reinforce performance change and improvement (Gilbert 1978; Rummler and Brache 1995);
- they are responsible for discovering efficiencies within an organization through analysis activities (Rossett 1999b; Swanson 1994);
- the principles and practices of human-performance technology (Jacob 1987), performance consulting (Robinson and Robinson 1996), and performance engineering (Dean 1999) are techniques used to enhance organizational performance.

Organizational Change

French, Bell, and Zawacki (1999) contend that organizational change is based on the principles and practices of organizational development, which require HRD professionals to adopt the role of change agent within the organization for the purpose of improving organizational effectiveness. According to Nadler (1998), organizational change is the pinnacle of a professional's effort, and organizational learning and performance often improve as a result. Burke (1992) contends that organizational change is a full-time activity requiring an independent group of practitioners responsible for its implementation, and is focused on permanently altering the organization's culture. Finally, organizational-change professionals believe that they can improve their credibility by bringing about change within the organization and by managing its implementation (Ulrich 1998).

Patterson (1997, 6) states that the principal responsibility of transformational professionals is to help organizations and their members absorb change without draining the firm or individual energies, which he refers to as *resilience*. Therefore, organizational-change professionals are challenged to strengthen employees' adaptability to change, both personally and professionally, so that they are "positive, focused, flexible, organized, and proactive" (Conner 1992, 238). Such employees demonstrate a special adaptability when responding to uncertainty. Thus, resilient employees have a high tolerance for ambiguity and engage change rather than defend against it. Resilient employees:

- take risks despite potentially negative consequences;
- draw important lessons from change-related experiences that are then applied to similar situations;
- respond to disruption by investing energy in problem solving and teamwork;
- influence others to resolve conflicts (Conner 1992, 240).

Transformation of HRD Programs: Using a Change-Alignment Model to Move from Activity-Based to Results-Driven HRD

Countless change-alignment models have been developed and proposed for guiding organizational change initiatives. Our preferred model was developed based on our direct experience with more than twenty major organizational change initiatives involving firms from several different industries (from financial services to fashion retailing) and with various sizes/ownership structures (Gilley et al. 2001). These include both publicly-traded Fortune 500 firms and privately-held fraternal insurance organizations. We believe the strengths of the model lie in its straightforward, compelling language, which is accessible by employees at all levels of an organization, as well as its universal applicability.

Guiding the transformation of HRD in any organization requires those responsible for leading the effort to understand, embrace, and apply the critical competency of change alignment (Quatro et al. 2002). It is the application of change alignment ("the how") that ensures that the redesign ("the what") takes hold, with the end result being successful HRD transformation.

Seven Keys to Successful Transformation of HRD

To reposition HRD within an organization and ensure that a results-driven HRD program emerges, the following seven keys must be employed.

1. Provide strong, highly visible, and personal leadership.

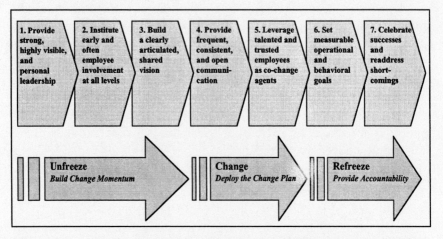

Gilley, J. W., et al. (2001). *The manager as change agent.* Cambridge, MA: Perseus Publishing.

FIGURE 2.2   Lewin's Model and the Seven Keys to the Transformation of HRD

2. Institute employee involvement early and often, at all levels.

3. Build a clearly articulated, shared vision.

4. Provide frequent, consistent, and open communication.

5. Leverage talented and trusted employees as co-change agents.

6. Set measurable operational and behavioral goals.

7. Celebrate successes and readdress shortcomings (see figure 2.2).

Conceptually it may help to connect the seven keys to Lewin's (1951) classic change model—the first three with "unfreezing," the next two with "changing," and the last two with "re-freezing."

Thus, we propose that an overarching strategy be used to transform activity-based HRD programs to results-driven ones. HRD professionals, acting as change agents, employ the seven keys to build momentum for the HRD transformation effort, deploy the change plan, and provide performance accountability for employees and the organization as a whole. These seven principles must be clearly articulated as nonnegotiable elements in the transformation of HRD. HRD professionals must remain unswerving as they employ the list and insist on the on-going commitment of their organization to the seven keys.

Key 1: Provide Strong, Highly Visible, and Personal Leadership

Kotter (1996) contends that, without a sense of urgency, the momentum for change never materializes. To bring about change, HRD professionals establish a sense of urgency to gain needed cooperation. This is very true when complacency is high and HRD practitioners are satisfied with their role in the organization. However, the transformation project depends on HRD leaders "burning the platform" so that complacent practitioners are willing to embrace needed change (Kotter 1996).

Next, the organization must ensure that a clearly dedicated and visible executive sponsor has ultimate ownership of the HRD transformation project and is driving it at all levels of the firm. Additionally, senior-level and HRD managers within the organization must display an unswerving commitment to the goals of the HRD transformation project at hand. Further, these same leaders must claim a personal stake in the success of the project and demonstrate a willingness to be held accountable for achieving that success through teamwork and inspirational leadership rather than through individual effort and coercion.

Establishing an Executive Champion. The first order of business for any HRD transformation effort is to carefully choose a well-qualified executive champion (sponsor). He or she must be selected with both position power and personal power in mind. From a position-power standpoint the executive sponsor must be in a role that ensures access to the resources (both human and capital) necessary to launch and sustain the transformation process, as well as the authority to make unilateral decisions regarding the allocation of those resources. Regarding personal power, the executive champion must be an individual with the expertise to lead the initiative, as well as the transformational referent power needed to energize others.

Given these requirements it is tempting to appoint the organization's senior HR executive to lead the transformation effort. After all, the senior HR practitioner is most often equipped with both ample resources and personal referent power as the main "employee champion" within the firm (*see* Ulrich 1997), and thus appears to be ideally suited to the role. Such a decision is faulty; we recommend instead establishing a senior manager from one of the line operations as the executive sponsor, and for two reasons. First, given the clear trend toward line ownership of HRD strategies and activities, assigning a highly visible and well-regarded senior-line manager as the executive champion adds instant business credibility and operational results accountability to the HRD transformation effort (Baron and Kreps 1999; Gilley and Maycunich 1998). Second, positioning the HRD transformation effort squarely in the camp of a significant line operation within the firm ensures that business unit–driven, short-term wins can be generated and given the necessary exposure to ensure on-going momentum for the overall effort. This is particularly critical in the transformation of HRD, given the ever-present challenge of demonstrating the bottom-line operational and financial benefits of HRD initiatives. These are further discussed within the context of the sixth key.

Driving Down the Initiative Through the Leadership Ranks. The overarching focus of the executive champion must be on driving enthusiasm and ownership for the HRD transformation effort down through the leadership ranks of the organization. This must be done aggressively and decisively.

In his recently published memoirs (Welch and Byrne 2001), Jack Welch reflects on the tremendously successful HRD transformation initiative that led to a "boundaryless" General Electric. This effort engaged all three domains of strategic HRD activity (Organizational Learning, Performance, and Change), which were firmly established as core areas of strategic focus for the entire firm. In his comments, Welch notes that his effort to drive down the initiative through the leadership ranks at GE was "a bit over the top." His behavior was purposeful, as he had learned that "for any big idea, you have to sell, sell, and sell to move the needle at all" (Welch and Byrne 2001, 186). It is only via such appropriately aggressive championing of the HRD initiative that the executive sponsor enlists the enthusiasm and coownership of the leadership ranks throughout the organization. The end result then becomes highly visible: personal leadership aligned with the HRD transformation effort is now dispersed on an enterprise-wide basis. Such an outcome is, of course, critical to the long-term success of the transformation of HRD.

Characteristics of the Leadership Team. Putting together a leadership team to direct the transformation effort requires the right membership. Four key characteristics essential to an effective leadership team are:

1. *Position power:* Are enough key leaders on board so that those left out cannot easily block progress?
2. *Expertise:* Are the various points of view—in terms of discipline, work experience, and so forth—relevant to the task at hand adequately represented so that informed, intelligent decisions can be made?
3. *Credibility:* Does the group have enough people with good reputations in the organization so that its pronouncements will be taken seriously by other employees?
4. *Leadership:* Does the group include enough proven leaders to be able to drive the change process? (Kotter 1996, 57).

Ensuring Transformational Versus Transactional Leadership. The organization, and specifically the executive champion, must ensure that leaders throughout the firm embody transformational as opposed to transactional leadership (Bass, 1985). A transformational leader focuses on creating dissatisfaction with the status quo, raising the aspirations of others, and shifting people and organizations into HRD-driven, high-performance models. In contrast, a transactional leader manages the status quo and holds others accountable to previously established objectives and norms, thereby solidifying the current state of the organization. Clearly, the latter leadership approach (in its pure form) is ill suited for leaders within an organization that is engaged in a significant HRD transformation effort.

Once again, Jack Welch reflects on this particular issue and how it emerged as a formidable barrier to the boundaryless HRD initiative. He discusses how GE came to the realization that their leadership ranks included what he called "Type 4" managers who "delivered on all the commitments, made the numbers, but didn't share the values—managers that typically forced performance out of people, rather than inspiring it" (Welch and Byrne 2001, 188). The key for the organization is dealing decisively with these Type-4 managers, through development interventions when possible, and involuntary separations when necessary. Only by facing this fact and making the appropriate yet difficult decisions regarding the transformational capacities of its leadership ranks was GE able to sustain the boundaryless HRD initiative and bring it to a successful completion.

Key 2: Institute Employee Involvement Early and Often, at All Levels

The organization must ensure that as many employees as possible, as early as possible, are actively involved in planning and conducting the HRD change effort in some capacity. It has been traditionally emphasized in the change management literature that employee involvement is critical to ensuring broad-based buy-in and support for transforming HRD from activity-based to results-driven both at the analysis/design stage and, even more important, at the implementation stage. The employees chosen for direct involvement must represent a broad cross section of the organization, both functionally and hierarchically. Although this traditionally emphasized benefit of ensuring broad-based employee involvement in the transformation of HRD is legitimate, and in and of itself a worthy purpose for employing the second key to this initiative, contemporary research is emerging that builds an even stronger case for doing so, which includes:

- facilitating organizational synergy by developing change-management competencies;
- understanding resistance and ambivalence toward change, specifically the HRD transformation initiative;
- demonstrating the application and integration of the three core domains of HRD.

The synergy created by soliciting the involvement of employees early in the transformation of the HRD process enhances the immediate transformation initiative and the long-term change management competencies of those involved via the creation of "knowledge reservoirs" for use at a later date. Employing this second key allows other employees to operate as change agents, thereby generating both short-term support for the HRD transformation initiative at hand and long-term capacity and competitive advantage for the firm as a whole. Increasing evidence indicates that knowledge transfer builds organizational competitive advantage (Argote and Ingram, 2000), which is reason enough for transfering the knowledge generated by this activity throughout the firm.

When employee involvement is truly broad-based and represents the direct involvement of employees from all functional and hierarchical levels of the organization, invaluable dialogue is generated throughout the organization. This dialogue can be leveraged to better understand the resistance and ambivalence that exists concerning the HRD transformation effort at hand, let alone toward organizational change in general.

Traditionally, HRD professionals would see this resistance and ambivalence as a threat to the change effort, and a target for quick elimination. On the other hand, contemporary thinking suggests that actually fostering this resistance and ambivalence during the early stages of the transformation of HRD is profitable (Piderit 2000). It is also a critical means by which an ultimately better solution will be developed for the project at hand, and serves as a developmental experience for building change competencies among previously change resistant employees.

Employing the second key to the transformation of HRD within their organizations enables HRD professionals to utilize all three of the core domains of HRD practice (*organizational learning, performance,* and *change*). By ensuring the implementation of this key within the context of an HRD transformation effort, organizations create a better, more comprehensively supported change solution while they build change capacity at the individual employee and aggregate organizational levels as well. In this way, talented and well-respected employees who are initially resistant or ambivalent toward an

HRD transformation effort can be identified and "converted" into highly leverageable supporters of the effort.

Key 3: Build a Clearly Articulated, Shared Vision

The organization must take the time to develop a shared and clearly articulated vision for the change effort at hand, and build support for it throughout the firm. *Vision* means a picture of the future with some implicit or explicit commentary on why people should strive to create that future (Kotter 1996). A vision is most often codified via a formal statement of purpose that serves as a consistent and compelling source of direction for the HRD transformation project (Jick 1992). This vision statement should be a natural output from the dialogue that occurs via the type of broad-based employee involvement discussed above, thereby ensuring that it is truly a shared statement of purpose and aspirations for the endeavor rather than simply a senior-management mandate. The final version of the HRD transformation vision statement must be simple but not simplistic, memorable but not gimmicky, specific but not overly technical, and challenging yet attainable.

Recently, we cofacilitated an enterprise-wide HRD transformation project for a state taxation agency that was guided by the following vision statement: "We will put the customer first, every time. We will develop and sustain a team environment. Our performance will be the benchmark for the nation." We believe this to be an excellent example of a formally articulated vision statement for an HRD transformation project; first, because it met all of the criteria listed above; namely, it was simple, memorable (without being trite), and easy for all HRD professionals to internalize and understand. Second, it was specific and challenging enough to be translatable into business-driven operational and behavioral goals that were eventually addressed via the three core domains of HRD practice (*see* Key 6: Setting Measurable Operational and Behavioral Goals). We further stress the importance of this connection between the formally articulated vision statement for the HRD transformation project and the specific performance goals defined in conjunction with the effort.

In the transformation process a good vision serves three important purposes; it:

1. clarifies the general direction for change;
2. motivates people to take action in the desired direction and helps overcome employees' natural reluctance to change;

3. coordinates the actions of different people by aligning individuals in a remarkably shared vision, and helps employees agree on the importance and value of change.

A shared vision clarifies the direction of change and helps employees agree on the importance and value of change without which interdependent people may constantly conflict. Kotter (1996, 70) contends that a good vision "acknowledges that sacrifices will be necessary but makes clear that these sacrifices will yield particular benefits and personal satisfactions that are far superior to those available today—or tomorrow—without attempting to change."

Key 4: Provide Frequent, Consistent, and Open Communication

The organization must ensure that as much information as possible is shared with all members of the organization at the appropriate times and in the appropriate manner. It is better to err on the side of providing too much rather than too little information, even if the details are still being developed. Several practical ways exist for doing this, including the establishment of twenty-four-hour telephone, voicemail, and e-mail services specifically designed for the purpose of gathering ideas/issues/concerns surrounding the HRD transformation initiative. Additionally, HRD professionals can write articles for all organization publications dedicated to outlining the current state and future plans associated with the project. Although these are worthy components of an improved communication plan and infrastructure, we propose that they are inherently impersonal, and as such they must be discussed during face-to-face interactions. This becomes particularly important as ambiguity and uncertainty surrounding the HRD transformation effort increase, the complexity of the messages that need to be communicated increases, and the potential for motivating positive behavior among the recipients of the messages increases (Lengel and Daft 1988).

Perhaps most important is the goal of remaining as transparent as possible regarding project-related information. The fear of the unknown is always greater than the fear of reality, especially among the frontline employee ranks within the organization. Thus, it is rarely profitable to intentionally withhold information pertaining to an HRD transformation effort (with obvious exceptions to maintain individual employee confidentiality as necessary). Too often, the purposeful "holding back" of HRD transformation project-related information threatens to undermine the confidence of the broader organization in the viability and even necessity for the project as a whole.

HRD professionals need to communicate short-term improvements (wins) that lay the foundation for sustainable long-term change. These help the transformation of HRD in at least six ways; they:

1. provide evidence that sacrifices are worth the effort;
2. reward change agents (HRD professionals and other leaders) by providing positive public recognition;
3. fine-tune vision and strategies by providing the guiding coalition with concrete data on the viability of their ideas;
4. undermine cynics and self-serving resisters by demonstrating the benefits of change;
5. keep organizational leaders involved and supportive by providing evidence that the transformation is on track;
6. build momentum, thus turning neutrals into supporters, reluctant supporters into active helpers, and so forth (Kotter 1996, 123).

Key 5: Leverage Talented and Trusted Employees as Co-Change Agents

As HRD transformation unfolds, the organization must identify those employees who have the highest level of credibility and influence among their peers and give them opportunities to lead the charge by modeling behavior. In this way, HRD professionals leverage the influence of these emerging co-change agents in support of the effort. Often the most powerful co-change agents are those employees or managers who had been staunchly opposed to the project during the initial stages of the project lifecycle. Having the foresight to identify these potential emergent change agents at an early point in the effort, and then intentionally and directly involving them in the analysis/design phase of the project is critical. Doing so often results in the *conversion* of these change resistors into enthusiastic and highly respected change leaders.

A traditional approach to change alignment would dictate executive coaching and concurrent reassignment to another functional area in the organization, giving the potentially troublesome supervisor an opportunity to become directly involved in the project only at a later date. Beer, Eisenstat, and Spector (1990) propose that such a solution is faulty and only serves to undermine further the project effort by focusing change-alignment efforts primarily on individual employee behavior rather than on roles and processes for a time-tested discussion of this common tactical mistake. Additionally, such action may simply postpone the inevitable should the change resistant manager prove unable to "convert" from being a "Type 4" manager, and thus need to be let go altogether. In this particular case, we strongly suggested and eventually prevailed in having the supervisor assigned to a key role on the design/development team. In the end, this "big risk" reaped "big rewards" for the organization in two specific ways. First, the supervisor responded to this developmental opportunity very positively, and the project experience served as a critical turning point in the acceptance of the HRD transformation and helped convert her into a transformational leader. Second, the accounts payable/receivable function led the charge for the HRD transformation effort as a whole. This provided two highly visible and credible early wins that would have been difficult if not impossible to achieve without the support of the supervisor in question, let alone the unified support of her peers.

Key 6: Set Measurable Operational and Behavioral Goals

A successful transformation effort requires the organization to develop meaningful individual and organizational goals designed to measure operational results and reinforce the development of the work skills, competencies, and behaviors consistent with the desired future state of the firm. Without operational and behavioral goals, the HRD transformation effort will simply be another example of *change for change's sake*, only serving to further reinforce the mindset that HRD is an inherently "soft" endeavor as opposed to a key driver of organizational strategy and bottom-line results.

Goals for the HRD transformation effort follow the classic SMART acronym; that is, the goals must be specific, measurable, achievable, relevant, and time-sensitive. Even more important, goals must be derived from the shared vision that emerged from extensive organizational dialogue and was codified through the formal HRD transformation's vision statement. Becker et al. (1997) believe that, without an alignment between the vision and the defined operational goals, the statement becomes empty propaganda and the goals run the risk of failing to address key strategic concerns. The result is a "deadly combination" that may lead to the demise of the HRD transformation effort altogether.

With these key factors in mind we turn our attention to our example. Recall that the formal vision statement for the HRD transformation effort was: "We will put the customer first, every time. We will develop and sustain a team environment. Our performance will be the benchmark for the nation." To achieve this vision, the HRD program identified several operational goals that included the following:

1. provide a single point of contact for individual income-tax customers within two years of project inception and within four years of project inception for business-tax customers;
2. redesign all "frontline" level jobs to emphasize task and team member interdependencies within four years of project inception, and
3. realize a 50 percent decrease in cycle time on individual income-tax accounts payable/receivable transactions within eighteen months of project inception.

These goals are precisely the type of operational goals necessary to provide (1) operational performance accountability and (2) strategic credibility for an HRD transformation effort. They support Becker et al.'s (1997) argument that it is essential to link an HRD program's vision statement to operational goals in order to demonstrate the "powerful connections" necessary for transitioning an organization's HRD practice from activity-driven to results-driven. The realization of these operational goals led to the state taxation agency in question being held as a benchmark for other state taxation agencies and all financial services firms (including those in the private sector). Eventually, the blueprint and methodology employed in conjunction with this HRD transformation effort became the road map for several other similar initiatives at different organizations around the nation.

Key 7: Celebrate Successes and Readdress Shortcomings

Although often overlooked, celebrating successes and readdressing shortcomings are a fairly straightforward endeavor. First, HRD leaders must hold its professionals accountable to its stated departmental goals while taking every opportunity to reinforce publicly and positively successes and readdress shortcomings in an appropriately aggressive manner. Second, HRD leaders need to take time to identify and celebrate legitimate successes, including holding plenary project-team celebrations and administering individual employee rewards such as project-related promotions or incentive bonuses.

Dealing with shortcomings is much more difficult, and ultimately more important, in terms of reinforcing the purpose and legitimacy of the HRD transformation effort. Handling an individual employee or team failure is simply an inherently difficult thing to do. However, it is critical for HRD leaders to take appropriate action when faced with performance shortfalls related to the HRD transformation effort.

HRD leaders need to identify performance shortfalls unless the executive champion or other members of an organization's leadership do so (Lupine and Van Dyne 2001). However, this approach may be less effective in terms of task performance and human resource maintenance among transformation team members. As with celebrating successes, several obvious and practical ways of addressing performance shortfalls are within the context of an HRD transformation effort, including breaking-up subinitiative project teams and replacing "Type 4" managers who are unable to convert to credible co-change agents. Such actions require courage and conviction, and will send a message loud and clear to the organization at large; that is, the HRD function has truly shifted from an administrative training function to a strategic and results-oriented driver of performance improvement and change.

Conclusion

HRD programs and their professionals are at a crossroad. They can maintain the status quo and be the organization's training partner or choose to become a strategic partner responsible for improving performance and facilitating organizational change. The former leads to business as usual while the latter opens the door to a new frontier for HRD professionals, one that positions them as important, influential, serious, and critical leaders within an organization. HRD professionals must choose the path they wish to travel. Choose wisely, for the path chosen will determine the destiny of HRD.

Managing the Human Aspect of Organizational Change

Jennifer V. Miller

The corporate landscape is littered with failed efforts at organizational change initiatives. From reengineering, to Total Quality Management, to Lean Manufacturing, leaders and employees alike have willingly (and not so willingly) entered into the latest "change initiative," only to emerge on the other side frustrated, demoralized, and embittered by the experience.

Why is this? A key factor is that leaders consistently underestimate the human response to change and its critical role in the ultimate success or failure of organizational change initiatives. Noted champion of corporate reengineering Michael Hammer recognizes the critical role that people play in a change initiative. In an interview in *The Wall Street Journal*, Hammer admitted that, in his enthusiasm to make companies more efficient and profitable, he forgot about people. "I wasn't smart enough about that," he conceded. "I was reflecting my engineering background and was insufficiently appreciative of the human dimension. I've learned that's critical" (White 1996, 1).

HRD professionals can play a strategic role in their organizations by positioning themselves with leadership as experts in the process of the human response to change. By doing so, HRD professionals provide essential expertise that increases the chances for a successful change implementation and thereby benefits the organization's health as a whole. To accomplish this task effectively, HRD professionals must be knowledgeable of the dynamics that humans experience as they move through change, be able to guide leaders successfully through a change process, and be prepared to deal with the inevitable setbacks that will occur.

Change as a Key Leadership Challenge

Drucker (1999, 5, 73, 92) takes a broad, historical view of the changes leaders will face in the twenty-first century. He compares and contrasts the industrial age of the 1800s and 1900s to the knowledge age that began late in the twentieth century. Drucker asserts that, just as traditional management was instrumental in increasing productivity for manual work, modern management must be transformed to play a similar part in increased productivity for "knowledge work," the biggest leadership challenge of the twenty-first century. "Unless it is seen as the task of the organization to lead change, the organization . . . will not survive," Drucker (1999, 73) states. Further, Drucker discusses the need for leaders to be "change leaders" who see change as opportunity. It is not enough to rest on an organization's past successes, because the changes that the twenty-first century will bring are vast, complex, and, as yet, unknown. Complacence could be an organization's Achilles' heel, Drucker warns. "It is futile to try to ignore the changes and to pretend that tomorrow will be like yesterday, only more so" (92), he says.

HRD as Strategic Partner to Senior Leadership

HRD professionals who position themselves as experts in the human-change process can provide an invaluable tool to senior leaders who are planning a change initiative. In order to give that advice, however, HRD professionals must be invited to the leader's table as an expert. In many cases, that invitation is still difficult to come by.

As with most occupations the role of the HRD professional has been a continually evolving profession, transforming from a mostly supportive and administrative role to a strategic role. Although the role of the human resource function is changing, there is still much progress to be made. Conner and Ulrich (1996) conducted a research study with mid- to upper-level human resource executives to evaluate the extent to which these executives were called upon to practice four primary roles—strategic partner, change agent, employee champion, and administrative expert.

The study showed that the strategic-partner and change-agent roles scored lower than that of employee champion and administrative expert, suggesting that HRD professionals are still not being called upon in great numbers to play a strategic role with leaders in their respective organizations. As such, HRD professionals must remain diligent in positioning themselves as valuable to their organizations beyond mere administrative functions. HRD professionals must be willing to understand both the core operational functions of their organizations, such as bill processing or customer service, as well as the strategic aspects of market positioning and future product developments.

It may appear to be an uphill battle, but there are actions HRD professionals can take to position themselves in a more strategic way. One action is to consciously develop strategic thinking skills. Linkow (1999, 34–37) puts forth seven competencies for the "strategically agile," two of which are critical for HRD professionals counseling executives: *multivariate thinking* and *valuating*.

Multivariate thinking is the ability to balance many dynamic variables simultaneously and discern the relationships among them. This holistic systems orientation sees the forest *before* the trees and also sees the trees, not to mention the spaces between the trees and the surrounding flora and fauna. People with multivariate thinking skills see the big picture, but they don't miss the details either. One HRD professional I know is masterful at this. He can always be counted on to ask unpopular questions like "What's the purpose for doing this? What are we trying to accomplish?" He continually acts as a beacon for senior management to help them keep their big-picture perspective. At the same time, he can describe in highly accurate detail the business and operational processes for any given project to which he's been assigned. It's the balance of a "helicopter viewpoint" and the understanding of line operations that gains this HRD professional credibility with senior management and makes his advice sought after time and again.

People who are experts at *valuating* seek to know and understand the underlying values, beliefs, and attitudes held by current and potential stakeholders. They are sensitive to the interests of others and can envision a direction that incorporates a balance of interests. Valuators tend to get a "gut feel" for how the stakeholders are seeing the situation and then they construct a consensus that optimally balances the range of stakeholders' interests. HRD professionals are often expected to play this role, which can be an easy one to fulfill. However, many HRD professionals can fall into a trap of seeming too "soft" or "warm and fuzzy" when they are seeking consensus. Many wise HRD professionals gather this information quietly by working one-to-one with key stakeholders. These HRD professionals then network outside their own organizations with trusted colleagues who act as sounding boards to help sort out the key issues. After receiving feedback from nonbiased listeners, the HRD professionals can then pitch their ideas to senior management. In this way, they have validated their "gut feeling" with objective outside opinions and are less likely to be focused only on the human elements to the detriment of business objectives.

Another way that HRD professionals can add value to a change initiative is to position themselves as experts in the process of change. Company leaders are very busy, with many competing demands on their time. Executives may have a desire to take the "human factor" into account, but in the day-to-day crush of a highly competitive environment, they may gloss over the human implications of initiating a change. HRD professionals can step in and offer assistance and advice in this topical area, providing much needed strategic information to leaders so that valuable time and money can be saved. It is up to the HRD professional to position this information as strategic—leadership may not see it as such. Therefore, by tying the change-process information to measurable results—a reduction in the number of sick days, a decrease in lost-time due to injuries, and improvement in productivity, the HRD professional will be speaking in a language that leadership is most able to understand. The next section outlines specific information that HRD professionals can use to improve their credibility when educating leaders on the dynamics of the human-change process.

What Is Change?

Numerous models of change and the change process exist to help HRD professionals understand the complex nature of the change phenomenon. Nearly all of the models have two primary components—organizational and humanistic—to help describe the change process. The next section defines change using these two broad categories.

Change Defined: Organizational Versus Intrapersonal

The *Merriam-Webster Collegiate Dictionary* defines *change* in a variety of ways: "to make radically different," "to give a different position, course, or direction to," and "to become different." Each of these definitions alludes to some type of transformation and insinuates that there are "before" and "after" aspects to the change. Although this is true, there is yet another element that HRD professionals must consider. In order to use the concept of change in a way that is meaningful and useful, one must draw a distinction between *organizational* change and *intrapersonal* change.

Organizational change occurs within an organization as a whole. It is a macrolevel view of change that takes into account the systemic nature of change. When referring to organizational change, one must consider the strategic aspects that a change may bring to bear on the organization. For example, if an organization is going to acquire a division of one of its competitors, the leaders of the organization must consider such issues as repositioning in the marketplace and the financial implications this change will bring.

Indeed, as the dictionary's definition suggests, organizations going through a significant organizational change will in fact "become different" in many ways.

Intrapersonal change, as the name suggests, is the highly personal, human aspect to the element of change. Intrapersonal *change* is the way that each person reacts when there is a connection to organizational change. This reaction is highly personal, and is as unique as a person's fingerprints. For every organizational change, countless intrapersonal changes occur. To follow the example listed above, when the company announces that it is buying a competitor's division, there will be many personal reactions to this news. These reactions may range from "Will I still have a job?" to "I don't agree with this decision" to "Great! A new opportunity!"

Change Versus Transition

Another important distinction that HRD professionals should draw in understanding the change process is that of the difference between change and transition. Bridges (1993, 3–4) contends that change is something that is external and situational. As such, change has a finite quality to it, with a definite starting point. This is the "before" and "after" aspect alluded to in the dictionary definition. In contrast, Bridges says that transition is "the psychological process that people go through to come to terms with the new situation" (4). He further asserts that unless a successful internal transition occurs, there will be no successful change.

Let's use this distinction between change and transition in an example. A company decides to move from issuing paychecks on a weekly basis to its salaried employees to issuing paychecks on a monthly basis. The "change" in this instance is the fact that the frequency of paycheck issuance will decrease. In fact, there will be a specific starting time to this change: "Effective April 1, we will begin to issue paychecks on a monthly basis . . ." The transition, however, is not as cut and dry. People will need to learn how to manage their cash flow differently. They may need to remember to change automatic bill-payment systems or to budget differently. Some people may experience anxiety over the change, whereas others see it as a temporary blip on their personal finance radar screen. Each individual will experience some sort of a transition as they move from the "old" system to the "new" one.

HRD professionals can help in two ways. First, they can ensure that there is an educational component to the communication of the change. For example, in the scenario of a changed payroll system, the HRD department can play a proactive role in the communication of the change by anticipating

peoples' reactions. Rather than assisting by simply posting the announcement in a company newsletter, they can feature a series of money-manage-
ment tips in the newsletter. Or, the HRD department can offer a series of fi-
nancial-planning seminars.

Second, HRD professionals can help by educating the champion of the
change in the actual change process. Whenever a change champion announces a change, HRD professionals must be ready to subtly educate executives. Let's say, for example, that the executive leading the payroll sends the
head of HRD an e-mail saying, "Would you please announce this payroll
change in your next newsletter?" The HRD professional could easily comply
and say, "sure" and let that be the end of it. In doing so, that HRD professional has missed a key opportunity to educate and influence a leader in the
organization. Instead, the HRD professional could engage the executive in a
conversation and say, "Sure, I'd be happy to post that announcement. Before I
do, I want to be sure I clearly understand the issue. My experience tells me
that people rarely respond to these types of changes without a few setbacks.
Let's cover all our bases to be sure that this transition goes as smoothly as
possible." The HRD professional then inquires about organizational change
factors and intrapersonal change factors to ensure that the transition will indeed go smoothly.

Organizational change, as defined earlier, is linked to Bridge's 1993 definition of change. It's the tangible, event-based aspect that is associated with
something that is about to become different. Intrapersonal change is tied to
Bridge's definition of transition. It takes into account the important humanistic aspects of change.

The Link to HRD

HRD professionals must be prepared to respond to all aspects of change—the
factual and logistical aspects that affect organizational change—and the psychological, human elements that are the hallmarks of intrapersonal change.
HRD professionals who can successfully coach leaders to understand both of
these phenomena will better increase the chances of a successful change initiative. The following sections elaborate on how to do this.

Organizational Change

Leaders are ultimately responsible for the success of their organizations. Often, changes must occur to achieve that success, and it falls to the leaders to
communicate and execute those changes. It's not a simple process by any

means. HRD professionals can help leaders sort through the complexities of implementing a large-scale change by helping them understand the overall architecture of a complex change.

Managing Complex Change

When coaching leaders, HRD professionals are often well served to have a simple, yet powerful tool to communicate the organizational aspects of managing change. Figure 3.1 can be a helpful visual aid.

Vision ➔ Skills ➔ Incentives ➔ Resources ➔ Action Plan ➔ Change

FIGURE 3.1   Five Factors of Managing Complex Change

As the diagram shows, there are five key elements to managing change.

Vision.   The leadership team must have a clear and inspiring vision of the change. The message must answer the followers' need to know "What's in it for me? How will making this change be better than staying the same?"

Skills.   Many times, a change requires the acquisition of new skills. The transition period must allow time for people to learn new skills and practice them.

Incentives.   Will it be worth people's time to do it the new way? What monetary and nonmonetary incentives and rewards will exist?

Resources.   Will people have the appropriate equipment, time, and other resources to do their jobs in this new environment? Or will they be asked to do "more with less"?

Action Plan.   To implement effective change, employees will need a plan of action. It must outline the goals in measurable terms and the consequences for not achieving those goals. In addition, there must be a system in place that allows people frequent and easy access to feedback so that they can gauge how well they are performing to the plan.

All five components must be managed well in order to have a successful change initiative. In addition, all five of these factors are external to employees. These are, by and large, the types of factors that leaders can control. Although leaders may not be able to control people's internal, psychological reaction to change, they can set the stage for an optimal reaction by managing these five factors.

Missing Factors in the Change Diagram

The Five Factors of Change diagram is a conceptual model that helps leaders see the big picture. In my practice, I have observed many smart, well-respected and talented leaders who take one look at the grid and say, "but we don't have time to _____." I have also found that the savvy HRD professional is prepared for this response and ready to speak persuasively as to why it's imperative to plan for all five factors on the grid. The following is a list of possible downfalls of not having each factor properly addressed. By helping leaders see the implications of ignoring one or more of the five factors, HRD professionals can help the leader ward off timely and expensive errors that could have been nipped in the bud with a bit of foresight. Figure 3.2 summarizes these pitfalls.

FACTORS					IMPLICATIONS
Vision ➔	Skills ➔	Incentives ➔	Resources ➔	Action Plan ➔	Change
_____ ➔	Skills ➔	Incentives ➔	Resources ➔	Action Plan ➔	Confusion
Vision ➔	_____ ➔	Incentives ➔	Resources ➔	Action Plan ➔	Anxiety
Vision ➔	Skills ➔	_____ ➔	Resources ➔	Action Plan ➔	Gradual Change
Vision ➔	Skills ➔	Incentives ➔	_____ ➔	Action Plan ➔	Frustration
Vision ➔	Skills ➔	Incentives ➔	Resources ➔	_____ ➔	False Starts

FIGURE 3.2   Missing Factors and Implications for the Change Process

Lacking *vision*, confusion reigns among followers. Research consistently validates that the communication of the envisioned new state is a critical factor in the success of any change initiative (APQC 1997; Kotter 2000; Senge 1999). Without a vision, people are unsure of the direction they should take. They know they should be moving, but toward what?

When *skills* are missing, people will most likely feel a sense of anxiousness. Even if the employees are excited about a proposed change, they will still feel concerned if they believe they lack the skills to perform in the new environment. A manufacturer that was installing a new computerized inventory system astutely managed this aspect of change. In addition to conducting computer-skills training on the new system for all employees, they assigned learning coaches and created learning labs where people could go to practice using the new software for two weeks prior to the system's implementation. The leadership understood that it wasn't enough to just "train" the people—the employees needed practice and reinforcement to feel confident in their newly acquired skills.

Lack of *incentives* to perform under the new change results in the failure to motivate employees to adopt the change, or the change will be gradual. Also, a high probability exists that people will revert back to familiar and possibly unproductive habits. Incentives can take both tangible and intangible forms. For example, a tangible incentive is that the "new" way will offer employees the option to go to a more flexible schedule. An intangible incentive is that the "new" way will allow people a better sense of accomplishment. Either way, these are powerful drivers of human behavior and must not be ignored.

Employees will be frustrated if *resources* are missing. When any type of resource—human, financial, or physical—is scarce or missing, people will be very agitated by the impending change. One midlevel manager once referred to all the changes she was asked to put her team through as "corporate whiplash." She said she'd no sooner tried to figure out the latest round of change, than a new edict would be issued. And with each new set of directions, came instructions to "do less with more." She was offered no additional resources to help implement the new change.

Change without an *action plan* will produce many false starts and wasted time. Some companies have a legacy of creating great ideas but fall short on the execution. One CEO recently confided to me, "We have no shortage of great ideas and a passion connected to those ideas. . . . where we fall down is we never seem to get out of the gate with half of these great ideas. I feel like our competitor is going to beat us to the market if we don't tighten up on our execution."

Intrapersonal Change

As mentioned earlier, the human response to change is a highly influential factor in determining the ultimate success of the change occurring in an organization. Ignoring or minimizing this aspect of change is one of the biggest mistakes that change champions make.

Emotional Responses to Change

Although leaders cannot directly control another person's emotions, they can be aware of these emotions and be prepared to help their followers through whatever emotional responses they are feeling in reaction to the change.

Many leaders are unable or unwilling to acknowledge or deal with the emotions of employees. Goleman (2002, 4–5) asserts that leaders often see discussing emotions in the workplace as inappropriate. He counteracts this view by saying, "research has yielded keen insights. . . . the best leaders have

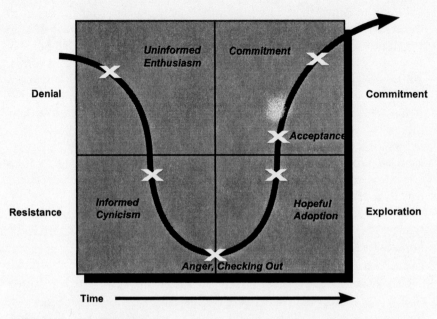

Denial

Commitment

Resistance

Exploration

Time

FIGURE 3.3   The Change Curve

found effective ways to understand and improve the way they handle their own and other people's emotions. Understanding the powerful role of emotions in the workplace sets the best leaders apart from the rest" (5).

HRD professionals have a distinct edge in this area. By nature of their training and daily experience, they are schooled to understand human emotions. This knowledge can be a powerful tool to HRD professionals who seek to counsel leaders who feel uncomfortable venturing into the complex territory of human behavior.

One such model of the human response to change is depicted in figure 3.3, the Change Curve. This diagram illustrates the typical emotions that people feel as they progress through some type of change. HRD professionals can use this diagram to help leaders understand the internal processing that nearly every person experiences when coping with a change. It's important to note that this change diagram illustrates typical human reactions to change. There is no "shortcut"—people must move through each of these phases at their own pace. Leaders who try to accelerate the process will only shortchange the entire effort.

In the upper-left-hand quadrant is the area of Uninformed Enthusiasm. This occurs early in the change process at a time when people are typically just hearing the news. The most prevalent emotion experienced during this time is "blissful" denial. People in this quadrant aren't truly in a state of mind to accept what is happening, so they reject any information that may cause them to behave differently. Phrases like, "Oh, it won't be that bad" or "Well, I'll be fine" are often heard in this phase.

In the second phase of the change curve, Informed Cynicism begins to take hold. More information has become available, and people are starting to sort out what the change means personally to them. They are comparing and contrasting what will stay the same and what will change. This is the point in the change curve where resistance happens. It's a natural part of the process. All "systems," be they human or organizational, are wired to maintain the status quo. Therefore, once people move out of denial and realize that there is a change, they begin to do things to preserve what they find comfortable. Phrases like "same monkey, different trees" and "it'll never work" are common in this phase.

At the low point in the curve is Checking Out. People have been resisting and now they're tired. They don't really accept what's going to change, but they don't have the energy to fight it any more. This makes them angry, and that's the most typical emotion found during this part of the change cycle. Typical phrases in this part of the cycle are "I give up! They can do whatever they want!" and "Whatever . . . just leave me out of it." Some employees will literally "quit" by leaving the company, but many stay on and quietly sabotage the change initiative. One company issued a new limit on daily meal expenditures. It was highly restrictive to employees who traveled to markets that were more costly than the average per diem. When traveling some employees sabotaged the new policy by buying their food at a local grocery store and then submitting expense reports for the total per diem and pocketing the difference. One manager, who traveled upward of 120 days a year, said, "If they [the company] won't pay to give us a nice meal, then I'll just go ahead and make a little profit. I don't mind eating in my hotel room."

As time progresses, the curve begins to swing upward into the quadrant of Hopeful Adoption. The anger passes, and now people are willing to take a look at other possibilities. The common emotion here is the willingness to explore. People are feeling that there is a possibility that the "new thing" will be somehow better than the "old thing." They are willing to listen to new ideas and perhaps even try out some new behaviors. They may say things like, "Well, it couldn't hurt to give it a try" and "What have we got to lose?"

Just over the border from Hopeful Adoption is Acceptance. This is a key transition point in any person's intrapersonal change journey. Once there is acceptance, people can move on to a much larger and stronger plane, which is

Commitment. But until there is acceptance, there will be no commitment. Leaders must beware of pseudo-acceptance statements like "Well, sure, I'll go along if you want me to," which is not a statement of acceptance. This person is giving conditional acceptance and is reserving the right to rescind acceptance at a later date. Many leaders have been lulled into a false sense of security in thinking, "my people are on board with this," when in fact their employees were still on the border of Hopeful Adoption or Acceptance.

The final phase of the change curve is found in the Commitment quadrant. At this point, true acceptance of the change begins. People are committed to it and are ready to move forward. They may still see pitfalls and have concerns, but they are truly ready to actively take part in the change. In many cases, people have been "testing out" the change and now see that it does indeed provide a benefit. This "seeing is believing" is often a key ingredient that's needed for people to become fully committed to a change. Phrases like "I wasn't sure at first, but now I'm sold" and "Let's get on with this" are signs that true commitment has occurred.

HRD plays a vital role in helping leaders understand the emotional and human aspects of change. When they educate leaders on change and use a specific change model, such as figure 3.3, HRD professionals do two things.

First, they position themselves as experts in the field of human nature. This allows HRD professionals to build credibility with executives in their organization. This credibility must exist in order for the HRD function to be seen as a truly value-adding function rather than a "nice-to-have" department or worse, simply a cost center.

Second, they provide specific and timely information that helps leaders make critical business decisions. In this way, HRD professionals are plugged into their organization's daily business. This focus on relevant issues ensures that the HRD professional doesn't get sidetracked by "nice-to-have" but irrelevant issues.

Guiding Leaders through the Change Initiative

Not only do HRD professionals educate leaders on the definitions of change, they serve as guides throughout the change process as well. It's not enough to simply say to a leader "Here's how we define change and the reactions you can expect from people—now get on with it." To do so would leave many leaders stranded; some leaders intuitively know how to execute the change, others do not. To be their most effective HRD professionals must be ready to play the role of guide, coach, and mentor with leaders who are championing a change. This section provides tools to prepare HRD professionals for these roles.

Key Elements of Successful Organizational Change

The first step in guiding a leader through a change process is to know the key aspects of effective organizational change. The American Productivity & Quality Center conducted a benchmarking study of "best practice" organizations in 1997. They found the following five factors to be consistently apparent in all organizations that had successfully implemented a large-scale change.

1. Committed and Active Participation of Leadership. For any change to be successful, a respected, credible leader must be at the helm. This is a consistent theme in much of the change literature (Collins 2001; Kotter 2000; Senge 1999). Additionally, the leader must be truly committed to, and a champion of, the change, not just offering lip service.

2. Culture Change. The APQC study highlights the transformation of an organization's "culture" as a distinguishing characteristic in successful change initiatives. They defined culture as "the collection of attitudes and behaviors embodied in an organization's work force." Their findings indicated that for a change to truly be lasting, a significant change in organizational norms, behaviors, and beliefs must occur.

3. Energetic Involvement of an Empowered and Educated Workforce. It is not enough to simply have a respected leader espousing a new vision. The workforce must be solidly behind any type of change. Change efforts will fail if there are only charismatic leaders trumpeting the change or announcing new change (of the month) programs (Collins 2001, 11; Goleman 2002, 232). Further, the workforce must be educated not only in the actual features of the change (the "what" will change), but in what they must now do differently (the "how" to make the change).

4. Effective Communication and Measurement. This is a multifaceted factor. In order to share the vision not only must leaders use communication, they must use it to signal progress and encourage employees to give feedback. It's also critical to communicate the progress the organization is making toward the change goal.

5. Aligning Human Resources Systems with the Goals and Objectives of Change. As noted in the section on managing complex change, there are various external factors that leaders can control that will increase the probability of success in a change initiative. When human resource systems such as compensation, performance reviews, and recognition systems are aligned with the change, corresponding changes in employee behavior are noted.

Senge (1999, 43) adds the human element to the mix. He contends that in order for any change to be sustained, there are three "fundamental reinforcing processes." The three processes must be in place in order for true, lasting change to occur.

The first fundamental process is that of *personal results*. People need to feel that their work matters on some personal level. They must feel connected to what they do each day and see value in it. This is the often heard "What's in it for me?" at play.

The second fundamental is a *network of individuals committed to the change*. These networks are typically informal in structure and are composed of people who have credibility with one another. These informal groups act as support systems and conduits of information, passing along tips of "what works" and "what doesn't," and providing encouragement along the way.

The third fundamental is linked to the *ability to produce results*. A lasting change will be more likely if it's seen as "worthwhile," and most worthy endeavors are somehow tied to the ability to improve results in some way.

Notice that of the three fundamentals, only the third, "demonstrating results," is directly related to organizational practices. The other two are rooted in human relationships—that of relationship to one's self and to others. This distinction is important, because leaders often focus on getting results and tend to minimize or diminish the importance of the human element.

How HRD Can Help Set the Stage for a Successful Change Implementation

Much of this chapter focuses on the strategic, educational, and advisory role that HRD plays with leadership when implementing a change. These are all vital aspects to ensuring that HRD is seen as a critical component of any change initiative. Let's take this one step further and assume that HRD has successfully educated leadership on an impending change and that leadership has listened and responded favorably. All of the strategic planning is in place—how can HRD set the stage for an upcoming change?

There are four ways in which HRD professionals can assist in a change initiative—*communicate, model the change, involve employees, and sell the change*. These aspects are derived from the successful elements of organizational change discussed earlier in the chapter.

HRD professionals can follow the example of their leaders and *communicate extensively* about the change in whatever venue is appropriate. One vice president of training and development was masterful at communicating change. She knew that the message must be heard several times and in multiple mediums for people to become accustomed to the change. Therefore, she worked with her entire staff (administrators as well as practitioners) to educate them on large organizational change. When the staff was conversant in the change, she then deployed her team strategically to "get the word out" in a variety of ways— a newsletter sponsored by the training and development department, group discussions held during workshops, and even "watercooler" conversations prompted by senior members of her staff. By doing this, she was helping senior management move the message into the mainstream. She also knew that her team was providing a valuable service to the company as a whole, by helping ease change concerns and moving people through the change curve.

The example above also demonstrates the second way in which HRD professionals can help set the stage for a change—*modeling the change*. By having a team well educated in the upcoming change, the vice president for training and development was demonstrating that her team could "walk the talk" of the new change. Not only did this demonstrate commitment to the change to the senior management, it also provided an example of a positive role model for employees.

The third way in which HRD professionals can set the stage for change is to *encourage employee participation*. This can be achieved in several ways. First, HRD professionals can encourage leaders to solicit input and feedback from employees on an upcoming change. This feedback is invaluable to leaders in refining their message and gaining buy-in from employees. Second, HRD professionals can encourage participation themselves by facilitating dialogue sessions (both structured and impromptu) when the need arises. One financial services company held "group gripe" sessions for employees when the organization initiated a new compensation plan to its sales force. The sessions were structured and led by a skilled facilitator from the HRD department. There were ground rules to prevent the sessions from becoming a free-for-all. Although the sessions were charged with volatile emotion, they did provide senior management with some key information that led to revisions in the system.

HRD professionals can also use impromptu opportunities to *sell employees* on the change. The HRD role often provides an opportunity that senior managers lack when dealing with frontline employees. One senior training specialist in the automotive supplier industry makes it a habit to circulate on the shop floor a day after any large changes are announced. He has no formal agenda; he walks through the shop floor, chatting with people and gauging their reaction to the change. "I find that if I'm casual about it, and neutral about my opinions regarding the change, I can get a lot of unbiased feedback," he says. He then takes that information and crafts a communications plan that includes clarifying misinformation, reinforcing key messages, and "fun facts to know" and includes that information on the company's intranet. This informal approach helps to "sell" employees on the benefits of the change without seeming to be "touting the party line."

Coaching Leaders Through the Change Initiative

Throughout this chapter, we have referenced the need for HRD professionals to be able to coach leaders throughout the change process. This is indeed a valuable skill and therefore is addressed more completely in another chapter of this book. It is important that HRD professionals understand that they can play a vital role with leadership by acting as a coach. In addition to the skills listed in chapter seven ("Performance Coaching"), it is also important to note that "coaching" in this context is that of adviser, sounding board, and confidant. In order for HRD professionals to be invited to play any of these roles, they must first gain credibility as discussed in the earlier section on becoming a strategic thinker. When leaders view HRD professionals as people who can help them sort through complex issues in an efficient manner, they will be asked to take on an advisory role.

Setbacks: Preparing for Pitfalls

Launching an organizational change, whether large or small, is a complex and challenging process. Even leaders with the best of intentions fall short in one or more areas. The following section outlines several potential pitfalls that leaders must consider.

When HRD professionals are aware of these pitfalls they can play a proactive role with leadership to help them ward off false starts and, ultimately, a failed change attempt. These pitfalls can be separated into two broad categories that correspond with the two types of change discussed earlier in this chapter. The first pitfall involves factors that correspond with organizational change and are *external* to an employee. Many of these external factors are things that leaders do or can somehow proactively control, such as access to financial resources or feedback on employee performance. The second pitfall concerns factors that are *internal* to an employee; these relate to the intrapersonal change discussed earlier.

Why Transformation Efforts Fail: External Factors

Most transformation efforts fail in large part because of the amount of time leadership estimates that the transformation process will take. Collins

(2001, 221) studied 1,435 established companies to determine what types of change initiatives made a company "great," as defined by excellent performance in several financial and human indices. In the top companies, his research indicated that a significant improvement in performance happened as much as a decade after what he calls the "transition point"—the point at which a senior executive at the firm made a conscious effort to enact a change. Further, Kotter (2000, 67) cites an example of a successful company that had its peak performance five years after the transformation effort began.

Kotter (2000, 61) proposes an eight-stage change process that is sequential. He calls this series of stages the "steps to transforming an organization." Kotter also presents a corresponding pitfall to each of the eight stages of transformation. If any of these pitfalls occur, they will undermine the success of the change being implemented. Kotter lists the following pitfalls as reasons why an organizational transformation may fail to occur. He says that leaders:

1. Fail to establish a great enough sense of urgency. More than 50% of companies in Kotter's research failed in their transformation due to lack of rigor in this phase. How urgent must things appear? Kotter asserts that at least 75% of management must be genuinely convinced that the danger of staying the same is more harmful than the change being proposed.

2. Do not create a powerful guiding coalition. A coalition in this case is a group of influential people who are committed to the cause. They are not all necessarily in executive positions, but it's always true that the head of the organization that is undergoing change (be it the CEO for a whole company, or head of a division) is on board. It is key in this phase to create momentum, and for a small organization this may involve five people. In larger organizations, the number is closer to fifty.

3. Lack a vision. People need to clearly see where the change will lead them. If the vision is detailed or blurry, people won't buy in. Kotter suggests that leaders be able to articulate the vision in five minutes or less and be able to elicit understanding and interest within that five minutes as well.

4. Undercommunicate the vision by a factor of ten. Leaders often think that if they hold a meeting and send out a few follow-up e-mails, that the communication will stick and that people will "get it." They underestimate how many times and in how many different formats people must receive information in order for it to sink in.

5. Do not remove obstacles to the new vision. Sometimes the obstacle is a resistant person in an influential position. Sometimes it's a process or

procedure that impedes progress for the new change. Leaders must be on the watch for everything that may challenge the fledging change from taking root.

6. Fail to plan for and create short-term wins. In order for most people to sign up for a large change, they need to see that there will be some evidence that the change is producing results. Leaders must plan for and then execute strategies that will allow people to see that progress is indeed being made.

7. Declare victory too soon. As mentioned earlier, leaders often underestimate just how long it will take for a transformation to occur. At times they see success and are satisfied that the change has taken place. It may have, but old habits die hard and declaring victory too soon will kill momentum.

8. Fail to anchor the changes in the organization's culture. Above all, it's imperative that all systems within the organization link to the new change. If the change runs counter to the organization's culture and norms, then the change will be doomed.

Challenges Impeding Profound Change: Internal Factors

In addition to leaders who set an appropriate context, vision, and support system for employees during a change, there are also internal, human reactions to contend with. Senge (1999) asserts that any change represents a threat to the "system"—in this case the organization. The organization will naturally "push back" on what it perceives to be a threat. Senge goes on to say that leaders who are trying to innovate typically focus on their innovation—what they are trying to "do," rather than on how the system's norms and culture will react to the innovation. "No progress is sustainable unless innovators learn to understand why the system is pushing back and how their own attitudes and perceptions (as well as other forces) contribute to the 'pushback'" (26).

Senge outlines ten challenges that are possible whenever a change is announced. These challenges appear in the form of typical human responses to an upcoming change. Although the responses represent a personal concern unique to each individual, addressing these challenges becomes a leadership task. Some responses require assurance and understanding on the leader's part, while others require a change in process or procedure. The ten challenges are:

1. Control over one's time. People are often not granted enough time to adjust to the change or practice new skills.

2. Inadequate coaching, guidance, and support. Often, a change is thrust upon employees with an expectation that they will somehow figure out how to cope.

3. The relevancy of the change. If people don't see the connection to how the change will make a difference to them personally, they will be less likely to adopt the change. It's often said that people don't change unless the pain of staying the same is worse than the pain of the change.

4. Management clarity and consistency of message. A huge gap often exists between what leadership asks of employees and espouses to be "the new way around here" and what the reality is. If leaders are not "walking the talk," then they can't possibly expect their employees to do so. A vice president of human resources was known throughout his company for giving stern lectures to new supervisors about the importance of conducting performance reviews. The irony is that none of the vice president's direct reports ever received timely performance reviews from him, unless each employee personally pestered the vice president into conducting a review.

5. Fear and anxiety. It's a natural human response to mistrust the announcement of a change. Many of these concerns will be unspoken and will masquerade as other issues, such as "We don't have enough time."

6. Negative assessment of the process. Often, people will use the same measuring stick to assess the new process that was used to evaluate the old process. This isn't always the best measuring tool and leads to erroneous conclusions that the new process "isn't working."

7. Isolation and arrogance. When people don't communicate across departmental boundaries (or even within work teams), they create invisible walls and an "us versus them" attitude. This leads to arrogance and a sense of "we're doing it the 'right' way, even if it's not the 'new' way."

8. Power struggles. A change often signals a transfer of power. People rarely enjoy relinquishing power, so there can be struggles between the old and the new regime.

9. Inability to transfer knowledge so others don't have to "reinvent the wheel." Even when a change is progressing fairly smoothly, there can be a stalemate as the pilot group or first adopters try to transfer what they know to new groups.

10. Clarity of organizational purpose and strategy. Although the vision may be communicated clearly at the outset of the change, people will need to stop along the way and periodically reevaluate the change in the context of their current situation. Change is a highly fluid and dynamic process—and what

often starts out as a clear direction needs clarifying and redefinition as the process progresses.

Conclusion

HRD professionals play a key role in guiding their organizations through change. To do so effectively, HRD professionals must understand the change process from both an organizational and a personal standpoint. Failure to account for both of these viewpoints results in unsuccessful change initiatives. HRD professionals help leaders be change champions by coaching them on (1) the change process; (2) the elements of successful organizational change; and (3) the challenges that threaten successful change initiatives. When HRD professionals position themselves as strategic partners to leadership, they provide a relevant and valuable service to the organization as a whole.

Globalization and HRD

Michael J. Marquardt

In considering the issue of globalization and HRD, one first needs to address a number of questions. Questions such as, Is globalization a benefit or a detriment to the development of human resources? Is globalization inevitable, and, if it is, how can the HRD profession maximize its benefits and limit its negative or exploitive elements? Where can HRD professionals have their greatest impact and place their priorities? Should we work in the political and public sectors as well as with corporations and private entrepreneurs? And should environmental sustainability and global ethics be a concern to HRD professionals? But before these questions are explored, let us first define *globalization* itself.

What Is Globalization?

Globalization is used to define a combination of factors—a single marketplace with growing free trade among nations; the increasing flow and sharing of information, connections or links of people around the world; the opportunity for organizations and people to shop around the world and not be constrained by national boundaries. A relatively new phenomenon that emerged in the last part of the twentieth century, globalization has caused and was caused by a converging of economic and social forces, of interests and commitments, of values and tastes, of challenges and opportunities. Four main forces quickly brought us to this global age—technology, travel, trade, and television. These four Ts have laid the groundwork for a more collective experience for people everywhere. More and more of us share common tastes in foods (hamburgers, pizza, tacos), fashion (denim jeans) and fun (Disney, rock music, television). Nearly 2 billion passengers fly the world's airways each year and more than 1 billion of us speak the global language—"broken English." People are watching the same movies, reading the same magazines, and dancing the same dances from Boston to Bangkok to Buenos Aires.

Globalization: A Force for Evil or Good?

Globalization is a highly controversial issue, and the concept has acquired a considerable emotive force. Some view it as a process that is beneficial—a key to future world economic development—and also inevitable and irreversible. Others regard it with hostility, even fear, believing that it increases inequality within and between nations, threatens employment and living standards, and thwarts social progress.

Opponents of globalization argue that it is overly profit driven, that it is a tool of the powerful to dominate and control the world. They also believe the benefits of globalization are reaped only by a few organizations from the richest countries in the West, and that there is no accountability in the process. They also believe that scarce natural resources are being exploited for the benefit of the industrialized economies and at the expense of future generations. Korten (1999) and Kaplan (2001) argue that globalization is merely a form of neocolonization or neoimperialism, a reemergence of a process that was started centuries ago.

Antiglobal proponents see people losing their jobs while facing the uncertainties and fluctuations of the global economic environment. They point out the inequity created by today's global economy. The world's richest 225 people have more assets than the poorest 3 billion people do. The top fifth of the world's people consume 86% of all the goods and services, while the bottom one-fifth subsists on a mere 1.3%. Antiglobalists are also worried about power passing to international organizations——like the mysterious, behind-closed-doors dispute-resolution mechanism of the World Trade Organization (WTO)—as well as to multinational corporations. There is the fatalistic sense that people can no longer insulate themselves, their children, and their families from an alien culture—largely from the United States—that embodies values and beliefs that they just find unacceptable.

Proponents of globalization, on the other hand, believe that globalization has made the world a better place, a world that will eventually lead to economic prosperity, political freedom, and world peace. Friedman (2001) noted in a speech at George Washington University that globalization is the result of the "democratization of finance, technology, and information, but what is driving all three of these is the basic human desire for a better life—

a life with more freedom to choose how to prosper, what to eat, what to wear, where to live, where to travel, how to work, what to read, what to write, and what to learn." A globalized world is one in which there is a free movement of ideas, people, values, and systems across the globe. Friedman further points out that globalization has provided the best opportunities for democracies and good governance—Mexico, Ghana, and Bangladesh are just a few examples. The poorest countries and the least democratic countries—North Korea, Burma, Cuba, and Sudan—are also the least globalized countries. "Their problem is not too much globalization. It's, in fact, too little."

The key attraction for globalization according to Micklethwait and Wooldridge (2000) is freedom. People bemoan restrictions on where they can go, what they can buy, where they can invest, and what they can read, hear, or see. Globalization by its nature brings down these barriers, and it helps to hand the power to choose to the individual. Global markets create competition that yields better goods and services at better prices. People all over the world will have opportunities and better-paying jobs that never existed in closed nonglobal economies.

Sachs and Warner (1999) of Harvard University discovered through their research that developing countries with open global economies grew by 4.5% per year during the past twenty years, while those with closed economies grew by 0.7% per year, thus doubling in size every sixteen years, while closed ones must wait a hundred. In the Republic of South Korea, for example, absolute poverty is now less than 5%, and the literacy rate has increased from around 30% in the mid-1950s to more than 95% today.

Globalization has been a prime force for spreading knowledge and technology. Foreign investment brings not only an expansion of the physical capital stock, but also technical innovation. Knowledge about production methods, management techniques, export markets, and economic policies is available at very low cost, and this knowledge represents a highly valuable resource for the developing countries.

Perhaps the greatest value of globalization is its potential in creating a world of peace. Economic growth has been identified as one of the strongest forces that turn people away from conflict and wars among groups, tribes, and nations. Global companies strongly discourage their respective governments to war against countries in which they have investments. Focusing on economic growth encourages cooperation and living in relative peace. Kofi Annan, secretary general of the United Nations, has noted: "Whatever cause you champion, the cure does not lie in protesting against globalization itself. I believe the poor are poor not because of too much globalization, but because of too little."

Critical Need for HRD in the Global Environment

Obviously, the pro- and antiglobalization forces disagree on the impact and value of globalization. There appears, however, to be little dispute on the inevitability of the forward march of globalization. There also is agreement on both sides that globalization can and does create pain and suffering, especially if the human side of globalization is neglected. Thus, the real issue is not stopping or promoting globalization, but rather how to ameliorate, lessen, or eliminate the negative effects of globalization and to enhance and leverage its powerful positive effects.

Thus HRD professionals have a responsibility to step in and take the leadership role, to be sure that globalization has a human face with long-term benefits for all of humanity. For isn't HRD, at its heart and essence, concerned with the learning and enhancement of individuals, of groups, of organizations, of communities, of nations, and, ultimately, of the entire world? According to McLean (2001), Bates (2002), and many others, the HRD profession must include not only economic development and workplace learning, but it must also be committed to the political, social, environmental, cultural, and spiritual development of people around the world. Global success depends upon utilizing the resources and diverse talents and capabilities of the broadest possible spectrum of humanity.

At no time in history has HRD been more critical in solving critical economic and social problems faced by a wide array of groups, communities, organizations, and nations. A growing number of people, companies, and countries are now beginning to look to HRD professionals for strategic thinking and for help in succeeding in the global arena. HRD can be a mediator mechanism where value and goal conflicts between work systems and sustainable human-development needs can be negotiated and resolved at both the micro and macro levels. HRD should be concerned about all humans, and thus become a key broker in developing a world that serves the interests of all.

Unless we act, human conditions will worsen on a worldwide basis. Unless we act, economic development and human development will not occur. The world would then face increased exposure to external risks of all kinds, including economic disruption, forced migrations, ethnic strife, cross-border health crises, famine, fundamentalism, regional conflicts over resource use, weakened states, and ecoterrorism.

Eight Areas in Which HRD Can Positively Impact the Forces of Globalization

There are a number of key areas in which HRD can maximize the beneficial elements of globalization and limit its dehumanizing forces. However, the most significant value and greatest leveraging emerges from focusing on the following eight areas:

1. Political Development;
2. Economic Development;
3. Human and Social Development;
4. Organizational and Workplace Learning;
5. Education and Vocational Training;
6. Global Leadership Development;
7. Technology and Knowledge;
8. Environment Sustainability.

Let's examine why each of these areas is so crucial for initiating and sustaining long-term and communitywide human development, and what are the most strategic and effective roles the HRD profession should play.

1. HRD and Political Development

HRD professionals are rarely involved in political development, in the development of democracies, in creating clean and transparent governments, in propounding fair, nondiscriminatory legal practices. However, there is certainly no more critical dimension that impacts human development on a local, national, or global scale. The failed efforts of assistance programs over the past fifty years, be they public or private, bilateral or multilateral, demonstrate conclusively that good government is absolutely essential for technical or financial assistance to have any impact. Hundreds of billions of dollars have been spent on development by the World Bank, UN agencies, governments, and religious groups on programs for the people living in dictatorships and closed government systems, and, without exception, the conditions and development of the people of these nations are worse today than before the aid was first offered. The training, technical support, and financial assistance have resulted only in supporting, strengthening, and maintaining corrupt and immoral governments. The people remained poor, powerless, and threatened.

Ethical, free, transparent government is the *sine qua non* of human development. In a recent speech Friedman (2001) noted that the secret for societies and organizations to capture the positive benefits of globalization is "all about the fundamentals. It's about . . . good governance, institutions, free press, and a process of democratization. If you get the fundamentals right, the [benefits] . . . will find you, and globalization will basically work. You get them wrong, and nothing will save you." Thus, unless there is political freedom, democracy and good governance, there is little or no improvement in the lives of its citizens.

Political development involves the collective development of institutions like schools, corporations, legal systems, banking systems, and health care systems. There is a symbiotic relationship between public government development and human development. For example, a country's literacy and mortality rates and the GDP are indicators of both economic and human development. In a society where personal development is a priority (high literacy, mortality rates), the chances of finding developed institutions are higher (high GDP and employment rates).

HRD can help governments create policies that will be expansive and not create reactive barriers that ultimately hurt their citizens. HRD should encourage and train political leaders and government officials on policies that encourage country integration into the global economy while putting in place measures to help those adversely affected by the changes. HRD should encourage policies that focus on several important areas:

- strong institutions and an effective government to foster good governance without corruption;
- structural reform to encourage domestic competition;
- macroeconomic stability in order to create the right conditions for investment and saving;
- outward-oriented policies to promote efficiency through increased trade and investment;
- education and vocational training to make sure that workers have the opportunity to acquire the right skills in dynamic changing economies;
- well-targeted social safety nets to assist people who are displaced.

2. HRD and Global Economic Development

The living standards in many poor countries are not catching up with rich ones. Today nearly half of the world's 6 billion people survive on less than two U.S. dollars a day. Thus, a prime goal for HRD worldwide needs to be the elimination of the persistence of such abject poverty. Poverty is such an important HRD issue because it deprives people of choices and significantly reduces the level of well-being, limits participation in political and development processes, and is associated with unemployment, underproductivity, poor health, nutrition, housing, and personal security.

Recent history shows that the common factor of successfully emerging countries is a shared openness to trade (Bhagwati 2002). If governments try to protect particular groups, like low-paid workers or old industries, by restricting trade or capital flows, it may help some people in the short term, but ultimately it is at the expense of the living standards of the population at large. Governments should therefore pursue policies that encourage its integration into the global economy while putting in place measures to help those adversely affected by the changes. The economy as a whole will prosper more from policies that embrace globalization and promote an open economy, and, at the same time, squarely address the need to ensure that the benefits are widely shared.

The traditional focus of most HRD efforts has been to improve the economic lives of workers, and this remains an important concern upon which to build upon benefits of globalization. The experience of the countries that have increased output most rapidly shows the importance of creating conditions that are conducive to long-run per capita income growth. Economic stability, institution building, and structural reform are at least as important for long-term development as financial transfers. What matters is the whole package of policies, financial and technical assistance, and debt relief, if necessary.

HRD can and must be a crucial tool for building and maintaining the reservoir of skills needed for economic and social development. Singapore, Korea, China, Ghana, and Chile provide examples where HRD has been a key part of the national strategy to foster sustainable economic development.

3. HRD and Human and Social Development

A number of human and social development areas have slowly improved over the past several decades. Infant mortality and maternal mortality have been brought down; the percentage of people suffering from hunger and malnutrition has likewise been reduced; food production per capita has grown by 25% during the past decade; access to education has been broadened worldwide, reflected in a 12% increase in the adult literacy rate since 1990 (up to 76% worldwide). Eighty-four countries (including 49 in the developing world) now have life expectancies of 70 or above.

Despite significant progress in many parts of the world, notably East Asia and China, the overall development picture over the decade is not a pretty one. We entered the new millennium with over 1.2 billion people in extreme poverty, more than 100 million kids not in school and nearly one in every three countries in the world poorer than they were at the beginning of the previous decade. More than 9 million people starve to death each year, 75 percent of whom are children under the age of five. (It should be noted, however, that twenty years ago nearly twice as many children died each year.) Health conditions are much worse in poorer countries. Half of the women in undeveloped countries are malnourished during pregnancy, resulting in weakened babies and lower IQs. Women generally receive lower wages, have low life expectancies in poor countries, work longer for less, and suffer a higher level of literacy.

Thus, much more needs to be done in each of the *basic human needs* (as defined by the UN Development Program—the lower two rungs of Maslow's hierarchy). Some strategic HRD roles could include the following:

Health—Development of national health policies; training of health aides, especially for rural areas; intensification of the population and family planning programs by strengthening all aspects of service delivery; priority attention to the provision of safe drinking water and proper sanitation; expansion and strengthening the quality of health services at all levels; consolidation and strengthening of basic health care services through synchronized measures; unified actions for the prevention and control of HIV/AIDS.

Housing—Generating safe affordable shelter for all citizens; encouraging simple but culturally appropriate housing; educating governments in recognizing that decent, energy-efficient homes contribute to social cohesion, improved health, and better use of fuel and other resources.

Nutrition—The Green Revolution has enabled dramatic increases of agricultural production. Former breadbasket countries have become food importing countries because of corrupt or shortsighted economic policies. Training agricultural extension agents as well as senior agricultural officials are necessary.

Transportation—Jobs as well as the distribution of foods and service require effective transportation and mass transit systems, thus HRD should assist in the transfer of best practices from around the world.

4. Organizational and Workplace Learning

Organizations will increasingly need to operate and compete for customers on a worldwide scale. They will need to use global sourcing of human resources, capital, technology, facilities, resources and raw materials. Global capabilities as well as local cultural sensitivity to employees, customers, and patterns will become critical to the success of organizations.

HRD can help to build successful global companies by developing globality in six areas:

Corporate Culture—establishing the global vision, mind-set, values, activities of the organization.

People—identification, recruiting, training, development, and global experiences for all workers.

Strategy—developing a global mission and philosophy; undertaking analysis and diagnosis of global opportunities and threats; establishing specific global goals and performance targets; forming strategic global contingencies and plans; implementing appropriate alignments and integration of resources; and evaluating, modifying, and reapplying global strategies.

Operations—globalizing all operations including research and development, manufacturing, quality, marketing, finance, administration, marketing, and personnel.

Structure—changing the spatial dimensions of the enterprise so as to create a more flexible organization.

Learning—creating the learning organization, globalizing training programs and the curriculum (Marquardt 1998; Marquardt and Reynolds 1994).
Specific HRD roles can include some of the following:

- preparing employees for overseas assignments; includes cross-cultural training, expatriation and repatriation support, language training;
- building global teams and enhancing their ability to work virtually across time and distance;
- creating systems for continuous quality improvement to meet global customer expectations;

- developing cross-cultural communication skills;
- developing abilities in learning how to learn through action-learning processes;
- building capabilities in knowledge management and technology systems.

Organizations need individuals capable of operating effectively in diverse cultural environments, using increasing complex organizational structures and communications patterns, and managing change using multiple integrative business strategies with an embedded global perspective. Sustainable development is possible only when human beings are properly educated and trained.

5. Education and Vocational Training

Changes in global market dynamics, technology, and the structure of labor have created work that is much more complex, abstract, and knowledge based, thereby increasing the number of jobs that require higher levels of reading, math, problem solving, interpersonal, and other workplace skills.

McLean (2001) notes that as unskilled and semiskilled work become less needed, it is important that countries put greater efforts into developing high-quality education systems so that students can be prepared for the more skilled jobs of the future. This requires that HRD professionals focus on both the training of teachers and administrators, as well as policy makers at local, state, and national levels. We should also utilize our organization development skills to ensure an environment in which professional education can work effectively and students can learn effectively.

The UN's Agenda 21 Forum noted that all forms of education such as formal education, public awareness and training, are processes by which human beings and societies can reach their fullest potential. Education plays a critical role in promoting sustainable development and building capacity for addressing environment and development issues."

Both formal and nonformal education are indispensable to changing people's attitudes so that they have the capacity to assess and address their sustainable development concerns. It is also critical for achieving environmental and ethical awareness, values and attitudes, and skills and behavior consistent with sustainable development and for effective public participation in decision-making. To be effective, environment and development education should deal with the dynamics of the physical/biological and socioeconomic environment and human (which may include spiritual) development, should be integrated in all disciplines, and should employ formal and nonformal methods and effective means of communication.

The demand for learning and performance improvement grows exponentially. Periods of rapid change create a premium on learning—for both individuals and organizations. Prosperity and growth are the rewards for those who are the fastest at learning and putting their learning into action; stagnation and decline are the penalties for delay. In an era when it is knowledge rather than physical assets that increasingly defines competitive advantage, the process of managing knowledge becomes a central part of the learning process.

As societies move from the industrial era to the global knowledge era, job requirements will continue to become more challenging (Drucker 2001). Employees will move from needing repetitive skills to knowing how to deal with surprises and exceptions, from depending on memory and facts to being spontaneous and creative, from risk avoidance to risk taking, from focusing on policies and procedures to building collaboration with people. Work will require "higher-order" cognitive skills—the ability to analyze problems and find the right resources for solving them, and often with both limited and conflicting information.

However, most of the world's potential workforce lack these new basic skills necessary for the modern workplace. HRD should assist vocational education programs to develop competencies that fill these emerging new gaps. HRD professionals should also help to:

- Establish or strengthen vocational-training programs that meet the needs of environment and development with ensured access to training opportunities, regardless of social status, age, gender, race, or religion;
- Promote a flexible and adaptable workforce of various ages equipped to meet growing environment and development problems and changes arising from the transition to a sustainable society;
- Strengthen national capacities, particularly in scientific education and training, to enable governments, employers, and workers to meet their environmental and development objectives and to facilitate the transfer and assimilation of new environmentally sound, socially acceptable and appropriate technology and know-how;
- Ensure that environmental and human ecological considerations are integrated at all managerial levels and in all functional management areas, such as marketing, production, and finance.

6. Global Leadership Development

HRD professionals should develop global leaders with a number of global capabilities, including skills for:

- understanding global business opportunities, the ability to recognize and connect trends, technological innovation, and business strategy;
- setting an organization's direction—for creating vision, mission, and purpose;
- implementing this direction in an ethical and culturally sensitive way;
- personal understanding and effectiveness with multicultural teams and alliances in a global context;
- thinking globally with a global mind-set.

Leaders with global mind-sets, according to Rhinesmith (1993), seek to continually expand their knowledge; have a highly developed conceptual capacity to deal with the complexity of global organizations; are extremely flexible; are sensitive to cultural diversity; are able to intuit decisions with inadequate information; and have a strong capacity for reflection. A leader with a global mind-set sees the world globally, is open to exchanging ideas and concepts across borders, and is able to break down provincial ways of thinking. Global leaders are able to balance global and local needs as well as operate cross-functionally, cross-divisionally, and cross-culturally around the world (Dalton, Ernst, Deal, and Leslie 2002).

HRD should also help prepare those global leaders with a strong sense of ethics and a concern for global sustainability. Twentieth-century cost-cutting, downsizing, and reengineering have cut out the "soul" of many companies. Many workers worldwide feel unfulfilled, unmotivated, and find little meaning in their work. Too often people have been seen as disposable in their jobs. Thus, global leaders need to help companies set off on journeys that are attempts to create a sense of meaning and purpose in the workplace and a connection between companies and communities. The combination of head and heart is a competitive advantage.

HRD professionals should encourage leaders to:

- institutionalize ethics throughout the organization via a proactive ethics program;
- set the organization's ethical tone by tying ethics to shared company values and goals. Employees are more likely to follow corporate ethics

programs and policies when senior management proactively endorses
and practices them;

- exhibit high ethical standards by leaders who set the example for all
  employees;
- create an ethical climate in the organization that accommodates
  differences in cultures worldwide;
- develop a reward system that encourages good ethical behavior,
  empowers employees, equates ethical behavior with success in
  business, and treats ethics programs as a continual learning process.

Leaders must be encouraged to look beyond their shareholders and economic growth toward stakeholders by improving lives, sharing wealth, and
shaping the future of the global communities in which they operate. Economic and social responsibilities of businesses should contribute to the social
advancement, human rights, education, and vitalization of host nations and
the world community. They should be protecting and improving the world
environment and avoiding participation in and not condoning unethical and
illegal business practices. HRD can thus help to serve as the conscience of the
organization.

7. Technology and Knowledge

Technology can powerfully propel peoples and nations to leapfrog intermediate, slower routes of development. Technology's lower costs and greater
widespread accessibility make its resources increasingly available to the poor
as well as the rich.

Perhaps the most valuable use of technology at present is its ability to
spread knowledge. The recent World Bank report "Knowledge for Development" begins:

> Knowledge is like light. Weightless and intangible, it can easily travel the
> world, enlightening the lives of people everywhere. Yet billions of people ev-
> erywhere still live in the darkness of poverty—unnecessarily. Knowledge
> about how to treat such a simple ailment as diarrhea has existed for cen-
> turies—but millions of children continue to die from it because their par-
> ents do not know how to save them (World Bank 1999, 1).

Poor countries differ from rich ones not only because they have less capital, but because they have less knowledge. Forty years ago, both Ghana and
the Republic of South Korea had virtually the same per capita income. By the

early 1990s South Korea's income per capita was six times higher than Ghana's, primarily attributable to Korea's greater success in acquiring and using knowledge.

HRD professionals should focus on helping nations and people to:

1. Acquire knowledge—encourage the creation of knowledge locally through research and development as well as tapping and adapting knowledge available elsewhere in the world;

2. Absorb knowledge—ensure universal basic education with special emphasis on extending education to girls and other traditionally disadvantaged groups; create opportunities for lifelong learning; support tertiary education, especially in science and engineering;

3. Communicate knowledge—take advantage of new information and communications technology—through increased competition, private-sector provision, and appropriate regulation—to ensure that all have access, including the poor.

8. HRD and Environment Sustainability

Globalization has already harmed the environment and still poses a threat to it in the future. Protecting the environment is one way in which the HRD profession can help develop the lives of, and provide equity for, future generations. We can undertake a number of activities such as:

- Advocate that governments and national professional associations develop and review their codes of ethics and conduct so as to strengthen environmental connections and commitment;
- Ensure the incorporation of skills and information on the implementation of sustainable development at all points of policy- and decision-making;
- Encourage national and educational institutions to integrate environmental and developmental issues into existing training curricula and promote the exchange of their methodologies and evaluations;
- Encourage all sectors of society, such as industry, universities, government officials and employees, nongovernmental organizations and community organizations, to include an environmental management component in all relevant training activities, with emphasis on meeting immediate skill requirements through short-term formal and in-plant vocational and management training;

- Strengthen environmental management training capacities;
- Establish specialized "training of trainers" programs to support training at the national and enterprise levels;
- Develop new training approaches for existing environmentally sound practices that create employment opportunities and make maximum use of local resource-based methods;
- Encourage nations to develop a service of locally trained and recruited environmental technicians able to provide people and communities, particularly in deprived urban and rural areas, with the services they require, starting from primary environmental care;
- Enhance the ability to gain access to, analyze, and effectively use information and knowledge available on environment and development;
- Prepare environment and development-training resource-guides with information on training programs, curricula, methodologies, and evaluation results at the local, national, regional, and international levels;
- Assist governments, industries, trade unions, and consumers in promoting an understanding of the interrelationship between good environment and good business practices (Arnold & Day 1998).

Planning and Implementing HRD Programs for a Global Future

HRD professionals need to be concerned with overall societal human needs. This new mind-set begins with how we assess the needs of the global work place and community, including political, economic, social, and cultural perspectives. We must develop a holistic, systems approach that recognizes how the worker and learner are part of an entire human-development chain.

In developing and implementing programs for improving the lives of people, a number of traditional as well as new strategies are available. Perhaps the most important trend in human resource development today is that of the changing relationship between the trainer and learner, the donor and recipient, the manager and worker. New methods of participation and association should emphasize joint action throughout the development cycle. The recipients (be they governments, workers, students, or citizens) now have much greater input on programs and projects, helping determine the needs as well as the means. The basic objective should be changed to reflect the increased capacity of communities to be the actors and craftsmen of their own sustainable development.

Establishing Societal Objectives in the Global Environment

HRD must move beyond its traditional individual and organization-centered foci to consider broader issues related to improving and sustaining socioeconomic progress. These include organizing educational systems to meet sustainable social and economic development, using education and training interventions to enhance political participation as well as address issues of health, nutrition, population growth, urbanization, and environmental degradation.

HRD is concerned not only with what is, but more important, with what should be. The inclusion of sustainable human development as a fundamental HRD objective is important because it makes explicit the normative component inherent in all HRD concerns and activities. The process of developing human resources should be action-oriented, practical, and aimed at solving problems in ways that enable individuals and organizations to reach their goals.

HRD, from a global perspective, also needs to extend and expand its objectives. At the *individual level*, HRD addresses the needs of individuals performing in a work system to enable them to improve and maximize their contribution to the overall work-system performance. The objectives are oriented to acquisition of individual expertise or potential. At the *performance level*, goals are set that are derived from and contribute to the mission of the overall work-system teams, production units, divisions, or departments. *Process-level* objectives focus on customer, administrative, and management processes to improve the way work gets done. *Mission-level* objectives are more universal and examine the relationships among HRD, long-term performance, work-system goals, and the work-system's external environment. At its highest level *mission-level* objectives seek to enhance learning, human potential, and high performance in work systems in ways that contribute to sustainable human development. HRD goals must both (1) bring about intergenerational equity (work-system goals and activities that are carried out in ways that preserve the precondition of development for future generations), and (2) achieve intragenerational equity (conduct of work systems in one community should not undermine the ecological, social, economic, or political ability of other communities to meet their needs or improve their quality of life) (Bates 2002).

There are a number of essential elements of planning for HRD as well as the benefits of planning for global and sustainable development. The most important planning element is that of individuals and organizations learning at the same time as they implement plans so they can optimize outcomes (that is, action learning). Planning contains the essence of what it means to be a global citizen. Planning in HRD maintains the vital element of redefining and improving the processes of work and living. HRD planning involves strategies for bringing out the full potential of people across the world as global citizens.

Conclusion: HRD and the Future

Humanity stands at a defining moment in history. We are confronted with a perpetuation of disparities between and within nations, a worsening of poverty, hunger, ill health, and illiteracy, and the continuing deterioration of the ecosystems on which our well-being depends. Without the development of human resources in societies around the world, the continued degradation of natural resources will occur, as more humans are not offered the resources and skills necessary for them to become productive constituents and contributors to world progress. Friedman (2001) warns that globalization can be incredibly empowering and incredibly disempowering. It can be incredibly enriching and incredibly impoverishing. It can enhance environmental preservation and turbocharge environmental degradation.

HRD is fundamentally concerned with the enrichment of the quality of human life. It can become the instrument that can break the cycle of poverty, and lead humankind to an era of global development and peace. HRD professionals must commit themselves to enable people everywhere to:

- have access to educational opportunities and becoming lifelong learners;
- be treated by all with respect in a socially equitable and dignified manner;
- have the ability to participate in governance decisions that affect their lives and the community in which they live;
- have the potential to earn sufficient income to supply themselves with ample nutrition and shelter, and other material and esthetic needs.

Human resource development truly has the power to lead global development, in which economic and technological development are also people-centered and nature-based. We must be on guard so that damage to ecosystems can be prevented, biological diversity and productivity are conserved, the entropic physics of energy and matter is moderated, and the economy is converted to rely on the perpetual resources and resilient technologies. Developed and sustainable societies communize civic order and decision-making, democratize capital creation and work, and vitalize human-need fulfillment, ensuring sufficiency in meeting basic needs. This is what human resource development, properly designed and implemented, can do for the betterment of people around the world.

5

A View to Human Capital Metrics

Gary D. Geroy
Donald L. Venneberg

The changing place of work in life, evolving value-laden views toward rules governing relationships between enterprise and individuals, nontraditional personal-life strategies, and intense competition for valued skills form a new and complex dynamic to be faced by managers and HRD professionals responsible for strategic responses to performance management and organizational change process issues. The psyche of human capital is changing, and it is shaping a world where its needs compete with that of the enterprise.

Human capital metrics, what it embodies, and how it engages these issues are critical questions for enterprise and its planners. Without a full understanding of the evolving views and potentially conflicting values held by human capital, enterprise and its planners may be doomed to inefficient and ineffective utilization, a more and more critical and increasingly elusive resource. Equally, unwittingly committing the enterprise to a direction that outpaces any potential of maintaining the necessary supply-side human capital is fraught with pitfalls.

Human capital metrics is not about formularization of skills and abstract attributes associated with task performance and behavior. Rather, it transcends these matrix creations and objectifying models; serves to organize a situational view to the relationships of these matrices; and provides understanding of the strategic "why" imperative.

Human capital metrics as a construct not only embraces human capital performance-capacity factors that are immediately apparent to the short-

horizon success of the organization, but also the long-term strategic imperative issues critical to transcendental accomplishments of the enterprise. More
importantly human capital metrics embraces both those human capital performance capacities variables that are both active and passive, and which influence individual behavior and views relative to enterprise versus personal-
need strategies.

Creating terms that are simultaneously pleasing; provide a sense of venera-
tion; and a belief of knowing and accomplishment is a frequent strategy for
simplifying and giving meaning to concepts that we believe we understand. It
is also a frequent strategy for giving meaning to concepts we don't understand, nor are able to describe. Does this mean we shouldn't do it? To the
contrary! Creating terms can be a catalyst for engaging in the debate, which
leads to ultimate understanding, structure, or description of the concept. And
so it is with the term human capital metrics. This is a term heard with increasing frequency, yet one which may not yet have universally accepted
meaning or description. In the discussion that follows, we will provide a lens
for viewing the concept of "human capital metrics."

Imaging

We can, and frequently do, turn to imaging as a means framing a concept. We
begin our discussion by reflecting on some of the imagery potentially con-
jured up by the term human capital metrics. For some, it might conjure up
the image of an outdoor chess board, with frozen-form people aligned by
rank and purpose, some in action poses wielding tools, others in solitude
poses of ponderance, others in animated interpersonal dialogue. For others,
the image might be more one-dimensional, taking the form of a chart whose
row and column titles suggest a summary of complex interplay between variables mated inside cells. Still others might conjure up the image of mathe-
matical formulas and equations not dissimilar to a Leontieff's input/output
model. So we are challenged to evolve our experiences, and knowledge, to
view human capital metrics as a concept which on one hand has universality,
and yet can be applied in ways that give localized meaning.

Although we will not suggest who (by role or occupation) might conjure
up these or other equally valid images, we will suggest that any image evoked
is grounded in part or whole in our training, philosophies, and experiences.
We further suggest that if any images we encounter are simple, and easily understood—the more likely we are to accept and adopt it, and conform our behaviors and cognitive processes to its norms as a means to deal with phenomena which is new our experience.

A universal view to human capital metrics embraces a view of a number of issues and their influence on strategic thinking regarding this concept. These include: capacity for task, organizational goal-setting rationale, role versus individualism and mobility, generational culture influence, and investment.

In the following, we will discuss influencing factors that frame human capital metrics as a dynamic, rather than a static image. With this understanding, decisions made by organizations and individuals about choice and investment can be improved. The chapter constructs the concept of human capital metrics by using the notions of human capital, goal norming, role transformation, and culture as building blocks. The chapter further presents metrics as a strategic imperative.

Building the Concept

Appreciating the value of human capital in the enterprise is well established. Equally valued is its strategic imperative. This strategic imperative is analyzed in classic processes that identify appropriate and needed human performance attributes necessary to address current and short horizon organization issues. However, this limited view may not be sufficient for understanding the evolving human capital complexities that will create the sustainability challenge for organizations.

An ancillary dynamic that is driving organizations to potentially outstrip their current or reasonably attainable human capital is the norm based marketing messaging concerning the who, how, what, and why of their existence. This is the false-norming phenomenon.

The Human Capital Component

In our view, concern for investment and management of human capital is grounded in several notions. The first notion is that contribution to organization bottom line through investment in the development of human performance capability is economically viable. This notion has been postulated from the early work in the area by Swanson and Geroy (1984, 1986, and 1987) to the most recent efforts by Phillips, Stone, and Phillips (2001) to operationally implement ROI analysis strategies for human capital expenditures.

Within this notion, the new view of human capital is reflected in several examples. First is the increased willingness of organizations to engage in knowledge and skill development that can address performance needs of the organization in a manner that is active and immediate. In addition, there is the considerable evidence that organizations that invest significantly in the development of their human capital gain the additional value of increased retention of their skilled employees. For example, in his book *Human Capital*, Becker (1993) found that,

> After a few years of frequent job changes, most workers settle down and remain with the same company for a long time. Workers and their employers get bonded together in large part because of the on-the-job learning and training. Therefore, it is not surprising that job changes are common among unskilled workers and uncommon among skilled workers (20–21).

However, the fact that we now want to measure the investment in economic terms, the efficiency and effectiveness of the acquisition of this skill/knowledge, and other intrinsic performance-enhancement capacities means that we view it as capital investment. In other words, decision makers are willing to invest in the types of business capital that are most likely to give competitive (short- and long-term) advantage or goal achievement. In the new view of human capital, this means a basic paradigm shift from one which views investment in human capital as a cost-only choice to one that suggests realization of return on investment that is measurable with quantitative data.

The second notion is that ongoing efficient knowledge management can provide the passport to success for organizations and people, and that strategic investment in the development or acquisition of knowledge and skill, as well as other intrinsic variables (such as attitude), is critical to organization performance. This notion embraces the view that there is more involved in task performance than just skill and knowledge, and that these dynamics must be strategically viewed and managed. Gilley and Maycunich (2000) discuss some of these notions as *performer development goals*, which are linked to organizational and strategic business goals. For example, some of these performer developmental goals are:

- Acquisition of new job skills intended to improve performance outputs and activities;
- Acquisition of new knowledge that will help employees with complex problem solving or decision making;
- Acquisition or improvement of attitudes associated with one's performance (Gilley and Maycunich 2000, 291).

The strategic process is associated with the determination of whether retention, establishing career paths, or outsourcing options (among other possibilities) are critical for creating a human capital response to task performance and accomplishment needs. Questions such as should we retain and retrain to develop the human capital capacity needed, fire and hire the capacity needed, or outsource for the capacity, become common and critical human capital, strategic choice questions. In any one (or combination) of these options, we are investing in human capital based on some strategic or normative bias.

These notions have extensive literature and investigation supporting the why, how, and when of their validity and utilization, and role in management-decision and performance-management processes. However, simply combining the two notions and their underlying principles into a term such as human capital metrics is not sufficient to provide an understanding for a broader universal view of what this embraces.

Setting the Imperative . . . The False-Norming Phenomenon

Human capital factors become complex when organizations become imbued with external constituents' marketing norms concerning organizations' correct place and processes. Positive outcomes can occur when visions representing norms are communicated to organizations, which may be within the organization's current or reasonably accumulatable human capital capacity. Complexity arises when organizations respond to norms marketed to the organization in "should be," "should do," "how to," and "need to" messages that require unreasonably extending beyond current capacities and comfort norms. Problems arise when organizations respond to an acquired responsive, self-imposed belief that they are substandard because they are not doing the things that idea-marketing identifies as success, and accept with shallow reflection that the espoused norm is the correct norm for them. Organization responses such as expansion, diversity of product or services, capital and technology acquisition, market expansion or new market venture, cutting apparent cost-only centers to show positive paper position or achieve high-expectation stockholder payouts, and the like, are not unusual.

One question that emerges is how the biases or norms for what are appropriate organizational behaviors and goals are established. To a very large degree this is established in response to norms held by various organization constituents' portrayals of what is valued evidence of what is arguably defined as easily describable indicators of success. This may lead to pitfalls when organizations evolve strategic thinking about human capital investment. The demand to achieve "success" as diversely defined by a number of constituents frequently provides conflict, and the development of some superordinate be-

TABLE 5.1   Organizations' Response Actions Relative to False
Organizational Norming

False Norm	Norm Response Action
Accepting what you *"should be"* to be successful	Market share and image adjustment
Accepting what you *"should do"* to be successful	Systems creation/modification
Accepting *"how to"* be successful	Behavior modification
Accepting *"need to"* be successful	Capacity and capability performance development

lief structure designed to satisfy all. This vagueness of the process of establishing this belief is proportional to the degree to which organizations accept performance norms, which are outside an organization's capacity—in human performance capacity as well as other terms. This phenomenon, which we refer to as "False Organizational Norming," manifests norm-response actions that are summarized in table 5.1.

To the false-norm response-action human capital question, the answer process then becomes one of developing a "matrix" of human performance capacity variables that directly and immediately address allowing organization metamorphosis into the form that illustrates as many of the defined success indicators as possible. As a management process, we determine what matrix of human performance capacity variables are needed to address achieving the success indicators. As with any matrix, interactive planning dimensions are created, and the intersecting cells completed. In the case of human capital planning, this matrix frequently intersects such things as roles with tasks, or tasks with job classification, and defines the skills set in the intersecting cell both in terms of type and quantity. The determination of shortage or surplus of needed skills leads to the previously discussed question options concerning human capital investment.

Though this approach may have served, and continue to serve, organizations successfully, changes in the supply/demand equation in the labor market may require further strategic considerations and modifications as to how we must view human capital. In this archetype, ROI is a piece of the picture, but not the whole picture. ROI for improvement of human capacity is at the task-apparent level only, and as such is a short horizon.

A matrix approach such as gap and task analysis, which identifies specific skills for each task or behavior attributable as an indicator of success, can be objectively determined. However, organization decision-makers often extend some normative-biased subjective judgment about ability or willingness of individuals to apply their capacity to task. Therefore, critical to addressing organization performance needs is the choice that may be made by potential supply-side members of the labor market about what abilities they may choose to develop to meet current or future professional and personal needs that they view as important.

Like organizations, individuals also are inundated with images associated with success, appropriate activities, acquisition imperatives, and behavior. As with organizations, individuals may be prone—to varying degrees—to extend beyond their capacity to respond to this norm marketing. This may take the form of debt, upgrading homes and cars for upgrading's sake, career shifts, or the like. What is critical in both the organization and individual scenario is the message that you "can have," "can do," and "can be" if only you do what we tell you—in other words respond to our norm for you.

These norms may not be what the organization—without the market pressure—would consider appropriate or consistent with their capacity grounded goals. While all organizations and individuals must constantly evaluate what they want to do in reference to their ability, values, and needs, to respond to the market messaging without serious analysis is dangerous business thinking.

Giving face validity by reacting to marketing norms creates the phenomenon of false norming, which can be destructive to both organizations and individuals. A false norm is a norm to which organizations and individuals respond that is beyond their current or readily/reasonably achievable capacity (in both passive and active terms), sufficiently outside their transformation and transactional ability as to be reasonably accomplishable without undue risk, or loss of sustainability.

Metrics Versus Matrix

To extend the horizon for human capital investment, organizations need to embrace the idea of a *metrics* rather than a *matrix* view of human capital investment. As previously illustrated, the matrix approach defines type and quantity of skill sets needed for immediacy of task application and accomplishment (short horizon). As such a matrix view of human capital is grounded in the construction of definable variables and is dominated by organization rather than individual choice. A longer horizon for structuring investment in human capital would embrace overarching dynamics, and be dominated by empathy for individual choice. We label this as a metrics view of human capital investment.

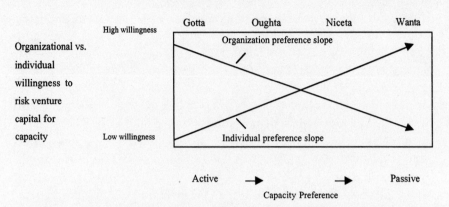

FIGURE 5.1   Composite Metrics View of Human Capital Development Issues

In this view, there are two important guiding principles. First is that human capital *capacity* is composed of skills, knowledge, and the influence of attitude and other intrinsic variables. Second is that human capital capacity is *passive* and *active*. Passive capacity is that knowledge that the individual gains and is available for potential/future use. Active capacity is knowledge that the individual gains and is available for immediate use.

Within the metrics construct of thinking, individuals and organizations differ on their view of the dimensions of *need* for active and passive capacity, and the characteristics of that need. The first dimension of *need* can be categorized according to the ". . . ta" phenomenon. This phenomenon suggests that degree of need can range along a continuum from "Gotta-have-it, Oughta-have-it, Niceta-have-it, to Wanta-have-it."

Within the metrics construct, individuals and organizations may not agree on active or passive capacity preference. Moreover, there may appear to be an inverse relationship between where individuals and organizations set the priorities of human capital investment relative to their view of the dimensions of need (the "ta" phenomenon). Figure 5.1 illustrates this notion from the point of view of both the individual and the organization. Finally, as noted, the metrics construct considers both active and passive capacity, and the willingness of individuals and organizations to risk venture capital to build these capacities.

The metrics construct begs reflection of the question: "*Why—given some satisfactory level of commitment of individuals to be positive contributing members of an organization, concerned for its welfare and success—would such dis-*

parity in preference potentially exist?" An answer may be found by a new way of viewing human capital investment.

Although the new perspective for the organization continues to embrace skill and the development of knowledge capacity for task accomplishment within defined roles (traditional view) as a priority, it also extends to integrate role diffusion and individual mobility within the organization and critical dynamics. In addition, the new perspective extends to considerations associated with intra-economy mobility of individuals currently in organizationally defined roles. Moreover, the perspective is no longer one-way. Rather, it provides for an organizational view of human capital that embraces the legitimacy of the individual's view of human capital investment from an equally valued—albeit opposite to tradition—perspective. In this latter scenario, individuals look for investment in them by the organization and through their own self-sponsored efforts for their own current or future betterment (passive capacity building).

Role Issues

A dimension that affects this new perspective of the development of human capital capacity is the shift over the past few years of the role behaviors of individuals in the organization.

Traditionally, the role of the individual in the organization was clearly and formally defined in the organization structure by such things as the organization chart, table-of-organization, job description, and so forth. In addition, the system, that framed the operational behaviors of the organization, also bounded the role occupied by individuals. These in combination offer little latitude for legitimized outside-the-role behaviors (*see* figure 5.2).

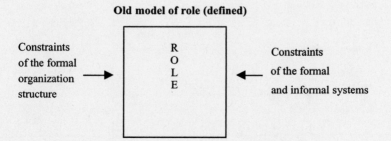

FIGURE 5.2   Traditional View of Imposing Constraints of Role Evolution

The Fuzzy Dimension: Role and Organization Value Systems

In recent years, more enlightened organizations have viewed the role of the individual in the organization as having a slightly broader, albeit fuzzy dimension to that historically defined by the enterprise. Frequently this includes both consideration of the individual's potential for growth through strategic career-path initiatives within an established role and experiments with activities ancillary to the role. This consideration embraces the notion of *role potential*. However, within the construct of human capital metrics, the new perspective provides that individuals equally embrace this notion.

The individual with the organization's acceptance of the "fuzzy dimension" of roles can strategically look to future roles in the organization for which there may be a need to evolve passive capacity for this future need. Additionally, the individual may see potential for new roles in other parts of the economy, which also may require development of passive capacity—from the current time reference perspective. This also fits the notion of role potential. The difference lies within the point of reference being utilized—that of the organization or the individual. This new role model based on role potential is illustrated in figure 5.3 as a strategic combination of strategic role-core (current matrix view and active capacity) and role-potential (metrics view and passive capacity). This could occur through vertical or horizontal integration. In the vertical integration, assumptions about need for skills and performance associated with roles that were above the current role are assumed. In horizontal integration, assumptions about need for skills and performance associated with roles that were lateral to the current role are assumed.

When organizations address human capital investment, they must be concerned with two dimensions. The first, current role-core capacities, and second the future role-potential. As previously discussed, one dynamic that is a poten-

Role Potential	Role Core	Role Potential
*Vertical integration	*Static integration	*Lateral integration
*Metrics view and passive capacity	*Matrix view and active capacity	*Metrics view and passive capacity

FIGURE 5.3   New Model of Role (Core and Potential)

tial pitfall for organizations is the degree to which there is incongruence between the organization and individual views of capacity needs for both the current and potential roles. However, another powerful dynamic also enters this mix. This dynamic is the generational cultural influence on views toward role accomplishment, and the place of role tenure as a life and professional strategy.

Depending on the values generational members hold toward this strategy, the desire for passive- versus active-capacity development and its content definition may be a point of conflict between organizations and individuals. Referring to the "ta" phenomenon, this means individuals and organizations could have differing views or preferences for investment in capacity development.

Among other dynamics, the generational value structure regarding the place of work in life will influence an expanded view of core plus potential. An important result will be a shift toward the value of individualism in society and organizations. This response to false norming—either social or organizational systems generated, externally defines role and conformity expectations.

Generational values of course will influence the individual's view of role, and will influence the degree to which that individual builds personal passive capacity to move between organizations for intra-economic mobility. This individualism will influence also the role of the individual in the organization. From the individual's point of view, they will aspire to perform current role effectively, and grow as much as possible within the organization, while simultaneously developing passive capacity for intra-organizational mobility (*see* figure 5.4). The cultural construct that will drive this shift is the impact of the change in generational values of the new workforce.

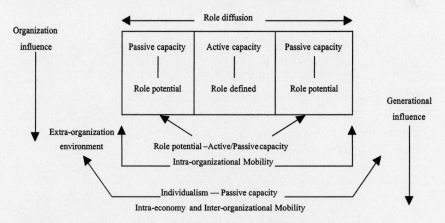

FIGURE 5.4   Organizational and Generational Influence of Role Diffusion and Capacity Building

In summary, role diffusion and emerging generational value systems will impact how both organizations and individuals view investment in human capital. The implications being that these two dynamics are part of the broader metric. The cultural construct that will drive this shift is the impact of the change in generational values of the new workforce.

Generational Values and the Need for Individualism as an Influence on Human Capital Metrics

The need for individualism as an influence for gaining performance capacity varies with the norms and values of each generational cohort in the current or future workforce (Zemke, Raines, and Filipczak 2000). Two generations, the baby boomers, who were born between 1946 and 1964, and Generation X, who were born between 1965 and 1979, dominate the current workforce. Just entering the workforce are the *Millennials*, the *Nexters*, or *Generation Y*, who were all born between 1980 and 1996. Those who were born since 1996, who will be the new workers beginning in the next decades, are currently labeled *Generation Z.*

The post–World War II baby boomers were born and raised in the heady years after the war when the economic outlook was rosy, and their parents (who mostly came of age during the Great Depression) were now doing well and focused on making sure that their kids had more than they, both while growing up and in terms of education and job possibilities. Not only did they receive a great deal of attention from their parents but, as the largest generation to date (76 million), they also were the focus of the media. It was "all about them."

The early members of this generation were imbued with their parents' value of working hard to get ahead, but just as important was the value of loyalty to the organization. Their paradox was that they also led the protests against the Vietnam War and the revolt against the authority of parents and political leaders. "Don't trust anyone over 30."

The baby boomers are now reaching maturity and some are even taking early retirement (or being laid off) from their companies and institutions. Those remaining in the workforce are fast becoming the "establishment" they railed against in the late 1960s and early 1970s. They now embody the statement by the late Walt Kelly's Pogo comic strip character: "We have met the enemy and he is us." Their values and norms now largely conform to those of the organization, and their desire for individualism and the development of passive versus active capacity is diminishing (*see* figure 5.5).

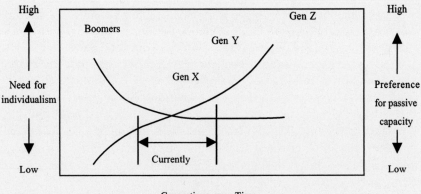
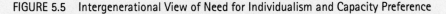

Generations over Time

FIGURE 5.5   Intergenerational View of Need for Individualism and Capacity Preference

Generation X (or Gen X), on the other hand, came of age in an era of economic decline and was the first generation in the twentieth century who expected not to do as well economically as their parents. They are part of the "baby bust," and represent a much smaller population (51 million) than the boomers. Unlike the boomers, the Gen X'rs had less time devoted to them by their two-income-generating parents. They were the first "latchkey kids," learning early on that they were largely on their own. As adults, unlike the boomers, they do not view the companies and institutions for which they work as a "home" or an extended family. They value independence and believe that they need to take care of themselves and are skeptical of, if not outright rebellious toward, organization norms, values, and goals, which suggest conformity. Their mantra: "What's in it for me."

Gen X'rs' need for individualism through capacity building is far stronger than the boomers' need. They focus primarily on developing passive capacity for future mobility (either within or outside the organizations) (*see* figure 5.5). As clearly articulated by Brown (1997, 2).

. . . knowing that they must keep learning to be marketable, Generation Xers are lifelong learners. They do not expect to grow old working for the same company, so they view their job environments as places to grow. They seek continuing education and training opportunities; if they don't get them, they seek new jobs where they can.

The leading edge of Generation Y is just now reaching adulthood and beginning to enter the workforce. This generation of 70 million is rivaled in size only by the boomers. According to some estimates this generation will represent more than 40% of the U.S. population within the next decade (DeRogatis 2001).

Gen Y'rs were raised almost totally during a time of economic prosperity. For Generation Y, nothing much was ever at stake. Significantly their generation has not experienced a defining social or political event, such as the Vietnam War was to the boomers. However, the September 11, 2001, terrorist attacks on the World Trade Center and the Pentagon may become defining events for this generation. Their values are reflective of this prosperity: optimism, civic duty, confidence, achievement, sociability, diversity and "street smarts" (Zemke 2000, 132). These values may result in a new generation of workers who want to inculcate the values of the organization.

Generation Y members also have grown up during the era of "the customer is king," and are used to customization in products and services tailored to their desires. It is likely that this will carry over into the workplace, where they will expect individual development tailored to them. Thus their focus will also be largely individualistic and toward the development of passive capacity (*see* figure 5.5). The good news for organizations is that Gen Y's are also likely to be more loyal to the organization than the Gen X'rs, and therefore they may be willing to use their passive capacity for meeting goals. The key for their managers will be to assure that they are given the maximum opportunity to use this capacity.

Generation Z (born after 1996) is still in the early formative stages. It is, therefore, too soon to tell how their values will translate into the workplace. However, one thing they do share with Gen Y is that they will likely expect customization and tailoring to their needs. This may result in an even greater individualistic outlook toward performance-capacity building (*see* figure 5.5).

The stronger value of individualism by the newer generations will result in a shift of their role in organizations. The need for individualism will result in a preference for developing passive capacity by individuals to build their portfolio. A common emergent strategy is to embrace growth within their current organization, and then to seek opportunity in the broader economy (*see* figure 5.5).

To address this change in generational values of the new workforce, organizations will have to embrace human-capital-metrics thinking to allow for the maximum individuality of its members for developing their passive capacity, as well as organization-driven active capacity, while retaining the talent of the members.

Metrics as a Strategic Imperative

A critical underpinning to metrics as a strategic imperative lies in a view put forward by Dr. Greg Wang of Performtech, LLC:

> People cannot be treated as assets because assets will depreciate over time. But the value of people will appreciate with accumulated experience and organization development strategies. Employees are the organization's investors. Employees as investors are expecting increased return from their investment. This is not only in the form of salary and benefits, but also in individual competency, development, and career growth (Wang 2002, 5).

This confirms that investment in human capital will occur at two levels. First is the individual, and, second, is the organization or sponsoring agency. The difference will lie in the preference of capacity building.

In the case of individuals, this preference will be dominated by passive-capacity building for "portfolio-construction." Portfolio construction will potentially benefit both the individual and the organization. The degree to which the organization benefits will be proportional to its understanding of its memberships' current passive capacity and how the organization is able to shift this to active capacity for achieving short- and long-term goals. One apparent strategy will be that of role diffusion. In addition, investment in passive-capacity building that addresses future needs of the organization will provide a potential response to the generational values that embrace role diffusion and the need for being valued.

Individual investment is dominated by a goal of building *passive* capacity, in terms of current task behavior, in portfolio for *mobility*; intra-role, intra-organization, inter-individualistic, and career. The strategic ROI view is long term.

The second level of investment will be dominated by the organization's need to develop primarily active capacity for current and short-range future needs. To a lesser degree individuals will also invest in this strategy, to ensure that they are better able to retain their roles, and to be able to successfully address role diffusion.

Organization investment is dominated by a goal of building *active* capacity, in terms of current task behavior, and limiting extra-organizational mobility. The strategic ROI view is short term. However, organizations that think in human capital metrics terms will risk "venture capital" to build long-term stability and provide for internal mobility. The ROI view is long term.

	Individual (*wanta*)	Group/Org. (*oughta*)
Individual View	**Individualism** (their view of their total self)	**Social role** (place as defined self by social rules and norms)
Organizational View	**Professional Role** (who you are as defined by professional standards)	**Formal role** (who you are as defined by workplace literacy and organization place in system)
	Passive (*needta*)	Active (*gotta*)

FIGURE 5.6   Role and Desired Capacity

Conclusion: Summary of Roles and Capacity

In summary, the new and future individual and organizational views of how roles should be defined and who or what drives the need for and emphasis on active and passive capacity can be thought of in terms of a two-dimensional matrix (*see* figure 5.6).

Individuals have a view of themselves and their potential in which they desire to develop more passive capacity to move both within the organization and to a new organization with more challenges or promotion opportunities (the *wanta* dimension in the upper left corner of figure 5.6). At the same time, individuals view their work role through their individualism; they desire to learn what is necessary to do their jobs well and grow within the organization and meet their social place and role expectations within the organization (the *oughta* dimension in the upper right quadrant of figure 5.6).

Individuals often also need to develop the necessary capacity to meet the requirements of, and to excel in, their professions. This knowledge is usually defined by the profession and may be passive capacity from the organization's point of view. (It is expressed as the *needta* dimension in the lower-left corner of figure 5.6.) In addition, individuals have to develop a capacity to fulfill their formal or systems roles in the organization. This is primarily active capacity (expressed as the *oughta* dimension in the lower right quadrant of figure 5.6).

Human Capital Metrics—The Imperative

Human capital planning is affected by false organizational norming at both the organization and individual levels. The organization can overcome the effects of false norming by embracing a metrics view to identify and optimize both norm preferences and capacity available. This provides the ability both to structure internal mobility to succeed with transformation and transaction processes and to develop an understanding of the external mobility variables employed by individuals.

Individuals utilize the metrics approach to develop their own transformation processes, which for the most part will be culturally influenced. For both organizations and individuals, viewing the environment with a critical awareness of attendant false norming through a metrics lens empowers organizations and individuals to better determine realistic potential and success strategies. The greater the degree to which disparity exists in philosophy or practice regarding investment in passive capacity between individuals and organizations, the greater the likelihood that critical human capital attrition will occur in organizations. Rather than continuing a matrix approach to human capital investment, organizations can benefit by embracing a human capital metrics approach.

6

Performance Management in the New Millennium

Ann Maycunich Gilley
Sharon K. Drake

Today's world is competitive as never before. Individuals and organizations face many challenges—a cyclical economy, global competition, local competitive pressures, recent accounting scandals, bankruptcies, layoffs—the list goes on. These challenges force organizations to demand the most of their personnel via activities that directly and positively impact the bottom line.

Survival and the ability to thrive require leaders, managers, and employees to think and act strategically. Today's customers are well informed, aware of their options, and demanding of excellence. Today's workforce is rapidly changing, information-savvy, and requiring flexibility and accommodation as never before. For these reasons, organizations must think constantly and strategically about how to build and grow an exemplary workforce capable of meeting the challenges of today and tomorrow.

Individuals at all organizational levels—from the executive offices to the front line—must be held accountable for their performance while being ready, willing, and able to improve continuously. Continuous performance improvement is a process, and one best facilitated through performance management.

The Changing Nature of Competitive Advantage

Traditional sources of competitive advantage include access to resources, technology, time, economies of scale, and regulatory environment. Historically, however, these sources have proven to be relatively short-lived, particularly in light of the information age. Competitiveness over time requires that sources of competitive advantage be difficult to imitate.

How can FedEx be "absolutely, positively" sure that a package will make it overnight, yet the airlines lose our luggage and the U.S. Postal Service takes days, even weeks? How can Swatch make a $5 watch that will last 20 years, yet a $5,000 Rolex can't keep accurate time? More and more, organizations are realizing that the changing basis of competitive success is people (Beer 1997; Pfeffer 1995). Ulrich and Lake (1990, 2) call this "organizational capability, or the ability of a firm to manage people to gain competitive advantage."

Take, for example, Southwest Airlines, one of the few success stories in the airline industry. Southwest enjoys no economy of scale, no technological advantage, exists in a highly regulated environment, is one of the least leveraged airlines in the United States, has a unionized workforce, and offers a no-frills, commodity product. Yet this airline operates with fewer employees per aircraft than the industry average, turns around nearly 80% of its flights in 15 minutes (compared to the industry average of 45 minutes), has the fewest passenger complaints, and an overall exceptional level of customer service. How is this accomplished? By way of a very productive workforce—and processes that focus on people (Pfeffer 1995, 114–15). "The strategic value and performance potential of the workforce can determine the relative success or failure of the enterprise" (Katzenbach 2000, 11).

As with any asset or resource, organizations are demanding that employees prove their worth on a daily basis. Employees are expected to add value (Ulrich 1997) for their employers through successful interactions with customers, creative research and development, and quality commitment to production. Value-added performance represents the application of one's knowledge, skills, and attitudes to achieving specific, measurable results that contribute to the bottom line in support of individual, unit, departmental, and organizational goals and objectives. The collective value of employee performance determines the success of the organization.

Performance management yields the vehicle for accomplishing goals and objectives at all levels within firms. Performance management systems provide supervisors, managers, and executives with a framework for interacting with and leading people through the maze of policies, procedures, politics, and expectations encountered on the job.

Benefits of Performance Management

Performance management systems drive the behavior and productivity of individuals and, thus, their organizations. Effective performance management systems help organizations:

- plan for future human resource needs;
- reduce turnover;
- provide environments conducive to growth and development;
- motivate employees;
- encourage individuals to take responsibility for their own development;
- reduce ambiguity;
- help managers develop their employees;
- encourage employees and managers to support continuous learning;
- provide managers with a framework for interacting with employees;
- clarify direction and expectations;
- develop and maintain competitive advantage/readiness;
- align employee and managerial efforts with organizational goals;
- enable employees to create meaningful, proactive growth and development plans;
- clearly link compensation and rewards to performance.

Why Don't Individuals and Organizations Perform as Expected?

Why don't individuals and organizations perform as expected and/or achieve desired results? Quite simply, within organizations:

- leadership often occurs in a vacuum;
- many managers are incompetent—lacking the knowledge, skill, and ability necessary to influence others;
- training and development are inadequate;
- stakeholder needs are not addressed;
- jobs are poorly designed;
- performance is not linked to organizational goals and objectives;
- barriers to good performance are established;
- a performance-management system is not in place;
- supervisors, managers, and executives don't know how to measure or evaluate performance;
- employees are not involved and supported;
- organizations focus on short-term, not long-term results;
- organizations reward wrong or inappropriate behavior (Gilley and Maycunich 2000).

Similarly, individuals:

- often don't know what is expected of them;
- don't understand their job responsibilities;
- lack support/encouragement from supervisors/managers;
- are faced with barriers/obstacles to good performance;
- don't feel safe asking for help;
- are not given feedback regarding performance;
- lack the knowledge or skills to do the job;
- think they are doing the job properly;
- allow personal problems to interfere with work performance;
- are not appropriately rewarded for doing their jobs;
- refuse to perform adequately (Gilley, Boughton, and Maycunich 1999, 14).

Setting the Stage for Performance Management

Developing a comprehensive, systemic, organization-wide performance management system seems a daunting undertaking. Where does one begin? Quite logically, at the beginning. Dynamic performance management begins by defining who we are.

Who Are We? Who/What Do We Want to Be?

Failure to clearly define the business prohibits organizations from effectively establishing goals and objectives, and from designing, implementing, and managing performance, structure, practices, and processes (Gilley et al. 1999; PWCIT 1996; Rummler and Brache 1990).

We recently facilitated a performance management workshop for approximately 30 mid- and upper-level managers. When asked who knew their organization's vision statement, not a single participant responded. Similarly, when asked their department or unit mission/goals/objectives, not a single response was made. This is not a unique occurrence. If we don't know the ultimate goal, how can we craft strategies to get there? How can we honestly evaluate our own performance or that of others when we have no basis for comparison?

Shortly thereafter we observed a meeting in which a dozen or so professionals, while attempting to recraft their vision and mission statements, were derailed by an individual insistent on arguing the difference between the two types of statements. The entire importance and focus of the meeting was lost as bickering and semantics ruled. How many times has this occurred in your organization?

What makes for a meaningful, effective mission? According to Garfield (1986, 78), the mission should motivate, challenge, inspire action, and strengthen individual characteristics such as leadership, collaboration, communications skills, and problem solving.

Katzenbach (2000, 26–27) identified conditions that reveal commitment to an organization's vision, mission, and goals: a rich history of which employees are proud, noble purpose in the eyes of employees, value-driven leadership, and ample team opportunities. Long-term success requires magnetic leaders who envision what can be, articulate what matters most to employees, and show employees their true value as individuals and organizational members.

Link Performance to Strategy

An organization's vision, mission, goals, and objectives define the heart of the business and lay the foundation for a strong structure. A clear strategy drives performance goals and objectives, which in turn supports the strategy.

All members of the organization must know the firm's vision, mission, and objectives, and must support them, *live* them. All work and subsequent goals, objectives, coaching, evaluations, and compensation must align with unit, department, and organizational objectives. Failure to do so makes one's work worthless. Linking performance to strategy separates successful from unsuccessful firms (Rummler and Brache 1990).

Focus on the Individual

To build a successful organization, "you must recognize that its fundamental building block is the individual employee" (PWCIT 1996, 20). Organizational performance is mediated through human expertise and human effort, that is, through the human lens. The performance scorecards available to organizational decision-makers, however, generally ignore these elements.

Outstanding organizations treat individual intelligence and human capacity as resources to be nurtured and cultivated, with as much attention as land and capital. Top organizations maximize performance by capitalizing on inherent talent and skills, passion, and preferences (Garfield 1986).

The Right People in the Right Place at the Right Time

The right people in the right place at the right time, doing the right things. An organization is only as strong as its weakest personnel link. All managers like to think they hire the brightest and the best fit for the job. In reality, the sense of urgency to find someone to "get the work done" often leads to hiring too quickly or simply filling the vacancy with individuals who don't fit the position or the organization. Results include low retention rates, job misfits, a loss in productivity, and poor customer satisfaction. A director of a Midwest search firm has estimated the cost of a bad hire ranges from two to three times that person's salary. Costs for replacing a mid-level manager add up quickly due to down time when a job goes unfilled, duration of the hiring process, training time, and how long it takes to get someone up to speed.

In his recent study of 1,435 firms (eventually narrowed to 11), Collins examined characteristics of successful companies, defined as those that cumulatively outperformed the stock market by 3 times for 15 years. Collins (2001, 13) writes,

> Good-to-great leaders . . . first got the right people on the bus, the wrong people off the bus, and the right people in the right seats—and then they figured out where to drive it. The old adage "People are your most important asset" turns out to be wrong. People are not your most important asset. The right people are.

This approach is particularly crucial for the management team (see below).

Great companies are not characterized by ruthless cultures that hack and cut in difficult times or maliciously fire without thoughtful consideration. Instead, they exemplify rigorous cultures that consistently apply exacting standards at all times and to all levels, particularly upper management. As a result, people need not worry about their positions and can concentrate fully on work.

Collins (2001, 54–59) extracted three practical disciplines to get and keep the right people.

1. When in doubt, don't hire—keep looking. Don't act just to get the position filled and get on with business. Growth and expansion will occur based on the ability to hire the "right people." Certainly having the specific knowledge, skills, and background are essential to a good job fit, but the "right" fit has more to do with character traits and innate capabilities.

2. When you need to make a people change, act. A hiring mistake has been made the moment the manager feels the need to tightly manage someone. Great people need to be guided, taught, and led, but not tightly managed. Often, system changes are created to accommodate the "wrong fit" and a great deal of energy is expended trying to remedy the situation. Too much is

invested in the wrong hire who, in the end, will leave or be let go anyway. To let the wrong people hang around is at personal expense of the manager and is unfair to the right people who end up compensating for the inadequacies of the wrong people. Hire the RIGHT people up front.

3. Put your best people on your biggest opportunities, not your biggest problems. Creative potential can be lost when the constant focus is on solving problems rather than seeing opportunities. At the very least, people become exhausted over time. Collins (2001) notes that creating a place for the best people to always have a seat on the bus will also increase the likelihood of support in the event of a change of direction.

Start with Management

The ability to build a talented, high performing management team determines the organization's level of success. Management is responsible for the actions of its organizational players. Management sets and enforces policies, creates culture, and "steers the bus," thus it is critical to have the right players "on the bus."

We often receive calls from potential clients seeking help for their frontline personnel. A division of a large computer manufacturer, for example, recently called in search of "customer service" training for its in-house maintenance division. Initially, the manager was convinced that this was a "personnel" problem—his technicians simply weren't treating their internal clients properly. Investigation revealed a personnel problem all right—although the individuals causing the problems were supervisors and managers!

The scene was typical; this organization had hired and promoted individuals who:

- possessed no skill in supervision or leading people. Although some had experience, that doesn't mean the experience was successful;
- had simply been around the longest;
- were incapable of securing results through people;
- created environments full of fear and mistrust;
- were incapable of developing synergistic relationships with their employees;
- were unable to model, train, or convey the requirements of the job;
- had failed to clearly define jobs, goals, and expectations;
- were unable to provide appropriate feedback.

And on, and on, and on.

These behaviors constitute managerial malpractice, a term introduced by Gilley and Boughton (1996). Managerial malpractice can be overcome by having the "right" people on board (Collins 2001).

Selection

Effective workforce planning transcends the typical search for sufficient knowledge, skills, and abilities to meet a current job requirement. Kochan (1997, 120) lists "attracting, developing, and retaining top talent" as one of the most significant challenges facing business. Seek individuals with compatible values, vision, qualities, teachability, propensity to grow and develop—assess the candidate's potential contribution to the organization's culture, values, developmental, and even attitudinal needs. Telling employees to value excellence, behave with integrity, or promote quality typically proves a futile effort. Hiring individuals who possess these views and characteristics makes sound business sense. "The selection process is critical to achieving the levels of workforce performance that organizations require" (Leibler and Parkman 1999, 351). An organization that cannot staff itself effectively will have little chance of success (Drucker 1988).

The traditional staffing approach matches individuals to specific, well-defined jobs. Because every job is located within a business process, care needs to be taken to ensure that the hiring and staffing process is also viewed as an important part of strategy. Gilley, Boughton and Maycunich (1999) link job design to the organization's strategic business goals and objectives. Their job-design model (43) has, at its core, the organization's strategic business goals and objectives along with interrelated components. These other components are performance outputs, performance activities, performance standards, and competency maps. All are key to good performance-management practices and the hiring process.

Effective hiring encompasses two critical elements: the demands and requirements of the job and the candidate's abilities and experience. If the job design has been well done, then matching the person to the job is the next step. A good job fit balances job demands with abilities (*see* figure 6.1). However, if the demands of the job are greater than the individual's abilities and experiences, poor performance will be the end result. Conversely, when one's abilities and experiences exceed the demands of the job, boredom and discontent will occur. "Effective managers effectively match individual talents with necessary tasks" (Fletcher 1993, 2). Those who choose and hire poorly cultivate a culture tolerant of poor performance and the resultant employee/manager conflicts that arise. To quote a client struggling with perfor-

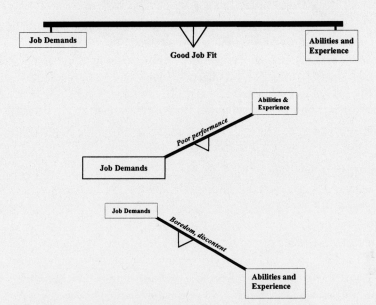

FIGURE 6.1   Balance between Job Demands and Abilities

mance issues stemming from poor selection, "ultimately, bad hires made good fires." Why not hire well to begin with?

Leibler and Parkman (1999, 351) believe that "the selection process is critical to achieving the levels of workforce performance that organizations require." They divide the selection process into four major tasks.

1. Describe the position in terms of specific functions to be performed effectively.
2. Specify the knowledge, skills, and personal characteristics needed to achieve desired performance.
3. Determine the selection criteria, including the characteristics a candidate must possess when hired, not those that must be developed on the job.
4. Develop a systematic, objective procedure for assessing each candidate with respect to the selection criteria. (353)

Ten Characteristics Managers Should Look For

One key to achieving superior performance involves hiring to competencies: knowledge, skills, abilities, and attitudes. Organizations can't teach attitude—

they must look for desired philosophies possessed by candidates. The Price Waterhouse Change Integration Team (1996, 80–81) identified ten personal characteristics that are becoming more important in selecting and evaluating people: integrity, initiative, intelligence, social skills, resourcefulness, imagination, flexibility, enthusiasm, a sense of urgency, and a "world view." These character attributes are proving far more important than mere skills, which can be taught.

Diversity

The need for shared values and beliefs has been stressed for individuals, work groups, and organizations. On the surface diversity appears lacking, although this may not be the case, for in addition to their values and beliefs, employees also bring their vast individual differences. Age, gender, race, religion, thinking style, learning style, family orientation, and physical abilities are just a few of the many differences that add a great deal of richness in an organization, along with plenty of opportunities for management problems in the work arena. Businesses that respond in a meaningful fashion to workers' uniqueness, talents, needs, and concerns obtain superior performance from the most capable and skilled people in the workforce. Certainly, attention to U.S. Equal Employment Opportunity guidelines is critical to keep an organization lawful in the hiring process. More important, aligning organizational and individual culture, fit, values, and beliefs—"getting the right people on the bus" —are the elements essential to effective performance management.

Proper employee selection builds the foundation for individual and organizational success. Next, we examine proven procedures and processes for maximizing one's potential—regardless of position or title.

Performance-Management Process

High performance has been defined as "producing results much better than expected in both individuals and organizations" (Fletcher 1993, 2).

A large number of performance management models have surfaced over the years. Although they differ slightly in construction, most agree on necessary components. The performance management process at the employee level consists of the following steps (*see* figure 6.2):

1. mutually set goals and objectives;
2. establish standards/expectations;

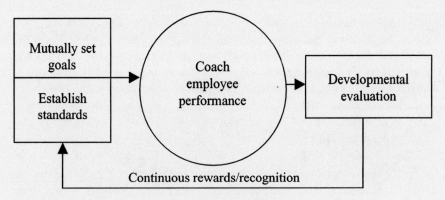

FIGURE 6.2   The Performance-Management Process

3. engage in performance coaching;
4. conduct developmental evaluations with growth and development plans;
5. link compensation and rewards to growth and development (Gilley et al. 1999, 49).

Mutually Set Goals/Objectives

Goals are established to support business processes and objectives. Goals drive organizational performance and form the basis of individual growth and development plans.

Performer goals encompass a variety of activities. They can be written exclusively to improve individual performance or quality, or in such a way as to improve employee growth and development. Performer goals are the backbone of the performance alignment process, serving as the individual targets employees shoot for on a daily basis. They should be written with the organization's strategic business goals and objectives in mind; thus performer goals are linked to business strategy (Gilley et al. 1999, 42).

Employee goals may include acquisition of new job skills or knowledge (e.g., computer software applications), gaining experience (e.g., the opportunity to supervise interns, new hires, temporary workers, or others), career enhancement (e.g., a promotion), personal development (e.g., attending a conference or training session, taking a class), and so forth.

Effective goals are established mutually by supervisors and employees; after all, we support and are committed to what we create. Both employees and supervisors should prepare for and contribute to the goal discussion. Each party identifies a few specific, challenging goals for the employee, which are discussed and honed to maximize potential performance, alignment with organizational objectives, and employee growth. This phase involves negotiation, flexibility, and the ability to envision the future needs of the employee, unit, department, and organization.

Goals should be challenging, yet achievable. Well-crafted goals encourage enhanced performance and a sense of accomplishment. Effective goals are SMART: specific, measurable, action-oriented, realistic, and time-based. Anemic goals fail to inspire or stretch the intellect and talents of workers. Unrealistically high goals only serve to de-motivate employees who, in response, will often devise ways to "get around" or sabotage what they perceive to be unreasonable expectations on the part of management.

We worked with a financial services corporation that was experiencing what they described as a "morale problem." Symptoms included increasing tardiness, sick time, and turnover, employees' stealing each other's clients and business, and a variety of passive and overtly aggressive behaviors. Management was convinced that their workforce was in dire need of "fixing," and had initially requested training. We quickly discovered that individual and departmental goals were unrealistic, set by a management team horribly out of touch with the realities of the front line. Employees were constantly warned that failure to meet goals would result in written reprimands, lost bonuses, and eventually, termination if goals were unmet for three consecutive months. As a result, employees felt pressured to "do whatever it takes" to meet goals—from stealing each other's business to manipulating or coercing clients into purchasing products they neither wanted nor needed. Those who lacked the energy avoided work by calling in sick, showing up late, or simply quitting.

Establish Standards and Expectations

Establishing standards and expectations profoundly impacts employee behavior. "Expectations of outstanding performance can actually increase people's job performance, while low expectations can diminish performance" (Pfeffer 1995, 107). Performance standards are the targets used to measure the efficiency and quality of outputs. Standards and expectations represent the best practices envisioned by the firm and desired of employees.

A few years ago we worked with a fifty-person insurance sales division experiencing production problems with a few personnel—a situation brought to light by a lawsuit. Policies were booked without clients' permission, non-essential coverages were added, multiple policies were appearing under individual client names—and this is just a sampling of the abuses that were occurring. Discussions with managers, supervisors, and employees revealed that at no time had standards or expectations for proper performance been shared. Employees had not been given guidelines regarding quality, customer expectations, or ethics. What's more, the organization had actually been rewarding unethical behavior with bonuses! A lawsuit finally caught management's attention. The relatively simple act of sharing acceptable guidelines and standards had an immediate impact on performance within the division. Employees reported "relief" that they now had guidelines for acceptable performance.

Coach

When asked to describe coaches with whom they've interacted, adults often use words such as trainer, mentor, feedback provider, demanding, cheerleader, encourager, team builder, friend, sets high standards, caring, pushes, results oriented—the list goes on.

Even though we're given strong feedback and may not always agree, we understand that the coach is concerned with our individual well-being and success, or that of the team.

In the work setting, performance coaches are viewed similarly. HRD contributes value by helping management understand the tenets of coaching and hone their coaching skills. Coaching allows managers and employees to assess the job/work's desired impact, and use coaching and evaluation to mold one's performance to that desired outcome. Coaches consistently evaluate performance and provide ongoing feedback to employees and work groups on their progress toward reaching their goals. Ongoing coaching provides the opportunity to check employees' progress toward meeting predetermined targets and to make changes to unrealistic or problematic goals or standards. By coaching continuously, unacceptable performance can be identified early and assistance provided to correct performance.

Gilley and Boughton (1996) identified four phases of performance coaching: training, mentoring, confronting (providing feedback), and counseling.

Training. As trainers, coaches teach. What better way to ensure that employees gain the information needed to be successful? This role allows supervisors/managers to model desired performance, establish credibility, articulate standards and expectations, assess employee knowledge and skill levels, and improve their interpersonal relationships with staff. Since managers are responsible for employee performance and appraisal, they, logically, should be the source of information for which their employees are held accountable. Evaluating the impact of training provided by others is a guess at best.

Some argue that managers, like all employees, possess specific strengths and competencies along with performance weaknesses and thus should not be expected to train in *all* aspects of the business. True. And in these areas managers should seek assistance, whether from colleagues, their staff, or the training department. Some of us, for example, lack sophisticated computer skills—turning us loose on an unsuspecting staff will cause needless pain and suffering. Enlisting the services of an expert makes sense. It is the manager's responsibility then, to be intimately familiar with the training content, objectives, and outcomes—particularly if these will constitute a portion of the trainee's performance evaluation.

Mentoring. Mentors are guides and confidants, who, by virtue of their experience with the firm, are able to help employees unlock the mysteries of the organization. What's really going on? Who can be trusted? What's the true political arena? Coaches as mentors take others under their wings to help them navigate turbulent organizational waters and avoid potentially damaging behavior that often occurs as a result of organizational ignorance.

Feedback. Feedback is information about employee performance and its consequences (Gilley and Maycunich 2000b). Purposeful feedback develops fluency and encourages performance improvement.

Providing feedback often presents the most challenging aspect of coaching. Positive feedback proves easy, and typically a pleasure to give. Who doesn't like to support or encourage successful performance? Many supervisors/managers, however, have difficulty with developmental feedback, or confronting, largely due to the natural tendency to avoid conflict. The desire to protect the self causes us to fear others' reactions to what is often perceived as negative news or criticism.

Summative, or evaluative, feedback assesses the quantity of performance, while formative, or developmental, feedback addresses quality (Tosti and Jackson 1999).

Many years ago, one of us worked as a sales representative for a large insurance company. After completing a telephone call that resulted in a sale, a supervisor who had monitored the call approached and said, "I heard your conversation. Unfortunately, it could have been better. I'm not certain what you could have said, I just know it didn't sound right." Was this formative feedback useful? Definitely not.

Helping supervisors/managers master feedback techniques enables HRD professionals to partner with all levels of the organization to improve performance. They can help managers (a) perfect their communication skills; (b) focus on behaviors and performance problems rather than the employee; (c) use feedback to maximize strengths, minimize weaknesses, and produce desired change without defensiveness; and (d) maintain positive, healthy relationships with employees.

Counseling.   Managers possess a myriad of experiences both on the job and off, which lends them a wisdom whose value manifests itself in sharing. Performance coaches often find themselves counseling those who report to them, typically in career-related aspects. According to Gilley and Boughton (1996, 37) performance coaches "guide employees through a relatively in-depth review and exploration of their interests, abilities, and beliefs regarding their present and future career path." Given the manager's wealth of career and organizational experience, this type of counseling makes sense.

Developmental Evaluations

Most organizations assess an employee's performance in a similar fashion to measures of financial performance—by summarizing the past. The measures themselves often pose problems in that they are often inadequate, outdated, not aligned with organizational goals, difficult to quantify, or biased. Without a doubt, successfully measuring performance depends on having or developing good criteria (Bates 1999).

In contrast to traditional forms of measurement, developmental evaluations focus on the future. Although many developmental evaluation sessions do include assessment of past work, the strength of developmental appraisals lies in planning. Developmental evaluations include goal setting, an assessment of employee strengths and weaknesses, and action plans for continuous improvement of skills and acquisition of new talent. Performance coaches and employees engage in "where/what/how" analysis: Where are you now? Where do you want to go? What must happen for you to get there? How can I (the manager) help? Ultimately, these evaluations frame future growth and development activities to enhance employees' abilities and advance their careers.

Developmental evaluations enhance strategic effectiveness by:

• providing a means for evaluating individual and organizational efficiency and effectiveness;

- providing information about employees' skills and capabilities;
- assessing individual and organizational dimensions that indicate capacity to grow, reinvent, and accomplish future goals;
- linking expectations to goals, feedback, and rewards;
- enabling the organization to make informed personnel decisions based on workforce knowledge, skills, abilities, growth plans, and goals;
- functioning as a control-system tool to influence the level and quality of employee behavior;
- providing a medium of communication through which organizations can drive change.

Future-building performance growth and development plans allow employees to maximize strengths while minimizing weaknesses. A common response to inadequate performance by employees is to punish them with training. In reality, training does little to remedy poor performance. At best, performance improves slightly or becomes merely adequate, but hardly the superior performance desired by organizations (Clifton and Nelson 1992). A wiser strategy involves matching employee talent to job requirements and enhancing existing skills with developmental opportunities. "People will produce better results if they are allowed, supported, and encouraged to work in the way that they work best" (Fletcher 1993, 17).

Obsessing over poor performance proves a waste of time for both employee and manager. "Because most training activities focus on fixing weaknesses, managers have the misguided perception that their job is to identify and isolate their employees' weaknesses" (Gilley et al. 1999, 129). Managers are responsible for securing results through people. Focusing on employee strengths and aligning talent with organizational needs drive success.

Rewards and Recognition

Rewarding means recognizing employees in a manner that meets their personal needs—both individually and as members of groups—for their performance, and acknowledging their contributions to the organization's mission. Recognition should be an ongoing, natural part of daily work.

Effective rewards are tied to individual growth and development plans, which in turn support unit, department, and organizational goals. Thus, compensation, rewards, and recognition are yet another aspect of strategy.

We hear laments from supervisors, managers, and executives such as, "You can't motivate a union workforce," "People only care about money," or "My organization won't allow me to give cash incentives." The list goes on. In reality, we each are motivated in different ways, and that's the key. The challenge to managers is to uncover these sources of motivation and create stimulating, healthy work environments that allow employees to fulfill their needs. How? Ask! "What motivates you?" "What do you enjoy doing and why?" Questions such as these surface drivers of individual behavior, which managers can then tie to the work setting.

A few years ago one of the authors had the pleasure of having an office on the third floor of a large corporate building. The man responsible for cleaning and maintaining the floor was fabulous—personable, cheerful, possessing a wonderful work ethic. When asked why he enjoyed his job so much he said, "The people." Also, he made a conscious effort to do his best and enjoy each aspect of his job. In return, he received numerous "Thank you's" and letters of appreciation from the day staff. That made it all worthwhile. The intrinsic challenges and rewards of his job were much more powerful motivators than extrinsic factors.

The Role of HRD

Effective HRD practices make employees and their organizations more flexible, responsive, and competitive. In his 1995 article in *HRMagazine*, Fitzenz stated that in "many companies, management does not see the value added by human resources (HR) in effectively managing the human assets of the enterprise" (85). Fitzenz is both right and wrong! Yes, it is true—many companies fail to see the value added by human resources. However, HR is not responsible for managing the organization's people—that's the responsibility of supervisors and managers. Employee "management" is an organization-wide phenomenon. Misguided thinking such as this epitomizes the problems surrounding HRD. Ultimately, human resource development is everyone's responsibility. HRD professionals add value to their organizations by helping managers and leaders do their jobs.

HRD professionals' primary roles include performance consulting and organizational development/change. Their responsibilities include developing internal partnerships with business units, leadership development, creating learning transfer plans, internal consulting, and overseeing and evaluating the performance-management process.

Change

Change is constant. Managers, supervisors, HR/HRD professionals, internal or external consultants . . . all are challenged to help individuals and organizations facilitate change. Performance management systems, by design, frame continuous change in the form of continuous growth and development, and constant improvement.

HRD has the potential to significantly impact an organization by helping all levels design and implement a performance management system. Managers should be the primary consumers of HRD services, which help them craft strategies to add value to the firm, and enhance its renewal capabilities and competitiveness. Furthermore, "Firms building organizational capability rebuild their commitment to and from employees" (Ulrich and Lake 1990, 14).

The strength of those who engage in HRD lies in the quality of their products and services. This quality is built on experience, attitude, involvement with people, and a strong theory to practice approach. HRD serves the firm strategically by working with managers to improve their skills and productivity. HRD as advisers, guides, and internal consultants help managers integrate organizational performance-management practices (goal setting, development standards, coaching, developmental evaluations, rewards) with strategic goals/objectives, business practices, and culture. These processes support sound business strategy while concurrently involving employees in decision making, making them responsible for their own behavior/performance, and raising loyalty and commitment.

Conclusion

Managing performance effectively proves a rare, often elusive talent. A critical challenge facing HRD lies in helping organizations design and implement performance-management systems that support the firm's vision, mission, and goals. We add value by sharing our performance-management expertise with supervisors, managers, and executives, and helping them execute each key component process well. Goals are established and work is planned routinely. High standards are set, but care is taken to develop the skills needed to reach them. Employees are coached as progress toward those goals is measured and they receive developmental feedback and evaluations. All five component processes work together and support each other to achieve logical, effective performance management—and ultimately, success.

Performance Coaching

Jerry W. Gilley
Nathaniel W. Boughton
Erik Hoekstra

One of the most overlooked problems facing organizations is a phenomenon known as *managerial malpractice*. Gilley and Boughton (1996, 4) define this condition as the practice of maintaining and using individuals who are unqualified, poorly trained, misguided, or inadequately prepared. This problem has plagued organizations for years and has become the Achilles' heel of literally thousands of firms. Managerial malpractice is a simple, subliminal problem that is seldom addressed by organizations—and if left unchecked, will prevent organizations from achieving the desired effectiveness and efficiency.

Performance coaching is designed to eliminate managerial malpractice and help organizations better manage performance. Unfortunately, some believe that the performance-coaching process is simply a formalized feedback approach (Peterson and Hicks 1996; Whitmore 1997). On the contrary, it is a complex process that includes several important roles and activities that managers must adopt in order to help their employees solve problems, improve performance, and achieve desired results (Bolton 1986). Thus, performance coaching is a critical issue facing those responsible for the growth and development of human resources.

Performance coaching is based on a person-centered management technique that requires face-to-face communications, personal involvement with employees, and establishment of rapport (Gilley, Boughton, and Maycunich 1999). It transforms managers from passive observers to active participants with employees, and is based on good questioning, listening, feedback, and facilitation skills as opposed to autocratic, controlling techniques.

Why Is Performance Coaching Important?

Whether large or small, manufacturing or service, every organization selects managers and assigns them the task of securing results through people. In theory, managers serve as guides, directors, decision-makers, and energizers for their employees, without which organizations struggle in mediocrity. They are the implementers of organizational change initiatives and developmental interventions. In reality, unfortunately, many are abusive and indifferent toward employees. They possess superior attitudes and poor interpersonal skills (the inability to listen well or provide feedback). Some fail to delegate effectively, develop their people, or conduct meaningful performance evaluations. Still others have little or no patience with their employees as they struggle to improve their performance. Some even criticize employees' personalities rather than confront their work performance. Typically, such managers create work environments full of fear and paranoia, and defy employees to challenge their authority. As a result of such behaviors, employee morale and productivity remain low, leading to poor quality products and services, and higher costs. As a way of overcoming this dilemma, managers can embrace performance coaching as an option.

What Is Performance Coaching?

Performance coaching involves creating a synergistic relationship between managers and employees; the primary benefit is the establishment of a collegial partnership between the two. Based on two-way communication, trust, honesty, and interaction, this partnership should be nonjudgmental, free of fear, and both personal and professional (Gilley and Boughton 1996). Additionally, performance coaching allows managers the opportunity to better serve their employees through performance coaching, developmental evaluations, performance growth and development activities, and rewarding and recognizing employees' accomplishments and development.

Peterson and Hicks (1996, 14–15) contend that performance coaching is the process of equipping people with the tools, knowledge, and opportunities they need for self-development and to become more effective. Simply, performance coaches do not develop people—they equip people for self-development.

Whitmore (1997, 27) believes that the first key element of coaching is *awareness*, which is the product of focused attention, concentration, and clarity. The *Concise Oxford Dictionary* defines *aware* as "conscious, not ignorant, having knowledge." *Webster's New World Dictionary* adds that *aware* "implies having knowledge of something through alertness in observing or in interpreting what one sees, hears, feels, etc." Whitmore (1997) suggests that awareness can be raised or heightened considerably by focused attention and through practice.

Further, Whitmore (1997, 31) stresses that *responsibility* is another key element of performance coaching. He asserts that responsibility is crucial for high performance because when employees truly accept, choose, or take responsibility for their thoughts and actions, the organization's commitment to them rises, thus, so does employees' performance. When employees are ordered to be responsible, however, their acceptance may be reduced, which affects their performance.

According to Hudson (1999, 15), a performance coach is basically a person that works with employees and organizations as clients, and finds bridges to the future—connecting what is to what might be—and works from what is possible, using imagination, vision, and motivation as resources. Performance coaches link inner purpose to outer work with persons, groups, and organizations, inspiring others to be more effective as leaders, teams, networkers, and managers, and guiding employees to high performance. They question the status quo; seek creative, transformative results, advocate, criticize, and extend corporate culture; and facilitate professional development and organizational system development. Performance coaches guide employees and organizations through necessary transitions; encourage networking through alliances and linkages with common goals; and, finally, serve as catalysts for renewal and resilience.

Peterson and Hicks (1996) point out that performance coaching is a continuous process, not an occasional conversation. They believe that performance coaches are like orchestra conductors in that they sometimes work one-on-one with a player; at other times they direct from afar, and, on occasion, they encourage employees to develop in areas completely outside their arena of expertise. As such, performance coaches encourage employees to learn and practice their skills, help them channel their passion to learn, and harmonize with other members of the organization.

Characteristics of Effective Performance Coaches

Hudson (1999, 18) believes that performance coaching is a process guided by core values, which demonstrates the characteristics of an effective coach. Additionally, he lists several tasks that a performance coach performs to demonstrate each characteristic.

1. Effective coaches are emotionally competent and are capable of:
   - sustaining intimate bonds and relationships;
   - providing an environment of caring;
   - maintaining high levels of self-confidence and self-esteem;
   - imagining, wondering, and envisioning possibilities;
   - listening intently and objectively to employees;
   - empathizing with and validating employees;
   - expressing feelings naturally and appropriately;
   - displaying gratitude and appreciation;
   - managing conflicts fairly and directly;
   - seeking and maintaining friendships that are mutually rewarding.

2. Effective coaches are mentally competent and are capable of:
   - possessing legitimate personal authority;
   - giving and receiving criticism fairly;
   - reflecting on sense of self and one's personal life course;
   - possessing legitimate personal authority;
   - negotiating useful and accurate coaching agreements;
   - distinguishing between trivial and significant problems;
   - distinguishing between situational and patterned distress;
   - providing accurate feedback;
   - observing and understanding the conduct of self and others;
   - knowing how to keep coaching relationships professional.

3. Effective coaches are action-oriented and are capable of:
   - discerning and clarifying personal values in self and others;
   - collaborating effectively and acting fairly as a team player;
   - celebrating, having fun, and pursuing affirmations and rituals;
   - planning and feeling responsible for making the future happen;
   - living his or her own beliefs and concerns;
   - challenging, testing, and expecting high performance from self and others;
   - looking for ways employees can experience their strengths;
   - looking for ways employees can learn to be self-directed;
   - looking for social settings and activities that can enrich the coaching plan;
   - validating and rewarding the efforts of employees;
   - embracing diversity in men and women and in people from other cultures.

Gilley, Boughton, and Maycunich (1999) believe that performance coaches need to be enthusiastic, self-controlled, impartial, honest, self-confident, genuine, friendly, optimistic, visionary, open-minded, flexible, and resourceful. Additionally, effective performance coaches must be willing to accept criticism, allow others to offer suggestions and recommendations, and to accept employees' successes and failures.

Frontiers of Performance Coaching

Peterson and Hicks (1999, 15) contend that three performance-coaching frontiers can be cultivated to improve a manager's ability to develop their employees. First, performance coaches can work one-on-one with employees, which is the most direct and personal approach. This provides managers an opportunity to provide firsthand feedback, challenge employees to take appropriate risks, and encourage workers when they experience setbacks and barriers. Second, managers can guide employees to learn for themselves because they are not always present when employees encounter an opportunity to learn something new. Consequently, managers need to arm employees as *crusaders on behalf of their own development.* Third, managers need to orchestrate resources and learning opportunities. As such, managers equip people to learn while still intervening with others on their behalf. This requires developing an environment that supports intelligent risk-taking. Additionally, managers must be willing to train and mentor employees, eliminate barriers that hinder continuous learning, and open doors to new experiences that are unavailable without assistance.

Myths and Misconceptions of Performance Coaching

Peterson and Hicks (1996, 16) have identified five common misconceptions about performance coaching that can affect its rate of success.

- Performance coaching takes a lot of time—it is common to assume that coaches deliver hours of private training and mentoring; a performance coach's primary responsibility, however, is to promote the development of others.
- Performance coaching is for fixing problems in behaviors—the real goal of performance coaching is to cultivate employees' capabilities and tap their true potential.
- Performance coaching means giving feedback and advice—performance coaches rely on many techniques to increase employees' insight into themselves and guide them to change.

- Performance coaching is the same as mentoring—mentors typically share experiences that enlighten employees and provide them direction, while performance coaching communicates the importance of the learning process and helps create the conditions for it to occur.
- Performance coaching is just a fad—actually, leaders throughout history have coached their employees to enhance their capabilities.

Peterson and Hicks (1996) contend that performance coaching equips people to develop themselves. Similarly, an old Chinese proverb states: "*Give a man a fish and you feed him for a day, teach a man to fish and you feed him for a lifetime.*" The same is true of the performance-coaching process because it is, indeed, a continuous developmental activity.

Purposes of Performance Coaching

Gilley and Boughton (1996) and Bolton (1986) state that performance coaching is designed to help *improve employee performance, solve problems, and secure desired organizational results*. Gilley and Boughton (1996) believe that improving performance is a five-stage process that begins by identifying the performance outputs required and communicating them to employees. Rummler and Brache (1995) contend that performance outputs are the business results required by the organization. These can include corporate profitability, the number of successful claims processed by a claims adjuster, or the revenue generated by a salesperson in the first quarter. In essence, performance outputs are the deliverables that employees are paid to produce.

Second, performance coaches identify employees' performance activities that are required to produce a given output. Performance activities include the step-by-step tasks or engagements (processes) necessary to produce a product or service, and reflect the best practices employees will use on the job (Rummler and Brache 1995).

Third, performance coaches identify performance standards that must be met or exceeded regarding performance outputs or activities. Such standards serve as criteria to be used when determining whether a performance output has been produced at an acceptable level or whether a job has been completed correctly. They serve as a blueprint in executing the job task or providing performance deliverables (Gilley 1998).

Fourth, performance coaches compare an employee's current performance with established performance and industry standards. This is done at both the performance output and activity levels, and helps determine whether there is a serious deviation in the execution of a given job or a difference between actual performance outputs and desired outputs. Once determined, a record should be kept for future reference and to serve as a baseline for performance improvement.

A deficiency in output or activities triggers the final stage. In short, this is where performance improvement begins. Sometimes change must impact the way a job is being performed or outputs are being created. Examples include changes in policies, procedures, or processes for executing performance activities, or establishing new ways of producing performance outputs. Although no significant difference may exist between actual and desired performance, it may still be appropriate to make adjustments in execution of performance activities to ensure continuous improvement. In other circumstances, actual performance may exceed performance standards. Typically, performance coaches are reluctant to make adjustments under these conditions; however, it is still important to examine possible ways to improve productivity to ensure that high levels of performance continue (Gilley, Boughton, and Maycunich 1999).

Another purpose of performance coaching is to help employees solve problems. Performance coaches can employ the creative thinking process to achieve this purpose. It includes:

- defining the problem;
- collecting all information relevant to the problem;
- identifying as many possible causes of the problem as possible;
- selecting the likely root cause of the problem;
- brainstorming as many solutions for removing the cause as possible;
- evaluating the solutions based on factors critical to success;
- selecting the best solution based on these factors;
- creating a plan of action to implement the solution;
- evaluating the action plan and the solution (Stone 1999, 58–59).

Although this approach has a proven record of success in solving problems, employees are also responsible to integrate the critical thinking process on the job. Thus, employees need to be taught how to effectively execute each step of the process. In this way, creative thinking becomes the responsibility of employees rather than a technique used to manipulate them.

Helping the organization achieve the results it needs is perhaps the most important aspect of the performance-coaching process. Organizational results can include increasing sales, obtaining more units of productivity, improving customer service, or rising market share. Performance coaches cannot obtain desired results by themselves—they need to rely upon their employees for assistance. According to Gilley, Boughton, and Maycunich (1999), this is where classic management techniques begin to fall apart as directing, organizing, and controlling employees may not produce positive results. Bolton (1986) contends that performance coaching offers the process necessary for securing results through people.

Core Values of Performance Coaching

Hudson (1999, 127–128) suggests that performance coaching is based on six core values, which are:

1. Personal power: claiming yourself. Includes self-esteem, confidence, identity, inner motivation, a positive sense of self, clear ego boundaries, self-love and courage.
2. Achievement: proving yourself. Involves reaching goals, conducting projects, working, winning, playing in organized sports, having ambition, getting results and recognition, and being purposive.
3. Intimacy: sharing yourself. Is loving, bonding, caring, being intimate, making relationships work, feeling close, nesting, parenting, and being a friend.
4. Play and creativity: expressing yourself. Means being imaginative, intuitive, playful, spontaneous, original, expressive, humorous, artistic, celebrative, re-creative, funny, curious, childlike, and nonpurposive.
5. Search for meaning: integrating yourself. Is finding wholeness, unity, integrity, peace, an inner connection to all things, spirituality, trust in the flow of life, inner wisdom, a sense of transcendence, and bliss.
6. Compassion and contribution: giving yourself. Entails improving, helping, reforming, leaving the world a better place, bequeathing, being generative, serving, social and environmental caring, institution building, and volunteering.

He believes that these core values compete for our loyalty and passionate commitment throughout our lives. Further, he argues that people often shift throughout the adult years from familiar, accomplished value areas to new, challenging ones.

The Performance–Coaching Process

According to Stone (1999, 14), the coaching process consists of five steps. The first is *gathering information*. An effective performance coach knows how to get information from employees without making them feel as if they are being interrogated. Such information is useful in making career- and performance-based decisions, such as identifying a skill deficiency, finding out an employee's interests and aspirations, or whether to promote an individual to a new job.

The second step is *listening,* which involves asking the right questions, recognizing nonverbal signals and body language, and analyzing the words spoken. An effective performance coach is able to determine the feelings behind an employee's response and knows how to use body language to communicate interest.

The third step involves *being aware of employee morale and motivation.* Again, effective coaches communicate frequently with their employees to determine whether morale problems or other circumstances or events are causing distress in the workplace, which can lead to lower productivity or generate attitudinal problems. To guard against such problems, effective performance coaches keep open the lines of communication.

The fourth step entails *instructing employees.* An effective performance coach conducts a needs assessment to determine gaps in knowledge and skills that must be addressed. Additionally, they can train employees and provide the learning transfer feedback needed to ensure that new knowledge is applied or new skills are used on the job.

The fifth step involves *giving feedback to employees.* Stone (1999) argues that an effective performance coach knows how important feedback is in improving employee performance. She contends that an effective performance coach "does not allow today's lean organizations to provide an excuse for not positively reinforcing good work or for not providing corrective feedback in a positive manner" (15).

Hudson (1999, 10) believes that performance coaching is a process in which a coach "plants the seeds" of democratic, collaborative processes in their employees by:

- emphasizing priorities, connectedness, balance, fairness, passion, purpose, vision, and planning;
- training employees to honor their core values, to articulate preferences, to negotiate differences, to compromise, and to manage conflict when necessary;
- encouraging debate about the wise decisions for challenging scenarios;
- advocating a collaborative decision-making process in which everyone affected by a decision has some way to influence the shaping of that decision;

• emphasizing personal empowerment.

Gilley and Boughton (1996) believe that performance coaching occurs whenever and wherever a need arises—bolstering the relationship between managers and employees. Consequently, the performance-coaching process's foundation is the coaching partnership that is fostered through the creation of a healthy, positive, synergistic relationship between managers and their employees.

Once a coaching partnership is established, performance coaches can address the performance problems within their organization. Gilley and Boughton (1996) argue that observation of employee performance remains the primary information-gathering tool of performance coaches. When an employee performs well, positive reinforcement is appropriate. Failing to perform adequately necessitates the performance coach to determine cause and furnish the employee with instructions that enable successful execution in the future. Performance coaches are further responsible for follow-up; that is, making certain that corrective action has been taken.

Effective performance coaches create environments that bring out the best of employees. To accomplish this, they need to meet or exceed the following criteria:

• establish clear performance goals;
• provide accurate feedback;
• be patient with employees who are experiencing difficulty on the job;
• create fear-free environments;
• expect success of employees;
• encourage excellence;
• ask questions;
• allow employees to make mistakes and govern their own performance (Gilley and Boughton 1996, 43–45).

Peterson and Hicks (1996, 14, 18–19) believe that performance coaching is a continuous process, not an occasional conversation. It is a process of equipping employees with the tools, knowledge, and opportunities they need to develop themselves and to be more effective employees. Moreover, they suggest that the performance coaching process is based on five strategies.

1. Forging a partnership—Building trust and understanding so people want to work with you.
2. Inspiring commitment—Developing insight and motivation so people focus their energy on goals that matter.

3. Growing skills—Building new competencies to ensure that people know how to do what is required.

4. Promoting persistence—developing a "never say die" attitude among employees.

5. Shaping the environment—Creating conditions that foster growth and development.

Roles in Performance Coaching

Hudson (1999, 16) suggests that the primary role in performance coaching is that of change agent. He argues that performance coaches understand that change is a constant in today's organizations. Moreover, performance coaches realize that helping employees improve their renewal capacity and resilience to change will improve organizational effectiveness.

He suggests that as a change agent, a performance coach should:

- question the status quo;
- feel challenged by the unknown;
- look at things from new perspectives;
- take risks;
- be willing to make mistakes and learn from them;
- bes driven by personal integrity;
- inspire others to be their best;
- be future-oriented and cautiously optimistic;
- look for new opportunities in the change process;
- pursue useful alliances and networks that enhance cooperation and results;
- rehearse scenarios thoroughly before making decisions;
- guide persons and systems into new developmental growth;
- imagine new ways to look at things;
- present ideas and make them convincing;
- confront behaviors that shut down human energy and hope;
- nurture employees in transition;
- facilitate learning, training, and referrals (16–17).

Gilley, Boughton, and Maycunich (1999) believe that performance coaching requires managers to be able to recognize varying situations and adapt to the behaviors and needs of employees. Under some circumstances, this requires performance coaches to be very directive and assertive with employees; at other times a supportive, amiable approach is more appropriate. Sim-

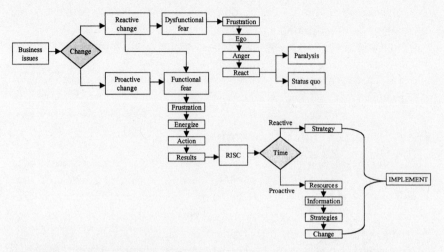

FIGURE 7.1   Change Model

ilarly, certain conditions and events require clear demonstration of leadership, while others call for operation as a performance partner for purposes of guaranteeing satisfactory organizational results.

As such, Gilley et al. (1999) believe performance coaching opportunities generally call for behaviors that fall along two continua. These two continua can be combined to create a working relationship that reveals the possible performance coaching roles encountered with employees (*see* figure 7.1). The horizontal continuum reveals assertive / supportive behavior with employees, while the vertical continuum expresses leader / partner behavior. Such a model illustrates four primary roles: trainer, confronter, counselor, and mentor. Each represents a different philosophical orientation toward performance coaching. For example, a directive approach with employees involves instruction, feedback, and confrontation, which can be represented by the trainer and confronter roles of performance coaching. Under other conditions this may be a supportive approach, represented by the mentor and counselor roles. Further, performance coaching roles are crystallized depending upon the performance coach's perception of whether to serve as a leader or partner with employees. Each role has a number of different outcomes associated with it.

As trainers, performance coaches are directive, but they operate as partners in performance improvement and use feedback and summary techniques to make certain that employees fully grasp the concepts being taught. In this role, performance coaches serve as one-on-one tutors with employees, responsible for sharing information that will ultimately impact employee growth and development. This traditionally comes in the form of on-the-job training, but can also include formal training activities.

As confronters, performance coaches are very directive and leader oriented. In this role, performance coaches' entire attention is focused on resolving performance problems. As confronters, performance coaches are responsible for identifying and addressing their employees' performance shortfalls, which are accomplished by identifying performance standards, communicating them to employees, comparing actual work to desired standards, and discussing results with employees.

As mentors, performance coaches are supportive and serve as leaders with employees. In this role, performance coaches share their experiences with them, helping employees gain additional insight, understanding, and awareness that will be invaluable in the progression of their careers. Mentors allow employees to benefit from their experiences, both the successes and failures—thus alleviating employees' fears, concerns, frustrations, and pains, while promoting celebration of successes, victories, and job accomplishments. Mentoring is a process of ultimate sharing, providing performance coaches with the opportunity to unlock the mysteries of the organization, which helps employees adjust to the firm's culture and better assimilate into the organizational work environment.

As counselors, performance coaches' primary responsibility is to help employees uncover underlying assumptions regarding their careers, and help them to analyze reasons for their current career plans. In the counselor role, performance coaches pose hypothetical questions to employees in order to expand their commitment to their careers, often presenting differing viewpoints in order to help them develop a more in-depth analysis of career options and decisions. And this role provides performance coaches with the opportunity to help employees make better career decisions and help the organization to better allocate human resources. As a result, employees gain greater insight into the organization, enhance their self-sufficiency, and better understand their feelings regarding their careers.

Responsibilities in Performance Coaching

Stone (1999, 16) contends that performance coaching entails several responsibilities. She believes that performance coaches are responsible for acting as a role model for higher performance, hiring the most competent and capable employees, and creating a work environment in which employees have reason to be motivated. Further, they are responsible for clarifying expectations—both micro-expectations associated with particular jobs and macro-objectives linked to the organization's overall strategy and mission. Performance coaches provide feedback to employees regarding their performance, and apply the performance evaluation process as a measurement tool tied to performance improvement and as a developmental process, both of which lay the foundation for growth and development plans (Gilley, Boughton, and Maycunich 1999). Additionally, performance coaches are responsible for providing the training and resources employees need to improve their performance and providing positive performance reinforcement useful in enhancing employee morale.

Unfortunately, many managers mistakenly believe that their employees know when they are or are not performing correctly. This is simply not the case. Therefore, it is the performance coach's responsibility to provide clear, concise, sincere, and timely feedback. A good working definition of feedback is *getting timely and specific information about job performance that includes praise or developmental direction*. By *timely*, we mean giving feedback on an ongoing basis, not just during annual performance reviews. *Specific* entails documenting exact performance behaviors that can be referenced when giving feedback to an employee, whereas *praise* and *developmental direction* involve providing feedback that relates to total job performance.

Competencies in Performance Coaching

Making the transition from manager to performance coach requires the development of several competencies. Hudson (1999, 17) believes that successful performance coaches must have well-developed communication skills. Specifically, an effective coach must be able to speak clearly and effectively one-on-one, in small groups, and in public meetings, as well as present ideas in a convincing manner. Effective performance coaches use a vocabulary rich in metaphors.

Next, performance coaches need to develop feedback skills, which are critical to enhancing employee growth and development. Regardless of its form, feedback is essential to employee growth and development because it helps employees know when they are producing the kind of performance outputs or activities needed by the organization. Gilley and Boughton (1996) suggest that feedback is a powerful motivator and source of encouragement for employees. Providing performance feedback helps performance coaches build synergistic relationships with their employees while reducing conflicts regarding performance. Feedback also helps employees better understand their strengths and weaknesses so that a plan of both growth and development can be created. Finally, providing timely and specific feedback leads to improved business results (Bolton 1986).

Using Performance Coaching to Facilitate and Manage Change

Organizational change is no longer an exception but a given in our global business world. The economic climate is as changeable as the seasons, and when resources are limited, inevitably, everyone is asked to do more with less. Survival in business depends on the ability to change rapidly. How can managers become coaches and promote growth within while responding to seismic shifts from without? Is there a magic pill or just a poison pill? What skills are necessary to create an organization of both flexibility and strength? The answers to these questions contain the blueprints of a successful transition from the standard "management team" to an innovative "coaching team."

Four essential focal points will be discussed in order to understand how coaches can deal successfully with change (*see* figure 7.1). First, there must be a distinction between two kinds of change, proactive and reactive. The second concern is the instinctive fear brought about by rapid change. The third focal point involves recognizing the need for caution and accurate risk assessment in order to successfully manage change. And, finally, a recent case study of a sales department implementing the principles of management transition will illustrate just how effective coaching can be when change does occur.

The first focal point is the difference between proactive and reactive attitudes toward change. Within organizations, a proactive attitude is significant in the development of visionary plans and policies that drive efficiency and create business opportunities. Proactive change builds momentum, and faces forward to meet the obstacles that challenge successful businesses. The terminology is explicit; the word *manage* conjures images of control and command, and, conversely, *performance coaching* embodies a collaborative spirit and a team mentality.

Coaches are the heralds of proactive change; they use a variety of techniques to initiate cooperation and encourage team members to buy-in. Buy-in means that each team member feels ownership and pride in knowing that his or her voice is heard by the team. The most effective way to accomplish team atmosphere is to use collaborative methodology. Collaboration is significant in that it fuels a proactive attitude toward change, that the framework is open and developmental, and that it allows individual employees to help direct the future of the business. Coaches rely on the input of employees to keep their fingers on the pulse of the organization. Who is deeply involved in the actual day-to-day business issues that impact revenue goals? The answer: your employees.

Too often when it comes to change the employees are the last to know. Is that smart? Absolutely not! Yet it is the norm. In a proactive environment, all of those who hold a stake must have active participation in—and get the real information about—the changes that are to be made. A team atmosphere ensures that the men and women who implement changes are invested and enthusiastic, sharing in the vision. Coaches that are successful realize that the acumen of employees is their best resource to discover the most reliable solution to any given issue in the business. Employees who are informed and invested will not fear change, and collaboration creates an environment of growth and openness.

The flip side of the coin, a reactionary attitude toward change, is what coaches see on a regular basis. Reactionary attitudes are a result of too little awareness. Anyone who has held a management position has experienced the infamous "fire drill." It is not surprising that employees balk when a sudden and overwhelming change is thrust upon them with little or no preparation. Fear of change is based in the confusion any employee feels when changes are mandated but not explained. For instance, an employee is engaged in his daily activity, which he believes to be an important piece of the organizational puzzle. Suddenly his supervisor orders him to drop what he is doing and focus on a new project, ASAP. Anyone in that position would be confused and more than a little fearful on being repositioned without notice or training. A former colleague and vice president was famous for this kind of reactive change; his employees were too afraid to speak their minds because of the fear caused by confusion and dysfunction. Even a routine request for a proposal (RFP) required all resources to be thrown at it while everyone abandoned their regular assignments and spent long hours responding in spite of the small chance that they would get the deal. When resources are deployed in this fashion, the building blocks of trust and teamwork crumble.

Reactive change that is not channeled in an appropriate fashion has extreme repercussions for a coach and his or her organization. Chaos and fear damage employee performance as unplanned urgency derails important strategic business decisions. The coach takes three steps backward and becomes an autocratic manager who is again flying solo amid dysfunctional fear. Undoubtedly, focusing on the urgent and forgetting about important business issues are the foundation for paralysis and a coach's decline. It is foolish to believe that there is any way to rid your organization of all reactionary attitudes toward change—some trepidation of the new and unfamiliar is, after all, human nature. A collaborative environment and a thorough risk assessment will provide the greatest opportunity for success and a team-driven initiative for change.

Whether proactive or reactive, the vast majority of the population equates change to *fear* (Block 1999). Fear is the pariah that causes personal dysfunction in the workplace, which leads to organizational dysfunction. Fear is associated with the unknown. Is fear only a negative energy that provides dysfunction, or can fear become a catalyst for successful interaction? We believe that there are two kinds of fear: the paralyzing fear that causes dysfunction and functional fear. *Paralyzing fear* can be defined as:

Frustration with people, places, or situations;
Ego gets involved because of our need for control;
Anger becomes the norm, and we have one of three choices:
Rage, resentment, or retreat.

Coaches desire to ensure individual and organizational success and therefore must eliminate the negative energy that drives dysfunctional organizational fear. We were brought in recently to a company where the vice president of sales was constantly firing people on his team. At first the dysfunctional fear was palpable. We interviewed and listened to members of his team, who felt that the pressure put on this leader from his own senior VP was creating so much fear that over 60% of the team members were looking for new jobs. When listening to call-center employees the desperation in their voices was amazing. This is a classic case of dysfunctional fear paralyzing a business that in the previous year tripled revenue. How could we change this autocratic manager into a coach who was able to turn the dysfunctional fear into functional fear? We will use this real-case scenario throughout the next several pages.

Functional fear we define as:

Frustration with people, places, or situations;
Energize your mind to winning;
Actively develop short- and long-term strategies;
Results will be delivered.

Using this definition of fear allows a coach dealing with change to optimize his or her workforce to execute appropriate strategies and successfully deliver all components.

Getting back to our example, the vice president was very close to losing his job. Transitioning him and his team from a place of dysfunction where fear was the norm, to functional fear that drove collaborative change, was not an easy undertaking. The pipeline for the next two quarters looked bleak: the sharks were circling, and the answers had to come quickly. The key involved the manager becoming a coach and change agent for his team. He was desperate, and for the first time in his career he asked for help and was ready to listen. One of the chief difficulties in consulting is getting someone, before it is too late, to understand and accept behavioral change, to check his or her ego at the door, and to be willing to listen and practice new behaviors. When he was able to evaluate his behavior and its impact on the team, we began to identify processes that would allow him to improve his credibility and move from dysfunctional fear and the associated paralysis to functional fear that energized and collaboratively engaged his team to drive sales. One of the processes that we incorporated in his organization was a risk-assessment tool, which is the other key component to coaching for change.

Risk is a four-letter word for most coaches because it means that they have to challenge the status quo. We define risk differently than most and believe that if you use the framework provided you will have a much better chance of managing change:

Resources
Information
Strategy
Change

Any time change exists, whether proactive or reactive, it is critical to assess the risk associated with making the change. The subtlety involves achieving a level where the change is reasonable and a worst-case scenario is one the organization can live with. Let's define the four terms.

Resources are needed to effect change and can be in a variety of forms, people, technology, and outside vendors. Coaches work collaboratively to identify each resource and the value it adds in reducing risk and resolving organizational issues.

The next step is to gather *information*. It is impossible to accomplish anything in a vacuum; external and internal factors are involved. Just as a golfer might throw grass in the air to see which way the wind blows, an organization must be aware and open. Due diligence is critical to successfully managing change, and the only way to ensure success is to gather as many data points as needed to reduce risk. Information must be gleaned from a variety of sources, such as internal polling of the key constituents (for example, executives, managers, and employees), assessing the customer base, gathering the opinions of the analysts, and observing the competition. Spending the time to ensure that all data points are thorough and accurate builds the foundation on which to develop appropriate strategy and initiate change.

Developing *strategy* is the third component in our RISC assessment. Strategy must be addressed and the right processes implemented in order to maximize return and minimize the cost of change. We use a variety of tools to address strategy. The General Electric corporation, for example, has built many exceptional tools. One such program, known as Work-Out, is a facilitation tool that identifies necessary changes through town meetings and then develops the best policies, change acceleration processes (CAP), and Six Sigma processes to dramatically address organizational change that impacts business results. Organizations and employees must take risks. The key component is that employees understand the value of risk-taking and the need to make appropriate and proactive decisions to ensure future growth and expansion of their business.

The final piece of our RISC Framework is *change*. Creating an intelligent framework for assessing risk allows organizations to build on past performance and focus on furthering the vision of the organization. By properly assessing the outcomes one can minimize the liabilities of the risk overall. Collaboration is the glue for using our framework successfully. Collaboration with all of the team allows an effective and efficient manner of risk assessment to minimize the liabilities inherent in change.

We have outlined a process that will help coaches manage and effect change, either in the proactive or reactive mode. By eliminating dysfunctional fear and focusing energies on collaborating and appropriately managing risk, one can successfully drive the business strategies that have been created. The vice president in our example was able over time to change his behavior and to release his team from the paralysis of fear. Through coaching techniques he was able to refocus his group toward a common vision: "to beat the competition." The business has been free to grow, and they will probably double revenue again this year. Through appropriate coaching on our end, the poison pill became the magic, and he is now a highly respected coach and leader within the executive team.

Using Performance Coaching to Facilitate Delegation as a Development Strategy

One of the lost arts in the process of performance coaching is that of delegation. Countless managerial surveys show that of all the skills that leaders wish they could improve, delegation often lands near the top of the list. Although this managerial recognition has been consistent for decades, the simple truth remains that throughout organizational life, not much has changed regarding delegation. Organizational improvement in the area of delegation as a performance coaching skill has been lackluster, at best.

Sadly, while skill-building in the area of delegation has been poor, the need for good delegation in the "flattened," "reorganized," and "right-sized" workplace of the twenty-first century has never been greater. To remain competitive, managers in every organization are being asked to do more with fewer resources, in less time, and at a lower cost. Without developing the skill of delegation, managers will simply face longer hours, longer to-do lists, increased stress, and possible personal burnout. All of this occurs while, under these same managers, the new workforce stands ready and willing to accept more responsibility.

Considering the demographic trends in the workforce today, Gen Xers are the predominant group in entry-level and middle-level management. Although many consider Gen Xers weak, uninterested, lazy, and self-centered, exactly the opposite is true if workers truly feel a part of the process and are given opportunity to develop their skills in meaningful ways. Delegation has the potential to solve both of these organizational ills, providing a way for managers to get out from under the tyranny of the to-do list and a way to develop lower-level subordinates who are "chomping at the bit" for such responsibility.

Lest you think that this particular issue is one new to modern-day organizations, just look back to the words of Oncken and Wass (1974) in their *Harvard Business Review* classic on delegation, "Management Time: Who's Got the Monkey?" In their introduction, they write "Why is it that managers are typically running out of time while their subordinates are typically running out of work?" They describe various scenarios and coping strategies for managers to get hold of their priorities and systematically move down the responsibility for results to subordinates. Although well-written and extremely helpful to managers, by focusing exclusively on the "time management" element of delegation, the authors miss more than half of the value in the delegation equation: to wit, the systematic training and development of subordinates to unleash the power of distributed work on the business goals and objectives of the organization. In good delegation, managers coach subordinates through the process of carrying out work on key issues to organizational performance without having to carry the load at the managerial level. Further, the organization builds performance capability through skill development, confidence building, and gained experience on the part of the subordinate.

Why Managers Don't Delegate: Fallacies and Rationalizations

If delegation is such a powerful performance coaching strategy, why do contemporary managers continue to struggle with the implementation of positive, developmentally based, delegation? Although the reasons may vary from manager to manager, the six key rationalizations below usually come to light when diagnosing the lack of motivation to delegate.

Fear of Poor Quality Work

Managers who do not delegate may believe that the quality of the work produced by subordinates will be of lower quality than if the manager were to accomplish the task. Although potentially true in the short term and when delegation is done poorly, if done well, delegation can produce higher quality work by enlisting the skills of more than one person in task accomplishment. Further, managers' time must be spent crafting good delegation and determining which tasks are appropriate to stretch and develop subordinates without putting key organizational deliverables at risk.

Perceived Insufficient Time Available to Delegate

Managers who show a lack of interest in delegation may believe that it takes longer to accomplish any given task by working through someone else. How often have you heard (or thought), "It will be quicker to do it myself"? Managers who succumb to this fallacy are under the "tyranny of the urgent" and are unwilling to prioritize the "important" work of people development above the "urgent" work of getting things done. Until such managers reframe their work as "getting things done through people," they will constantly be faced with the prospect of carrying the load themselves. Although delegation is not a quick fix, akin to hiring a bunch of temporary workers, it is the only solution to increasing the organizational capability and competency for the long run.

Managerial Feelings of Inadequacy

Most often, managers have been promoted due to their ability to personally "get work done right," not typically for their ability to build teams, work with others, or supervise. Thus, when elevated to the managerial ranks, most believe that delegation is a sign of weakness and fear loss of status or importance if they delegate work to underlings. Organizations that truly want to dispel this delegation fallacy need to develop managerial competency models that include emotional development as a part of the qualifications for supervision. Too often, promotions are given to the most productive or strongest "doer" in the department, without regard to the likelihood of success in getting work done through others. Managers presently suffering from this delusion must wake up and realize that future promotions will hinge on their ability to effectively delegate as a performance coach.

Fear of Being Overshadowed

A twist on the above "inadequacy" response, this rationalization for not coaching comes from managers who are afraid that trained, developed, and empowered subordinates will surpass them in the organizational hierarchy. Here too, organizations must consider the sturdiness of managerial ego. Maxwell (1998) calls this tendency on the part of managers "*The Law of the Lid,*" referring to the fact that organizations will not be successful as long as managers "hold back" true performers entrusted to their care. Organizational rewards must be in place for those managers or departments known as true people-development machines.

Fear of Organizational Poaching

Particularly self-centered and selfish managers worry about the long-term implications of using delegation as a development tool. The example, "If I train and develop my people to take on real responsibility and have real skills, they will be recruited from me by other departments or other organizations," seems to sum up this rationalization. Although all of the above rationalizations stem from selfishness on the part of the manager, this one is particularly troubling. Managers who subscribe to this error in thought are not acting with the organization's best interests at heart. Only by taking on a true "developmental" mind-set will managers enjoy the benefits of empowering and unleashing people's potential, without obsessing about if, or how long, they continue in their present role.

Perceived Insufficiency of Skills in Subordinates

A manager we recently worked with stated, "If I had stronger people, I'd delegate more to them." This sentiment is all too prevalent in managers who lack the skill to improve people through the delegation process. An honest and well-meaning manager we worked with actually spoke these words during a performance-consulting discussion. One of the ills he struggled with in the department was turnover and the inability to attract qualified candidates, because potential hires knew of his reputation as a poor people-developer. This delegation fallacy is particularly dangerous as a self-fulfilling prophecy; that is, managers who believe their people are weak and incompetent and, thus, don't delegate real work in a developmental way, are sentenced to always working with weak, incompetent people.

Dismissing the above fallacies and rationalizations about why managers don't use delegation is the easy part. Understanding just how deeply these beliefs are held in organizational life today is the humbling part. Assisting managers with changing these long-term habits to develop the potential of their people and to get more work done is the difficult task.

We believe that most managers hold these beliefs and that these managers are not, in and of themselves, bad people. The traditional managerial competencies of *planning, organizing, staffing, directing,* and *controlling* were built in the early industrial period of organizational life, when work knowledge was the domain of the managerial ranks and lower-level workers were discouraged from developing skills beyond being compliant and following instructions. Thus, today's cadre of managers who suffer from poor delegation are not solely liable for such inadequacy. Simply put, for more than 100 years much of management thought and practice was not designed to encourage effective, developmentally based delegation. Clearly, in today's knowledge-based service economy and quality-based continuous-improvement-driven manufacturing environment, the antiquated managerial tool kit can no longer afford to be absent the critical skill of delegation. Rather than a "human resource," today's worker must be viewed as a volunteer, able to find meaningful work in a variety of contexts and desiring to be developed by the organizations in which they choose to belong.

If most managers are not bad people, and delegation, if done well, is supposed to be "Good," and "Good for you," why don't more of them use delegation to its full potential? Our view is that no one yet has delivered to the managerial ranks a clear paradigm for developmentally based delegation. Much of the literature simply deals with the "why" of delegation, rather than moving beyond to deliver the "how" of effective delegation. To move organizations ahead, HRD must provide a more compelling and pragmatic answer to managers struggling with the delegation task of becoming a performance coach.

Outcomes of Performance Coaching:
Enhanced Self-Esteem and Improved Business Results

Performance coaching helps employees improve their self-esteem by providing challenging and rewarding assignments, positive feedback, and encouragement. It provides managers with an opportunity to better serve their employees through training, confronting, mentoring, and counseling. Consequently, performance coaching is a developmental process by which employees grow and enhance to improve their performance and advance their careers.

Performance coaching allows managers to increase their involvement with their employees, energize them, motivate and challenge them to become the best managers they can be. Performance coaching encourages managers to take on increasingly difficult assignments, which initiate change within an organization.

The ultimate outcome of the performance coaching process is to help performance coaches get results through people. For some, desired results could include increased revenue, improved quality, greater market share, or increased profitability. Quite simply, performance coaching helps managers and employees resolve problems, improve performance, and most important, achieve desired results.

Conclusion

Successful organizations have managers who motivate and inspire their employees, not discourage or beat them down. These individuals see themselves not just as "bosses" but as performance coaches, who take responsibility for: (1) providing employees with training that applies directly to the job; (2) helping employees enhance their careers and solve problems; (3) confronting employees in positive ways to improve performance; and (4) mentoring employees to help them become the best they can be. Performance coaches, ultimately, help employees grow and develop to their fullest potential.

Developing human resources is a managerial function, and the responsibility of supervisors, managers, executives, leaders, and HRD professionals. Performance coaching is one activity that enables those responsible for employee development to fulfill their obligations to individuals and their organization. The result is motivated, productive employees ready to accept challenges and take initiative.

Performance-Focused HRD

L. Michael Wykes

HRD professionals today are increasingly being asked to perform a broader role in helping their organizations reach business objectives. In order to do this, they have to be able to see the big picture, help business and organizational leaders and other employees determine what prevents top performance and what enhances performance, in the most efficient and cost-effective ways possible. HRD professionals who can't adapt to this paradigm will soon be at a disadvantage. Those who are able to implement all facets of HRD, including this expanded view (performance-focused HRD), will thrive.

Implementing performance-focused HRD means using a competence set that can be referred to as "performance consulting" or "human performance technology" to help internal or external clients achieve results quickly, efficiently, and effectively.

This focus is based on the simple fact that internal and external clients want results . . . their results. They need their problems solved. They want to hear things in their language. They are interested in the results of a process, not in the process itself. That's the world in which one must live.

Key Tenets for Performance-Focused HRD Practice

Solving problems by identifying gaps between actual and desired conditions and figuring out how to bridge the gap are pretty simple in concept but not always so easy in practice. There are a few key ideas to be considered in any real-world engagement of this sort, regardless of the exact methodology used. These include alignment, leverage, solving meaningful things, competence, simplicity, and speed.

Alignment

The tie to corporate/organizational strategic issues is critical. Any methodology used by an HRD professional must have the capability of assuring appropriate alignments and linkages throughout the organization.

Leverage

Leverage involves continually seeking the optimal solutions that present the best "bang for the buck."

Solving Meaningful Things

Internal business clients generally know what they want to do (for example, meet their goals) although they may not always have an idea of what is really wrong. HRD professionals and consultants have to play both sides of a fine-edged sword by making sure they deal with things of tangible value to their clients in the short term while focusing on root causes to solve for the longer term.

Competence

Competence means accomplishing "worthy" performance . . . performance that accomplishes a result valued by the organization but also does not cost too much, where cost includes financial issues, value issues, moral issues, and other relevant factors (Gilbert 1996, 29).

Simplicity

Albert Einstein is often attributed with saying that everything should be as simple as possible—but not simpler. Simple doesn't mean simplistic. Knowing what is important to clients helps define the level of detail to be used to classify problems and recommend solutions.

Speed

Effective HRD consultants and professionals always plan to deliver results to clients quicker than they expect. Being timely and accurate are two critical dimensions that will build HRD's reputation as an effective business partner.

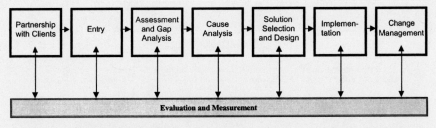

SOURCE: Based primarily upon *Performance consulting: Moving beyond training*, by D. G. Robinson & J. Robinson, 1995, San Francisco: Berrett-Koehler

FIGURE 8.1   The Performance-Consulting Process

Performance Consulting: Doing the Work

Performance-focused HRD relies on performance consulting to uncover needs and craft solutions for effective change. A paraphrased version of a typical project will be used as an example to illustrate how the consulting process works.

Figure 8.1 illustrates a combined process flow that integrates the best parts of models listed by several well-regarded sources (for example, Robinson and Robinson 1995; Rothwell 1996). Each phase of the process flow is discussed in turn.

Partnership with Clients

The partnership phase stresses the formation and growth of strong internal partnerships. Usually this means partnering at the highest possible level in the organization. Strong relationships are important to continued trust and credibility. These partnerships are generally ongoing and can be independent of any particular performance-consulting project (Robinson and Robinson 1995; 1998).

Effective HRD professionals engage in prior contacts with executive-level leaders to define worth. It's best if one has already performed several major projects successfully within the past several years or was brought in to help facilitate completion of a project to meet a specified business need.

Entry Phase

This phase entails entering into an agreement with internal clients to begin an actual project (Robinson and Robinson 1995). During this phase HRD

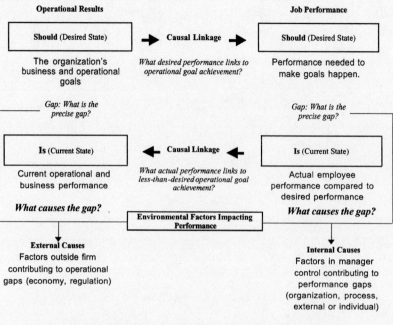

Operational Results

Should (Desired State)

The organization's business and operational goals

Causal Linkage

What desired performance links to operational goal achievement?

Job Performance

Should (Desired State)

Performance needed to make goals happen.

Gap: What is the precise gap?

Gap: What is the precise gap?

Is (Current State)

Current operational and business performance

What causes the gap?

Causal Linkage

What actual performance links to less-than-desired operational goal achievement?

Is (Current State)

Actual employee performance compared to desired performance

What causes the gap?

Environmental Factors Impacting Performance

External Causes
Factors outside firm contributing to operational gaps (economy, regulation)

Internal Causes
Factors in manager control contributing to performance gaps (organization, process, external or individual)

Adapted primarily from *Performance consulting: Moving beyond training* by D.G. Assessment and Analysis

FIGURE 8.2 Simplified Relationship Map

professionals or consultants define corporate business issues and projects during meetings, interviews, or executive focus groups. The main output for this project phase is a "project charter," which includes a "relationship map" to help link performances to measures and objectives (*see* figure 8.2) and a timeline definition document that defines two basic phases: (1) solving existing issues to improve immediate and long-term customer service concerns, and (2) developing and implementing an ongoing improvement process to continually enhance customer service and order-management services.

For example, in step 1 we may assume that business conditions dictated the need to use superb customer service to differentiate the company in the eyes of customers and dealers (for a product sold mainly through dealer channels). We are challenged to focus on critical activities that allow the company to win orders, manage orders, and follow-up on orders. Our client may desire more specific efficiency and effectiveness goals to:

• create organizational structure, process and job/performer clarification that reduces redundancy, achieves operating and expense

reductions and other expenses associated with winning projects, managing orders and performing corrective actions as needed; and
- reduce the time it takes to respond to customer inquiries regardless of topic, and consolidate the number of customer-contact points to increase levels of customer satisfaction.

In step 2, which is focused on the longer term, for the newly instituted process, organization, and job/performer functions the order management team would develop, own, and run continuous improvement activities to enhance the performance of selected employee groups and processes.

Assessment and Gap Analysis

During this phase, the consultant analyzes current performance compared with desired performance in order to identify the gap. Often this gap is presented in financial or business terms, and in terms of the performances needed to reach business goals. Goals that define where things should be (the "SHOULD" condition) are compared with actual accomplishments (the "IS" condition) to define the gap. Performances are examined in terms of what is needed to obtain desired performance and compared with what people are actually doing, which results in less-than-desired results. It is critical here to show the relationship between performances and obtaining objective goals. It is also critical to show linkages (or nonlinkages) of goals, objectives, and strategies. A key output of this stage includes clear identification of performance gaps.

In this phase, HRD professionals often form a team to accomplish the objectives as defined by the project charter. This team should be comprised mostly of high-level directors and others, including the performance consultant or HRD professional.

We've often spent several facilitated sessions defining and visually documenting current processes. At the same time, we engage in identifying the "disconnects" (things that didn't work) within the process and the barriers that appear to prevent people from working as efficiently as they should.

We then decide which disconnects are the most meaningful in terms of scope, potential, cost, and capability of being addressed within the time frame of the project. Our group then narrows the key disconnects into a series of "must-solve-issues" on which to focus. These could include statements like "we have too many contact points for customers and need one essential point for order management," "groups do redundant tasks continually," or "we have no efficient way to gather information and perform corrective actions."

The output is typically a report that includes a process document that specifically identifies barriers and disconnects, prioritizes them in order of importance, and lists potential solutions.

Cause Analysis

Output of this phase is the clear identification and presentation of key causes for gaps and their relationships. These causes can most effectively be grouped into six categories illustrated by Gilbert's (1996) Behavioral Engineering Model. He suggests that performance is the result of the interaction of a number of factors including:

1. Environmental factors—such as information flow (information and feedback); supporting systems, processes, and tools; rewards, incentives, and consequences.
2. Individual factors—such as skills, knowledge, attitudes, capabilities, and motivation of employees.

Figure 8.3 displays the relationship among these factors. The top row represents *environmental* factors (provided by the organization) and the bottom row depicts *individual* factors (provided by individual performers), which must be addressed and work together to provide an environment allowing high levels of performance. If any factors are not tackled appropriately, performance is likely to suffer. These factors are interdependent (Dean 1999; Gilbert 1996).

Gilbert's Behavioral Engineering Model works best when combined with Rummler and Brache's (1995) concepts and definitions concerning levels within organizations and the needs that must be filled for performance to

Environment Factors: *(What the organization provides)*	1. Information: expectations and feedback *(Clear expectations and appropriate feedback)*	2. Tools, systems processes, resources, space, and technology	3. Incentives: and rewards consequences *(Financial and nonfinancial)*
Individual Factors: *(What the individual provides)*	4. Skills, knowledge, and attitudes	5. Individual capacity	6. Motivation *(Intrinsic—within the person—and Extrinsic)*

SOURCE: Based primarily upon Gilbert, T. (1996). Human competence: Engineering worthy performance (Tribute Edition). Washington, DC: International Society for Performance Improvement.

FIGURE 8.3 Factors Needed for Top Performance

happen. Rummler and Brache view each organization as a system that must continually adapt to numerous forces from outside and from within in order to survive and grow. It can only do this if a number of performance variables are aligned and addressed (Rummler and Brache 1995; Rummler 1998). Rummler (1998) usually defines these components in the form of a matrix that has two dimensions: (1) the three *levels* of performance, and (2) the three performance *needs* that must be satisfied within each of those levels.

Three levels—organization, process, and job/performer levels—must be aligned. Within each level, three types of needs must be aligned:

1. Goals—all three levels need clear goals and standards that reflect customers' expectations;
2. Design—All three levels must have structures that enable goals to be met; and
3. Management (and Measurement)—Each level needs a management system and practices to ensure focus and progress toward goals.

Combining the three levels with the three types of needs yields a matrix that is made up of nine performance variables (*see* figure 8.4).

Rummler (1998) suggests that alignment among all of the levels and needs is critical for performance improvement to take place. The matrix, as a performance-consulting tool, helps to ensure that the necessary performance variables are satisfied. It also provides a convenient framework from which to design and ask systemic organizational diagnosis questions. Figure 8.4 illustrates how this "level-and-needs thinking" can be applied to help identify and categorize key barriers to performance in a systemic way. The following example is an abridged version of a categorization that can be used by performance consultants during a consulting engagement.

First, an HRD professional may hold several focused sessions with the development group to define the scope and levels of the key barriers. They specifically categorize the barriers and disconnects into categories corresponding to those defined by the Gilbert performance-factors grid and the Rummler-Brache performance-variables grid. This is done mostly to assure that a complete picture is viewed.

These categorizations help define which issues should be addressed and what issues need to be addressed to allow them to happen. For example, to address an issue on lack of communication due to physical separation, the solution would need approval at higher levels to allow physical changes to take place (for example, budget). Therefore, "gaining the approval" would be

	Focus Issues	Design Issues	Management and Measurement Issues
Organiza-tion Level Barriers	Lack of clarity about org. strategy Many different initiatives at once	Lack of role clarity among functions Too many points of contact for customers Redundant positions exist	Incentives are functionally focused, not process focused
Process Level Barriers	Process goals have internal focus vs. final focus on satisfaction	Complexities exist in the order management process itself	Tools (especially, electronic – for capturing data) not linked
Job Performer Level Barriers	Job goals not linked to integrated process standards Individual measures inconsistently linked	Department representatives lack decision authority	New jobs not clear. Integrated tools not complete at representatives level (note: other factors related to performance)

Adapted from "Barriers to Performance" by L. Michael Wykes, 2000, unpublished table. Based primarily upon upon Rummler G.A and Brache, A., (1995). *Improving performance* (2nd ed.). (p. 27) San Francisco: Jossey-Bass

FIGURE 8.4   Performance Variables: Simplified Version Showing Location of Key Disconnects and Barriers

built into the project plan for making any physical moves. This move, of course, would be only one part of a larger solution mix designed to address key issues systemically.

A basic version of a "should" process is employed—one designed to eliminate many of the key barriers and disconnects identified. For example, a key barrier may involve no efficient way to capture and use order-by-order customer data to "pass on" and assure that all players involved with it can be connected. In this case, the client group decided to utilize an existing customer software program and add a few enhancements to allow continued use for another year to eighteen months before the implementation of a large-business systems software was implemented. This particular part of the solution was relatively inexpensive to accomplish when compared to other possible alternatives since the capacity to run and alter it existed in-house (through a combination of IT professionals and order management professionals). Again, output is a cause analysis document that includes specific recommended solutions.

Solution Selection and Design

During the solution-selection and design phase, HRD consultants work with client representatives and subject-matter experts to select an appropriate mix of solutions designed to effectively lessen performance gaps. Typical solutions may include varied interventions based on barriers to success uncovered during the causal analysis. Solutions often include a mix of policy changes, clarifications, staffing, training, technology solutions, and changes to measurement and reward/consequence systems. The output of this phase often includes a simple, clear executive summary and documentation, including prioritized solutions that are matched with the problems they are designed to solve, cost/benefit analysis, resource needs, and other details as needed. The quality and comprehensiveness of the solution mix is directly related to the quality of the outputs generated during the analysis phase.

In this phase we develop a list of prioritized potential solutions with our group, using criteria within the desired time frame such as feasibility, cost, scope, difficulty of completion, readiness, and simplicity. We take care to avoid "analysis paralysis."

In a recent engagement, our solution mix included:

- Defining public agreement and statements from the executive-management team that showed the depth and measure of support for the project's objectives;
- Creating a new process that treats customer service as a single process (this included clear measures);
- Defining specific roles and responsibilities (who does what and when) to reduce existing ambiguity. This includes clear measures at the corporate, process and job/performer levels, job descriptions (approved by HR and Legal), basic performance models, job aids, and role, responsibility, and accountability/authority clarification. These documents help to clearly define levels of authority and accountability;
- Moving groups that perform closely related process functions into the same areas to facilitate easier communication and process. For example, making sure that customer-service representatives were located near both those who help get the order and those who help follow up on orders;
- Defining key points of contact for customers to eliminate confusion caused by multiple points of contact. This included only two key contacts (rather than many, as in previous iterations) to act as information and implementation contacts for dealers/customers throughout the order-management process. For example, once an order was entered into the system, specific customer-service representatives served as contacts for dealers throughout the rest of the process. Key ownership was assured by using a common, simple database to be accessed throughout the process to track order activities and gather information for potential long- and short-term corrective actions;

- Clarifying leadership for the new group(s) formed and assuring that leaders have the authority to do what it is they must do. In this case two basic groups were formed, one focused on "getting the sale—getting an order" and the other assured that the order was managed through delivery, billing, and—if necessary—corrective action;
- Assembling an aggressive but attainable implementation schedule;
- Learning and training interventions to assure that all "players" are fully aware of the process and tools necessary. This included several learning interventions, job aids, and defined coaching from management and others;
- Meeting regularly to discuss issues and solve them as they arise.

Implementation

During implementation the consultant works with the client to help ensure that solutions are carried out efficiently and effectively. It is critical in this phase that the client actually owns the benefit derived from the solutions. If clients feel that solutions are being done *to* them, the chances for successful follow-through are far less likely than if they perceive that solutions are being done *with* them or *by* them.

Key outputs of this phase include attainment of project-plan steps and measures and the ultimate increases in performance as outlined during the entry and analysis phases. Most of the work—especially the detail work on an overall performance-improvement project—occurs during the implementation phase. If done correctly, diverse and specialized teams comprised of client representatives and intervention specialists do this work. The performance consultant often acts as a process consultant and confidant to the chosen project leader.

This phase can cause concern among HRD personnel. Much of the actual expertise for implementing a particular solution, or mix of solutions, lies outside of the skill set that many HRD professionals possess. During this phase, the performance consultant often acts as both an intervention broker and a project manager, helping make sure that individual interventions combine to solve issues systemically.

A well-implemented plan shows a direct correlation between the major barriers uncovered during the performance analysis and the specific mix of interventions chosen to eliminate those barriers to allow for improved performance.

We recently implemented the process and a new customer-service system for a couple of months before the second phase of the charter began to assure that a continuous improvement system was in place. We began by choosing the department/function that was most ready to begin continuous improvement. In our case that proved to be the function that dealt with "order management," because its leadership indicated readiness and it contained the single largest number of employees (customer-service representatives) that could be focused on to begin the improvement process.

We began a subproject to help improve the performance of a preselected group of employees (customer-service representatives). At this point it was critical to ensure the project was "owned" by the function's leaders and group members.

Once the basic charter was developed for the subproject, we performed an analysis of current performance to identify key barriers to performance and to develop a specific performance model for the customer-service representatives. This took place during a two-week period during which the performance consultants and order-management trainers interviewed nearly forty individual customer-service representatives (exemplars—high performers), managers, and representatives of selected dealers using specifically defined questions. Key questions included:

- What do you expect of "good" customer service?
- How do you describe an ideal customer service representative?
- (For exemplars) How do you accomplish good customer service (speed to response, follow-up, and so forth)? Note: the resulting performance model was based on behaviors performed by exemplars (*see* Gilbert 1996 and others).
- What things get in the way of providing good service?

We then documented and categorized the information into barriers defined as factors (performance grid and performance factors grid). A rough model of key behaviors exhibited by exemplars was also defined.

The information was revised in the form of an executive report and a performance model, then reviewed with the management team. We then selected focus groups comprised of exemplary customer-service representatives, trainers, and two management representatives to meet several times to refine the model and develop a list of potential solutions to increase performance. Figure 8.5 displays a sample performance model.

To set the stage for acceptance we sent a memorandum to all order-management employees giving an update on the project and a time line of what was to happen next.

CUSTOMER SERVICE REPRESENTATIVE: PERFORMANCE MODEL (SIMPLIFIED SAMPLE)			
Result Area ...what must be accomplished?	Competencies Required	Best Practices ...how it can be accomplished	Result Area Measures ...criteria for excellence
Building customer loyalty	• Analysis • Decision–making • Relationship building	Definition: Providing quick, honest response to dealers' questions. 1. Provide timely responses to dealers (as perceived by them); return calls promptly (80% of answers to be provided within 3 hours). 2. Provide status to dealers regularly even when the final answer is not yet available. 3. Present options to customers in situations where their initial request may not be able to be met.	Σ 80% target met or exceeded. Σ Dealer survey indicates satisfaction. Σ Options provided.
Teamwork / Collaboration	• Organization • Relationship building	Definition: Help to accomplish team, group goals by performing appropriate actions 1. Helps teammates without prompting, whenever necessary 2. Perform regular, formal preparation for others who will be covering the phones and email when you are absent 3. When covering for another person, cover as if things were your own	Σ Peer survey and observation indicate helpfulness. Σ Checklist information indicates appropriate coverage preparation. Σ Customers indicate no drop in service levels during coverage situations. (Surveys)

SOURCE: Adapted from Wykes, M., March-Swets, J., & L. Rynbrandt, (2000). Performance analysis: Field operations management. In Phillips, J., (ed.), *In action: Performance consulting and analysis*, Alexandria: ASTD, (pp. 135–153).

FIGURE 8.5   Sample Performance Model

Once the basic model was approved, we defined a list of potential solutions. These included things like approving and implementing the performance model, defining key measures to be used for performance improvement to "set the expectations," developing appropriate job aids, surveys, and other methods to gather performance information, and performing appropriate "tweaks" to an existing software program. The performance model was communicated to the group at large and to customer-service representatives in particular. Several discussion meetings with various customer-service groups were held to answer questions and provide clarity. We then deployed the continuous improvement process to work on other job/performer functions.

Change Management

This "step" of the consulting process is not called out separately in many models—it is often incorporated into the general implementation phase. Rothwell (1996) and others, however, find it significantly important to distinguish. Managing the change process with the client is often the most difficult step to complete successfully. During this step, the HRD consultant monitors progress and helps ensure that individuals and groups get the information they need. Consultants also guarantee that key stakeholders are continually involved in the process. The best consultants are able to consistently maintain relationships with clients at the highest levels, build helpful support, and gain buy-in from executives and other corporate leadership.

During this phase, we hold regular weekly updates, reviews, and discussion sessions with senior management and employees to ensure that the project's goals remain in alignment with corporate goals and are acceptable to employees.

Evaluation and Measurement

This phase is really both an ending and a beginning. It puts a cap on the current engagement and sets the stage for possible further interactions. During this step, the HRD consultant compares actual goal-and-objective attainment with specific accomplishments that were defined in the entry and assessment phases. This phase asks the questions: Did you get the results you wanted? If not, why? What needs to be done now? The consultant uses a variety of qualitative and quantitative data collection and analysis techniques to perform measurement and evaluation. Evaluation is actually planned during the assessment phase but is carried out during the performance-consulting process. Evaluation can be done during the process to guide and shape the ongoing actions (such as formative evaluation). It is also performed after an intervention has been completed to gauge the intervention's impact on critical measures (such as summative evaluation).

Effective HRD professionals design evaluation components into the system near the beginning of the project. These contain breakdowns of objective measures (for example, cost reductions due to efficiencies, quicker response times to dealers, enhanced confidence indicated by customers and dealers, perceived better service, increased accuracy in identifying and solving problems both proactively and reactively, fewer dollars being paid out due to errors, and increased productivity of customer-service representatives).

Conclusion

Naturally, each consulting or performance improvement project in which you engage will have unique elements. This chapter presented a basic road map to follow. It is up to HRD professionals, managers, and consultants to use Performance-Focused HRD for strategic thinking and planning and for specific projects to meet or exceed your client's needs quickly, efficiently, and completely.

They will reap the benefits . . . and so will you!

Organizational Learning: A Reflective and Representative Critical Issue for HRD

Jamie L. Callahan

The concept of organizational learning began to emerge in scholarly literature in the early 1950s with Herbert Simon's work on adaptation processes in organizations (Cangelosi and Dill 1965). Since then, interest in the phenomenon has steadily grown; in fact, popular interest exploded with the practitioner work, *The Fifth Discipline: The Art and Practice of the Learning Organization* (Senge 1990). Crossan and Guatto (1996) note that the total number of articles dedicated to organizational learning or learning organizations went from a mere three in the 1960s to 184 in just the first few years of the 1990s. Some scholars (for example, Easterby-Smith and Araujo 1999; Prange 1999) have even suggested that learning is a core component of understanding organizational life and that organizational learning itself has become a focal point in organizational theory.

Organizational learning is an area of both research and practice that contributes to the survival, growth, and future of HRD as a field. As such, it meets the criteria established in the introduction of this book to be considered a critical issue for the HRD profession. However, organizational learning has even deeper importance because it is also important for the survival, growth, and future of organizations. This chapter explores organizational learning as a critical issue for both HRD and the individuals and organizations served by HRD.

Background

The twentieth century marked an increase in the rate of technological and so-cietal change the likes of which had never been experienced before; that rate of change continues today, and will continue to increase. Gilley and Maycu-nich (2000, 16) point out that "organizations will no longer remain competi-tive with informal approaches to knowledge and learning." While organiza-tional learning is crucial to maintain competitive success, it has also become essential to the very survival of organizations in our rapidly changing world (Schwandt and Marquardt 2000). Sustained performance in and by organiza-tions simply can no longer be achieved without learning.

Mindful learning systems—formal and informal, embedded throughout the organization—provide the tools for successfully navigating a host of con-temporary challenges. The rapid increase in technology is the classic example why organizational learning is the wave of the future (Schwandt and Mar-quardt 2000). Technology can maximize learning potential by increasing ac-cess to information, opening markets previously unattainable, and improving production processes. In order to take advantage of these opportunities, however, organizations must be prepared to learn about applicable technol-ogy and to then embed systems for capturing the cumulative learning associ-ated with the technology of today. But technology is not the only contempo-rary challenge facing organizations.

For example, the workplace is becoming more global and diverse (Bierema, Bing, and Carter 2002); we all have to learn how to work with people from different countries, cultures, races, and ethnicities. Organizational learning systems can provide the tools necessary for connecting to new and different environments and people. Organizations also face a workforce that is increas-ingly contingent and temporary, without the psychological contract of life-time employment (Bradach 1997). Employees who rotate in and out of orga-nizations on a regular basis certainly need to know how to learn as individuals. However, organizations can optimize a temporary workforce by having organizational learning systems in place that distribute broad-scale learning and shorten the time necessary for employees to "learn the ropes" in their new organizations.

The top trends facing organizations that emerged from the ASTD/AHRD 2001 Future Search Conference suggest that we live in a short-term world. The increasing demand for a just-in-time workplace and increasing stake-holder pressure for short-term profits are two of the top trends (Bierema et al. 2002). This focus on short-term-performance gratification may preclude investments in learning how to most effectively achieve organizational goals.

Performance creates immediate changes in activity, but it is learning that creates fundamental changes in structures and systems that can be used to attain goals (Parsons and Shils 1951). As the rate of change continues to increase, our rate of learning must also increase; thus, organizational learning is a critical issue for the success and survival of contemporary organizations.

Both organizational learning and its counterpart, learning organizations, are not only critical to organizations confronting endless and radical change, but they are also quintessential HRD issues. Organizational learning is both representative and reflective of HRD. *Representative* means "to serve as an example or specimen of; exemplify" or serve "to express, stand for . . . or symbolize" (Urdang 1988, 1120). Organizational learning is representative of HRD because it exemplifies the most historically important underlying theories of the field—learning theory and organizational theory. *Reflective* means having the ability "to give back or show an image of; mirror" (Urdang 1988, 1108). Organizational learning is reflective of HRD because the conflicts and difficulties encountered by those who study organizational learning mirror those experienced by the field of HRD.

Organizational learning and learning organizations both represent the intersection of *learning* and *organizations*. Because the unique characteristic of HRD is the application of learning theory to help organizations and people who work in those organizations, "learning" and "organization" theories and practices are the very foundations of the field. Thus, the concepts of *organizational learning* and *learning organizations* are critical to HRD because they are representative of the foundations of the field.

Not only is the issue of organizational learning representative of HRD, this field of study is also reflective of the struggles encountered in the development of HRD as a field of research and practice. The study of learning and organizations has been besieged by false dichotomies that set scholars against one another. In its search for identity, the field of HRD encouraged a culture of debate. Although this culture initiated the exploration of critical issues in the field, one of the negative consequences of such debates has been the emergence of false dichotomies. The most damaging dichotomy has been whether the nature of HRD is about learning or performance. Thus, the struggles in the study of organizational learning are critical to HRD because they are reflective of the struggles for identity in the field.

This chapter explores organizational learning as both a representative and reflective critical issue for the field of HRD. First is a review of the historic and enduring HRD connection to learning that makes organizational learning *representative* of HRD. The chapter then compares experiences in the field of HRD to those experienced in the study of organizational learning in order to highlight how organizational learning is *reflective* of HRD. The chapter concludes with a practical application section that addresses key operating conditions for organizational learning and presents a framework developed to incorporate the perspectives of both learning and performance in the study and application of HRD.

Organizational Learning as Representative of HRD

Although "organizational" disciplines may have other agendas, for the most part they purport to help organizations improve performance. What differentiate these disciplines are both the manner in which they attempt to accomplish this task and the theories that inform their practice. I suggest that the distinguishing characteristic of HRD is our historic and enduring connection to processes and theories associated with learning; no other "organizational" field or discipline can make that claim. To support this argument, this section briefly traces the central role that learning has played in HRD.

Although it is possible to suggest that the origins of human resource development can be traced to antiquity, the field as a distinct activity is more accurately traced to World War II and its aftermath (Nadler 1985). The need to quickly prepare a productive homefront workforce to replace American soldiers during the war spurred the growth of formalized HRD activities. In particular, Training Within Industry (TWI) was a specific project established by the Council of National Defense in 1940 to find ways to speed production and lower costs in the war effort (Ruona 2001). By the time World War II had ended, the concept of formal and informal training as mechanisms to improve organizational performance was widely recognized. Indeed, by the 1960s, a wide variety of human resource activities were emerging, largely in response to legislation and government-sponsored programs (Nadler 1985). To help industry meet the growing need for human resource development professionals, Nadler established the HRD graduate program at George Washington University in the mid-1960s (Nadler 1985; Swanson and Holton 2001).

This first HRD graduate program was, and still is, situated in the Graduate School of Education and Human Development at George Washington University because the key characteristic that distinguished HRD from a host of other "organizational" fields was *learning* (Nadler 1985). The focus on learning, or similar concepts, such as education, training, or development, has remained an important component of HRD programs throughout the country. Kuchinke (2002b) points out that three dominant HRD programs in the United States are not only situated in colleges of education, but they also incorporate learning and training as part of their curriculum. Despite their different roots and curricular structure, these programs recognize the fundamental importance of learning in HRD. Further, a survey of eighty-three HRD graduate programs revealed that courses associated with adult learning or education dominate the general HRD curriculum (Kuchinke 2002a).

This connection to learning and related concepts also can be seen in the evolution of HRD definitions. Weinberger (1998) lists sixteen definitions of human resource development that span from 1970 to 1995.* Most of these definitions (thirteen of sixteen) explicitly include "learning" or "training"; two, however, are more implicit. One definition refers to HRD as an "expansion . . . of work-related abilities" (Jones 1981 as cited in Weinberger 1998, 77), which could be considered some type of learning. The other, Nadler's seminal definition of HRD, highlights "behavioral change" but does not explicitly use the terms *learning, training,* or *development.* Nevertheless, it is widely accepted that Nadler believed learning to be the essence of HRD and "behavioral change" is a common descriptor of learning. Of the sixteen definitions of HRD, only Swanson's definition fails to mention concepts associated with learning, training, or development, focusing instead on capability and performance. Thus, of the sixteen definitions of HRD spanning twenty-five years, fifteen either explicitly or implicitly refer to learning, training, or development.

Leaders of the field also refer to learning as a fundamental component of HRD (Ruona 2000). A common theme that emerged from her in-depth interviews with ten widely recognized scholarly leaders of HRD was that learning, among other factors, is a part of the field's endeavor to serve both individuals and organizations. This connection of learning, individuals, and organizations might be seen as the unifying coordinate of HRD; indeed, the tie that binds HRD as a unique field of study is the concept of learning. The foundational pillars of the field of human resource development are the concepts of people, learning, and organizations (Callahan and McCollum 2002).

If one accepts that people, learning, and organizations are core elements of human resource development, it is easy to see that organizational learning and learning organizations would be critical areas of study that are representative of the field of HRD. Organizational learning offers an avenue of study that moves learning solely from the individual to include the collective level.

---

*Weinberger (1998) lists a total of eighteen definitions in her article. However, McLagan's definition explicitly states that she is defining training and development, and Jacobs's definition explicitly states that he is defining human performance technology. Neither "training and development" nor "human-performance technology" can be considered the equivalent of HRD. Because I am specifically concerned with definitions of HRD as a unique field of inquiry, I have excluded these two definitions from my discussion.

In other words, it opens a path for expansion and growth for research and practice in HRD—important criteria for critical issues.

Organizational Learning as Reflective of HRD

Not only is the combination of organizations and learning an area of study that is representative of the underlying theories of HRD, it is also reflective of HRD. The debates that have framed the dialogue about learning and organizations are similar to some of the core debates that have framed HRD as a field. As an area of research, organizational learning, and its counterpart, learning organizations, have suffered from the same "false dichotomization" dilemma as the field of HRD. Both HRD, as a field of research and practice, and organizational learning, as a subject of inquiry, have encountered debates about means versus ends and micro versus macro. The common experience of these debates makes organizational learning a reflection of HRD. This section will explore each of these debates.

Means Versus Ends

The study of learning and organizations is typically approached from either an organizational-learning perspective or a learning-organization perspective. The field of HRD has been besieged by debates about whether the role of HRD is to enhance performance or learning. As the following sections will highlight, each of these debates is fundamentally about the distinction between means and ends.

Organizational Learning and Learning Organizations.   Organizational learning and learning organizations are two distinct, yet complementary, areas of study. In general, the literature on organizational learning focuses on describing the nature and process of learning while the literature on learning organizations focuses on identifying prescriptive characteristics of learning in and by the organization (Easterby-Smith, Burgoyne, and Araujo 1999; Tsang 1997). The concepts of organizational learning and learning organizations have multiple definitions. Indeed, almost every author offers a new and different definition (Tsang 1997) and the literature generally has not been cumulative (Prange 1999). Many authors have engaged in dialogue about the distinctions between organizational learning and learning organizations (Easterby-Smith et al. 1999; Schwandt and Marquardt 2000; Tsang 1997). This chapter will only highlight some of the definitions of each construct and provide an overview of the key distinctions.

Some common definitions of organizational learning include:

- "Organizational learning refers to the process by which the organizational knowledge base is developed and shaped" (Shrivastava 1983, 15);
- "An entity learns if, through its processing of information, the range of its potential behaviors is changed" (Huber 1991, 89); and
- "A system of actions, actors, symbols, and processes that enables an organization to transform information into valued knowledge which, in turn, increases its long-run adaptive capacity" (Schwandt 1995, 370).

Some common definitions of learning organizations include:

- "an organization that is continually expanding its capacity to create its future" (Senge 1991, 14);
- "The critical characteristics of a learning organization [are]—that learning occurs at four interdependent levels—individual, team, organization, and society—and that learning transforms or changes the organization" (Watkins and Marsick 1993, 9); and
- "A learning organization is seen as a form of organization that enables the learning of its members in such a way that it creates positively valued outcomes, such as innovation, efficiency, better alignment with the environment and competitive advantage" (Huysman 1999, 61).

These definitions highlight that organizational learning is a process of some sort while learning organizations are those that are characterized by the existence of learning processes. As research in both of these areas has continued, overlap between the two areas has become more evident. Clearly, research in organizational learning processes has begun to reveal normative models of the learning process. Research on the learning organization often relies on theories from the process-oriented organizational learning literature. When taken together, these two bodies of literature help us understand both the processes that lead to learning in, by, and among organizations and the characteristics that identify those organizations. In other words, organizational learning is a means to achieve the end goal of becoming a learning organization. While organizational learning does not *necessarily* lead to becoming a learning organization, organizational learning must occur in order to achieve and maintain the characteristics of a learning organization.

Learning and Performance. The Watkins-Swanson debate at the 1995 Academy of Human Resource Development Conference (Swanson 1995; Watkins and Marsick 1995) spurred an ongoing debate about the nature and purpose of HRD. Since then, the field has been engaged in a sometimes heated dialogue about whether HRD is "about" learning or performance as an end goal. Much like the constructs of organizational learning and learning organizations, learning and performance are complementary constructs.

HRD professionals often use learning as the means to achieve performance when they practice their trade for organizations. As Parsons and Shils (1951) point out, the reverse is often true as well; performance can be a means to create learning. Because of the background in adult learning theory that HRD professionals (should) have, we are often influenced by theories that encourage us to focus on the inherent good of our interventions for the individual despite perceived or real conflicts with the performance goals of the organization. Some of the theories that are particularly focused on the meaningful consideration of the individual include radical, humanistic, and critical theories of adult learning (for a description of these and other learning theories, see Bierema 2001; Bigge and Shermis 1992; Merriam and Caffarella 1991). Thus, although performance is often (but not always) an end goal in our service to organizations, learning can have other ends that are valued by HRD professionals in their service to individuals. This is an important factor that actually helps HRD professionals behave ethically and, in particular, avoid the trap of what Jerry Harvey (1988) calls the Eichmann defense.

HRD professionals are regularly called upon to engage in practices that deeply hurt individuals in the name of profit and performance. Harvey suggests that, like Adolf Eichmann, we auction our souls by participating in these activities. The result is that "we destroy the delicate threads of human fabric that are required not only to make those organizations function effectively but also to allow them to survive" (Harvey 1988, 78). Our exposure to and awareness of humanistic, radical, and other similar learning theories helps provide a moral compass that allows HRD professionals to balance the needs of the organization with the needs of the individual. In order to account for this perspective as well as the more traditional perspective of performance, the end goal for HRD is perhaps best seen as "improving the human condition."

Although Swanson and Holton (2001) suggest that the paradigms of HRD are "about" performance and learning, that is a restrictive and divisive perspective. As a field that works with organizations as social systems, HRD is necessarily about *both* learning and performance. The paradigms in HRD are about the different aspects of improving the human condition we hope to achieve in our application of learning theory.

Micro Versus Macro

The debate about micro versus macro has its roots in distinctions between psychology and sociology and the underlying philosophical perspectives that guide each of those disciplines. In essence, the debate among organizational learning scholars has been about the nature of the construct itself. In other words, the issue is whether organizations, as non-human entities, can actually "learn" or if it is only individuals within organizations that can learn. The debate among HRD professionals seems to be about the focus of service. In other words, does HRD serve the individual and, therefore, construct interventions at the individual level; or does the field serve organizations and construct interventions that also target the organization as a whole? Both of these debates are about micro and macro issues that are associated with the level of analysis deemed most useful or appropriate.

Organizational Learning or Learning within Organizations?

The second primary area of debate among scholars of learning and organizations is whether "learning" that takes place is seen only at the individual level or whether it is somehow manifested at the organizational level. Those scholars who begin with a micro approach of learning *in* organizations often come from an adult learning or human resource development perspective (Finger and Brand 1999). On the other hand, those scholars who take a macro approach of learning *by* organizations as systems often come from an organizational theory perspective.

Those who believe that organizational learning is an individual phenomenon would typically argue that to suggest that organizations are entities that learn is anthropomorphism. Organizations can't learn, only people in organizations can learn. Huysman (1999) suggests that the organizational learning literature has a bias towards viewing learning as an individual phenomenon. However, while many management scholars certainly hold this belief (see Antonacopoulou 1999; Dodgson 1993), it is more common to see adult learning/HRD scholars explicitly apply learning theory as they explore the micro level of organizational learning. In perhaps the best example of this type of application, Bierema (2001) outlines the philosophical underpinnings of organizational learning by providing an in-depth overview of the major theories of adult education that could inform the construct.

The macro approach often does not include an explicit description of learning theory; this, in particular, provides fertile ground for future HRD research. Those who take the macro approach to organizational learning either look at organizational learning as a metaphor or as a phenomenon independent of individual organizational members (Huysman 1999). The perspective of individual learning as a metaphor or means to describe the collective phenomenon of organizational learning seems to be the most prevalent in the scholarly literature (Fiol and Lyles 1985; Hedberg 1981; Huber 1991; Schwandt 1994). These scholars suggest that organizational learning is something beyond the cumulative effects of individual learning. While most recognize the individual as a learner within organizations, they focus on the synergistic level of learning beyond individuals.

Thus, organizational learning and learning organization scholars are interested in two primary elements of learning. They typically either focus on the individual as learner within the context of organizations or on the organization as a social collective that can learn in its own right beyond its individual members. These differing perspectives represent differences in level of analysis. The two perspectives do not have to be diametrically opposed. Like the debate about means versus ends, each level informs the other.

HRD: Individual or Organizational?

As in the study of organizational learning, in the field of HRD similar micro-versus-macro issues arise. HRD scholars often fall into two general level of analysis groups—those that focus on serving the individual and those that focus on looking at the organizational level.

Although the earliest definitions of HRD included the organizational level, HRD was typically associated with training and development without consideration of the organization development component of the field. Many HRD professionals became expert in the application of learning theory through training interventions for organizations. Swanson and Holton (2001) point out that the focus on the individual level encompassed both the performance and learning perspectives of HRD. This was natural, they suggest, "because HRD has its roots in individual learning" (184).

The organizational perspective is considered key to positioning HRD as a strategic partner in organizations today (Gilley and Maycunich 2000). The organizational level of analysis in HRD began with the study of organization development and has continued through the study of organizational learning, performance, and change. As an independent field, organization development emerged on a parallel track with training and development (Swanson and Holton 2001). Together the two fields comprise the broader field of HRD. Thus, the very identity of the field is linked to the false dichotomy of the micro-versus-macro debate; HRD is necessarily about both the individual and the organization.

Like the field of study of organizational learning, the scholarship and practice of HRD struggles along several lines of debate. Organizational learning is reflective of HRD because it, too, has conflicts over the process-versus-ends and individual-versus-collective levels of analysis. Again, however, these debates are based on false dichotomies. Neither organizational learning as an area of inquiry nor HRD as a field of practice can be confined to singular perspectives represented in a dichotomy. As a result of these conflicts, both areas attempt to identify their unique contribution to scholarship and practice. This common thread merely highlights how the field of HRD struggles for a sense of identity.

The Struggle for Identity

HRD is struggling for a sense of identity; this struggle was made even more apparent by the debate topic at the 2002 Academy of Human Resource Development conference—renaming the field of HRD. The core of this argument was that the field does not have a sense of its own identity and that, perhaps, a change in the label we use to identify ourselves might help the field and its clients better understand what we "do" and who we "are." Ruona (2000, 2) claims that "as a profession, we have not done a very good job of working to identify who we are, what we stand for, and what we can do for those we serve." This struggle for identity can be seen in the way HRD has approached the construct of organizational learning.

Interest in organizational learning began to emerge in the field of management about the same time that HRD appeared as a distinct field itself. Although a few HRD scholars have engaged in the study of organizational learning, the field of HRD has never fully embraced the concept. The primary scholarly publication for HRD, *Human Resource Development Quarterly*, published only five refereed journal articles on organizational learning or learning organizations from 1994 to 2002. When considered against the vast number of publications on this topic discussed earlier in this chapter, this is a mere fraction of the dialogue on organizational learning and learning organizations. If organizational learning and learning organization represent two of the core theoretical foundations of HRD, why do we see so few refereed articles, and even fewer empirical articles, on the topic in the core journal of the field? The reason for this resistance to organizational learning can be found in the field's attempt to create a distinct identity as a valued strategic partner with organizational leadership.

It is not uncommon to hear people associate HRD with "training." As a field of practice that goes far beyond "training," HRD and its practitioners have struggled for decades to move into a more strategic position in organizations. Our approach to accomplish this goal has been to emphasize how

HRD contributes to performance (Gilley and Maycunich 2000; Swanson and Holton 2001). Organizational leaders certainly understand and value contributions that improve the "bottom line." As a field, we will only succeed if the organizations for which we work can value what we bring to them. However, while HRD must contribute to organizational performance in order to be a truly strategic partner, the path to partnership for HRD is through the emphasis on learning in, by, and among organizations.

Reconceptualizing HRD as a System of Action

The struggle for identity and recognition faced by HRD highlights the need to create new ways to conceptualize the field. The debates about "means" versus "ends" and "micro" versus "macro" that are mirrored in the critical issue of organizational learning should encourage us to find ways to reduce dichotomization. If we advocate a systems perspective for HRD, we should embrace the perspectives of both means and ends, and micro and macro.

American sociologist Talcott Parsons (1951) argued that social systems consisted of multiple levels of individual and collective action; he also argued that performance and learning were both necessary components of all systems of action. Each has a different role, however. Performance processes "transmit changes . . . without changing the structure of the system" (Parsons and Shils 1951, 123). On the other hand, learning processes can be seen as "changes in the structure or pattern of the system itself [that] are occurring all of the time along side of (and partly determined by) the performance processes of the system" (Parsons and Shils 1951, 123).

In other words, learning and performance are complementary actions that create changes in organizations. A singular focus on performance lacks reflection in, and on, action; true learning necessarily incorporates reflection that can serve to accomplish many goals, including performance improvement. Learning in and by organizations is informed, in part, by the desired performance goals of the organization. In turn, learning creates the opportunity for more lasting and effective change; it deepens performance.

In this spirit, I suggest using a holistic framework that captures both the individual and the organization, and performance and learning. It is a heuristic for categorizing both the theories that inform the field of HRD and the actions taken as a result of incorporating those theories. The framework is a simplification of the action-classification system developed by Parsons (1951) and applied to the field of HRD. The underlying Parsonian theory for the approach presented here has been used in a wide variety of studies of organizational phenomena. For example, it has been used as part of transformational leadership

Purpose of Action

	Means	Ends
Internal	**Identity** Performance and learning actions related to how an individual or collective can maintain a unique culture and identity	**Integration** Performance and learning actions related to how an individual or collective can create a common sense of identity
External	**Adaptation** Performance and learning actions related to how an individual or collective interacts with the external environment	**Achievement** Performance and learning actions related to how an individual or collective can use resources to accomplish goals

(Row label on left: **Orientation of Action**)

FIGURE 9.1   Purpose of Action

theory (Sashkin and Rosenbach 1993), in studies of organizational culture (Frank and Fahrbach 1999; Sashkin 1996), in research on emotion management (Callahan 2000), and as part of theory development and research on organizational learning (Schwandt 1994; Schwandt and Marquardt 2000). As a heuristic device, the framework is important because it helps us to identify issues and intervene based on *action* that includes both learning and performance.

The framework presented here is a multilevel systems approach that incorporates both the means and ends of action in a social system. As such it provides a framework for looking at both the individual and collective levels of a system while incorporating both performance and learning as part of the same system of action (*see* figure 9.1). Perhaps most important, such a framework offers a strategic tool for HRD professionals as they consider what actions to take within an organization. The most effective systemic approach would be to ensure that each component of the framework is addressed in the constellation of HRD interventions.

The model allows us to focus on learning as one of the key underlying theories of HRD, while continuing to recognize that performance is one viable outcome for HRD interventions. These four quadrants are collections of actions that occur in all social systems. The four function quadrants are identity (I), integration (I), adaptation (A), and achievement (A) and collectively comprise the I-A Model of HRD. Each quadrant represents a set of theories and actions that collectively comprise the field of HRD. Neither learning nor performance is the goal of action in this approach. Rather, both learning and performance are embedded in the actions that occur in each of the functions of the system.

It is important to emphasize that this framework is a systems approach to HRD. As such, these quadrants can be viewed from multiple perspectives while still framing theories and actions associated with HRD as a field of practice. In keeping with Parsons's approach to social systems, this is a nested framework for HRD. In other words, the four quadrants can be used to look at actions taken by individuals, departments within organizations, organizations, and the larger community. The I-A Model could even be used as a framework to explore HRD as a profession.

The *identity* quadrant includes those actions that help organizations maintain a shared sense of uniqueness. For example, theories about organizational culture and identity inform actions taken in association with this quadrant. In its role of serving organizations, HRD professionals might take actions to maintain identity such as:

- holding orientation seminars for new employees to socialize them into the organization;
- developing succession plans for organizational leadership;
- building organizational histories;
- inviting employees to regularly held social functions, such as retreats, holiday parties, or hail and farewell gatherings;
- creating logos or other symbols that represent the organization.

The purpose of actions associated with *integration* is to help organizations actually create a sense of common identity. In other words, these actions integrate the separate parts of the organization into an identifiable whole. Theories about organizational size, structure, and communication would help guide actions in this category. Some of those actions might include:

- publishing a newsletter for the organization;
- modifying the organizational structure to better facilitate communication;
- setting up an employee break room to encourage interaction;
- holding team-building workshops;
- investing in diversity training.

Achievement is about setting and reaching goals; actions here are focused on how to mobilize resources in order to achieve the desired goals of the organization. Theories about motivation, transfer of learning, reflective practice, or decision-making would be helpful in understanding this category. Actions might include:

- setting up reward systems;
- holding training sessions for skills;
- establishing a learning resource center;
- encouraging inquiry and reflection on the job.

Adaptation is about interacting with the external environment. It is focused on obtaining resources that would include people, information, and technology. Theories that would inform adaptation would be about environmental scanning, organizational adaptation, or innovation. Actions might include:

- recruiting new employees;
- benchmarking with other organizations in the industry;
- managing external continuing professional education activities;
- attending conferences or conventions;
- surfing the Internet for relevant new information.

All of the functions of the I-A Model include activities that most, if not all, organizations engage in. The role of HRD professionals is to help organizations balance the actions of each of these quadrants in order to achieve the goals of the organization. The I-A Model is a systems tool that HRD professionals can use to describe processes, diagnose areas of need, and implement appropriate interventions for the larger organization. For every action taken in association with one quadrant, the other three quadrants will be affected. In other words, the I-A Model represents a system of interconnected actions; changing one piece creates a change throughout the system. A heuristic, such as the I-A Model, simply makes it easier to identify the source and nature of changes throughout the system.

Conclusion

Ruona (2000, 2) quite rightly contends that "professions are forced to defend their contributions and often fail and fade because they do not do the work of differentiating, legitimating, and protecting the integrity of the profession." She calls on HRD to identify its unique contributions. I argue that "learning" is the most important unique contribution offered by the field. HRD is poised to lose its foothold in an area of research that is an ideal reflection of the philosophical and theoretical foundations of the field itself—organizational learning. For that reason, organizational learning, and its counterpart, learning organizations, are critical issues for the field of HRD.

The field's overemphasis on performance at the expense of learning obscures the uniqueness of HRD and may even contribute to the field's demise. Performance is one of many goals of HRD, but it cannot be the distinguishing characteristic of the field, and, without learning, it will not move HRD to strategic importance in organizations. As a field, we need to celebrate the application of learning theory beyond training and development. We need to show how learning can be meaningfully used at the individual and the organizational levels. The I-A Model can be our starting point into more mindfully considering learning as part of our actions and interventions as HRD professionals.

Applying the concept of organizational learning helps move HRD to a strategic level. It allows practitioners to use their skills and knowledge more systemically instead of focusing on improving organizational performance through learning at only the individual level. It opens HRD practice to both the individual and the organization. Organizational learning also opens new research and practice territory for HRD. It highlights a wide variety of managerial and organizational cognition issues that can be informed by HRD research and practice. In turn, those areas reciprocally inform HRD. Organizational learning offers a path for future development of core foundational areas of HRD. Thus, by changing the nature of practice and the scope of research for HRD, organizational learning is an issue that contributes to the growth of the field.

However, HRD has not pursued the study and practice of organizational learning as fully as it perhaps could have. Other management disciplines have actively engaged in this arena of research and practice; these other disciplines have begun to recognize the importance of learning in, by, and among organizations. We have not staked our claim to the expertise we, as a field, have cultivated for decades; as a result, we may lose our field because other management disciplines are beginning to stake a claim to our unique characteristic of learning as applied in organizational contexts. Thus, a focus on organizational learning may even represent the survival of HRD as a distinct field of research and practice.

Survival and growth—the two key characteristics of a critical issue as indicated in the introduction to this book. Because organizational learning is associated with both the survival and growth of HRD, it represents a critical issue for this field. The I-A Model presented here offers us a way to include performance in HRD interventions without sacrificing the critical component of learning. The model allows us to focus on one of the key underlying theories of HRD—learning—while continuing to recognize that performance is one viable outcome for HRD interventions. By shifting our focus away from performance versus learning as the ends of our interventions and by recognizing that HRD is necessarily concerned with both the individual and the organization, we reframe our understanding of the field of HRD to one of action instead of outcomes. This reframing of the way we look at our field and the nature of the theories that inform our field creates an opportunity to not only help the field survive but also help it flourish.

Training Transfer: Progress and Prospects

Reid Bates

Training can do little to increase individual or organizational performance unless what is learned as a result of training is transferred into on-the-job behavior. Unfortunately, research has documented that large numbers of employees do not apply learned knowledge, skills, and abilities (KSAs) when they return to the workplace (Baldwin and Ford 1988). Such findings have led to estimates that as little as 10 percent of the investment in training pays off in performance improvements (Garavaglia 1993). The dramatic discrepancy between what is learned and what is applied on the job represents a massive transfer problem (Ford 1994) so pervasive that there is rarely a learning-performance situation in which such a problem does not exist (Broad and Newstrom 1992).

Knowledge has been limited with regard to questions about when, why, or how the dynamics of training transfer work. Examination of these issues requires both a clear understanding of what transfer means and the factors that can influence transfer. The purpose of this chapter is to provide an overview of what is known about the nature of transfer, trainee characteristics, training design, and work-environment factors that influence it, and advancements and needs in learning-transfer research. In general, the review indicates that some progress has been made with regard to modeling, theorizing about, and analyzing different transfer-related processes. There are also some new tools for measuring and diagnosing learning transfer systems. Despite this promising progress, we still know only a little about a great many factors that have the potential to influence learning transfer and perhaps even less about how this complex of factors and processes works together to facilitate or inhibit learning transfer. In short, there is a good deal of room for more research and better practice in training transfer.

The Nature of Training Transfer

Transfer of training refers to the degree to which knowledge, skills, and abilities learned in training are applied to the job (Wexley and Latham 1981). This relatively straightforward definition masks what has increasingly been recognized as a complex, multidimensional process. For example, transfer can vary from positive (facilitating job performance) to negative (inhibiting job performance), from general (content independent) to specific (content dependent) (Cormier and Hagman 1987). Transfer is also seen as having dimensions of time that differentiate between transfer initiation (degree to which the trainee initially attempts to apply learning), maintenance (degree to which the trainee persists in applying learning) (Laker 1990), and the pattern of maintenance over time (Baldwin and Ford 1988). Transfer can also be characterized along a continuum of distance of generalization from near transfer (the degree to which the stimulus-response dimensions of the transfer task mirrors those of the learning task) to far transfer (the degree to which the learning and transfer task stimulus-response dimensions are different) (Butterfield and Nelson 1989).

Others have suggested that transfer can be further distinguished on the basis of the type of task being transferred. Gagne (1985) argued that task complexity is a critical dimension of transfer. He distinguished lateral transfer (performance of a task at the same level of complexity as the task learned) from vertical transfer (performance of a task at a more advanced level of complexity than the task learned). Salomon and Perkins (1989, 118) differentiated between low and high road transfer. The former refers to the spontaneous transfer of highly practiced, automatized skills requiring little or no cognition and the latter to transfer requiring "explicit conscious formulation of an abstraction in one situation that allows making a connection to another situation." Schmidt and Young (1987) suggested that the primary task for trainees transferring motor tasks is determination of *how* to produce a given behavior whereas transferring cognitive tasks implies a need to determine *what* to do. Cormier and Hagman (1987) also believed that distinctions between different classes of behavior (motor, cognitive, and metacognitive) play an important role in a comprehensive understanding of transfer. They noted that, although it is not entirely clear how learning occurs with each of these types of behavior, some research suggests that motor and metacognitive responses are less susceptible to negative transfer than is cognitive behavior (for example, there is less forgetting). More recently, Yelon and Ford (1999) presented a multidimensional view in which transfer is seen as the interaction between the nature of the task (open tasks are those which can be adapted to varying job circumstances versus closed or highly prescribed) and the degree of worker autonomy (highly supervised versus highly autonomous). Kozlowski, Brown, Weissbein, Cannon-Bowers, and Salas (2000) consider a variety of environmental and design issues that influence vertical transfer or the upward generation of individual transfer outcomes to team or organizational outcomes.

It should be clear from this brief discussion that it is very difficult to take a narrow view of training transfer. Transfer itself is a multidimensional construct whose complexity is compounded by the nature of the tasks involved. These factors alone make answering questions about the how, when, or why of transfer a daunting challenge. However, this challenge is further complicated a host of other input factors including pre-training influences, trainee characteristics, training design, and work environment elements that can interact in different ways in varying circumstances (Ford and Weissbein 1997). It is to these factors that we now turn.

Pre-training Influences on Transfer

Research on pre-training influences on training effectiveness indicates that an individual's beliefs and cognitions about an upcoming training event can significantly influence his or her readiness to enter and actively participate in training. For example, Tannenbaum, Mathieu, Salas, and Cannon-Bowers (1991) found that when pre-training expectations about training were met trainees showed greater post-training commitment, self-efficacy, and motivation. Dov Eden (Eden and Ravid 1982; Eden and Shani 1982) demonstrated a Pygmalion effect in which trainees whose supervisors expected more of them displayed more favorable attitudes toward training and had higher training achievement. Other research has shown that appropriately framing the purpose of training (Quinones 1995), labeling training as an opportunity for performance improvement (Martocchio 1992), demonstrating organizational support for training (McFarlane, Shore, and Wayne 1993), discussing negative pre-training events (Smith-Jentsch et al. 1996), providing trainees the opportunity to be involved in training design (Clark, Dobbins, and Ladd 1993), providing trainees with advance information about upcoming training events (Baldwin and Magjuka 1991; Hicks and Klimoski 1987; Tannenbaum et al. 1991) or about the about the skill improvement and job survival value of training (Haccoun 1996) can also influence expectations, motivation, and subsequent training performance.

Baldwin and Magjuka (1997) synthesized this and other research into a model of pre-training influences on training effectiveness. The model, grounded in social learning theory, suggests that training is best viewed as a socially constructed episode in which a person's cumulative training experience, the organizational environment, and stage of the training process influence the meaning individuals attach to training and the motivation they will carry into the training event. Their model includes factors such as the training program status (voluntary versus mandatory), level of participation by trainees in the training process, goal orientation, training group composition, and organizational transfer climate.

Although this research and thinking has expanded our approach to training effectiveness by underscoring the potential value of creating "training friendly" contexts (Baldwin and Magjuka 1997), the challenge for practitioners and researchers concerned with transfer is to carefully consider how events and cognitions that take place prior to training can be managed in ways that enhance transfer outcomes. For example, trainee expectations have been shown to be relatively open to pre-training manipulation and therefore offer the potential for dramatically enhancing transfer with interventions that are straightforward and inexpensive (for example, supervisors communicating persuasive messages to trainees about the skill improvement and survival value of training). It is therefore important to understand more clearly what individual (for example, self-efficacy beliefs, previous training experience, goal orientation) and situational factors (for example, work group norms, rewards) contribute to the formation of positive transfer expectations and how these contribute to the initiation and maintenance of transfer behavior. In addition, the other side of the expectations coin may be equally important. Frustrated expectations are a part of everyday organizational life but questions about the nature and extent to which negative or unmet pre-training expectations influence training transfer have yet to be fully addressed.

Trainee Characteristics

A variety of trainee characteristics can contribute to training effectiveness and are potentially some of the most important determinants of learning transfer. These include cognitive ability, personality, job attitudes, and motivation.

Cognitive ability. One trainee characteristic that emerges as important across tasks and contexts is general cognitive ability. General cognitive ability is seen as a potent predictor of job performance and training success because it reflects the ability of individuals to employ the major cognitive processes (for example, evaluation, planning, judgment, recognition, memory) that are used in day-to-day job performance (Ree, Carretta, and Teachout 1995). A large number of studies have demonstrated that general cognitive ability is a valid predictor of job performance ratings, objective measures of job performance, as well as success in training (Colquitt, LePine, and Noe 2000; Kaemar, Wright, and McMahan 1997; Warr and Bunce 1995; Hunter and Hunter 1984). This research supports the view that no other predictor of job performance or training success has the "pervasive predictive validity" of general cognitive ability (Hunter 1986).

There are, however, at least three important caveats to keep in mind with regard to the role of general cognitive ability in learning transfer. First, this variable is seldom measured in studies evaluating transfer. Although there is some indication that cognitive skills may influence an individual's perception of transfer-related factors in the workplace (Bates and Holton 2000), little is known about how or the extent to which cognitive ability can influence learning transfer. For instance, most jobs include task components that go beyond cognitive ability (psychomotor or affective elements, for example). This suggests the nature of the job or transfer task may play a role in determining the extent to which cognitive ability can reliably predict transfer (Salas and Cannon-Bowers 2001). Thus although general cognitive ability has been shown to reliably predict learning it may not be as efficient at predicting transfer. Finally, it appears that learning transfer is dependent on a number of other factors (individual characteristics and environment elements) that may interact with cognitive ability. The nature of these interactions and an understanding of which interacting factors may be most important in which transfer contexts is far from clear and represent promising prospects for future research.

Personality. The congruency interaction (Joyce, Slocum, and Glinow 1982) posits that performance is maximized when there is a fit between the person and the situation. This and similar perspectives (Schneider 1983, for example) suggest that trainee personality could play a significant role in learning transfer. For example, observing that most jobs are composed of varying degrees of both task and people requirements, Day and Silverman (1989) suggested that personality may be a more robust predictor than cognitive ability for jobs that emphasize people requirements (such as the ability to cooperate).

The most widely used personality framework in organizational research, the Five-Factor Model, suggests that the personality hierarchy is dominated by five broad trait categories: neuroticism, extraversion, openness to experience, agreeableness, and conscientiousness. Research using this model has shown these personality dimensions to be valid predictors of job performance (Barrick and Mount 1991; Day and Silverman 1989); teamwork (Barrick et al. 1998); motivation to improve work through learning (Naquin and Holton 2000); and training proficiency (Barrick and Mount 1991). Although little work has been done to link these personality dimensions to transfer, traits such as conscientiousness and openness to experience may be particularly important because of their consistent association with learning-related achievement and motivation (Barrick and Mount 1995; Colquitt and Simmering 1998).

One personality trait that has shown promise as an important transfer-related factor is locus of control. Locus of control describes "the extent to which people attribute cause or control of events to themselves (internal locus of control) or to environmental factors" such as luck or fate (external locus of control) (Kren 1992, 990). Past research has linked this personality dimension with academic achievement (Bar-Tal and Bar-Zohar 1977); job success (Andrisani and Nestel 1976); performance (Spector 1982); application of new knowledge gained in training (Baumgartel, Reynolds, and Pathan 1984); goal attainment (Hollenbeck and Brief 1987); "anti-output" behavior in the face of situational constraints (Storms and Spector 1987); and motivation and effort (Kren 1992). There is also speculation that locus of control may also interact with certain transfer-design methodologies (such as relapse prevention) to influence the level of transfer that occurs (Tziner, Haccoun, and Kadish 1991).

Self-Efficacy. Based on a relatively substantial body of research linking it with behavioral choices, goals, effort, persistence, and performance self-efficacy has been identified as a potentially important factor in learning transfer (Holton, Bates, and Ruona 2000). Self-efficacy refers to an individual's belief in his or her ability to mobilize personal resources and courses of action to meet specific situational and task demands (Gist 1987). This construct is seen as a potent intervening variable between training and performance, and its role in individual performance has been established by a number of studies (Hill, Smith, and Mann 1987; Ford et al. 1992; Frayne and Latham 1987; Latham and Frayne 1989). For example, Eden and Kinnar (1991) showed that boosting individuals' self-efficacy regarding a specific future behavior significantly increased the likelihood of their undertaking that behavior (the Galatea effect). Other studies have demonstrated that successful performance can enhance the development of self-efficacy (Bandura 1991; Mathieu, Martineau, and Tannenbaum 1993) suggesting the presence of a reinforcing feed-

back cycle between self-efficacy and performance: Initial self-efficacy enhances performance, which, in turn, enhances subsequent self-efficacy. This
has led to suggestions that self-efficacy may most usefully be considered a
valuable process target during training as well as a desirable outcome of
training (Tannenbaum and Yukl 1992).

Goal Orientation. Goal orientation refers to the cognitive framework used by
individuals to interpret and guide behavior in achievement-oriented activities
(Salas and Cannon-Bowers 2001). Goal orientation differentiates two different
types of goals: (a) learning or mastery goals that focus on the acquisition of expertise or competence; and (b) performance goals that focus on favorable performance evaluations (or performing better than others) as a means of con-
firming one's competence (Dweck and Leggett 1988). Research suggests
mastery goals are related to more effective learning (Fisher and Ford 1998), efficacy beliefs (Phillips and Gully 1997) and persistence (Dweck 1986). Performance goals, on the other hand, are associated with a focus on ability, lack of
ability subsequent to performance failures, and the avoidance of difficult tasks.
Research addressing the role of goal orientation in learning transfer has yet to
be done. However, it is possible to speculate that individuals with a mastery-
goal orientation may be better able to transfer learning successfully, especially
in challenging situations, than those with a performance-goal orientation. On
the other hand, the promise of goal orientation as a transfer facilitator would
be at least partially dependent on the capacity to modify an individual's orientation prior to or during training (for example, to move him/her toward a mastery orientation). But the extent to which an individual's goal orientation is
malleable is still open to question (Salas and Cannon-Bowers 2001).

The relationship between job attitudes and transfer of training is one of
the least explored areas in HRD. However, research suggests that at least two
job-related attitudes may attenuate or enhance the impact of training on
learning transfer.

Job Involvement. Noe (1986) developed a model of motivational influences
on training effectiveness that suggested employees' motivation to improve
work-related skills may be a function of their involvement in their job. "Job
involvement" refers to the degree to which people identify psychologically
with their work and the importance of work for their self-image (Lodahl and
Kejner, 1965). Thus employees who are highly job involved would be expected to be more motivated to participate, learn, and use training because
such efforts would improve skill levels (and performance) and enhance feelings of self-worth. Only two studies have examined the relationship between

job involvement and training outcomes. Noe and Schmitt (1986) found a significant positive relationship between job involvement and learning. Mathieu, Tannenbaum, and Salas (1992) attempted unsuccessfully to replicate this finding and suggested that their failure to do so may have been a function of the type of training studied. More research is needed to confirm the value and delineate the role of this attitudinal variable in training transfer.

Organizational Commitment. Organizational commitment has long been recognized as an important attitudinal variable to be included in modeling and researching employee behavior in organizations. Organizational commitment has been defined in a number of ways, but all definitions share the common theme that organizational commitment represents a bonding of the individual to the organization (Mathieu and Zajac 1990).

In general, the research on organizational commitment demonstrates that when commitment reflects an attitudinal (versus a calculative) involvement in the organization, a payoff in the form of increased motivation may result. For example, research has shown that committed employees are more likely to expend greater effort in performing work-related tasks (Steers 1977), to engage in creative and innovative "extra role" behaviors (Katz and Kahn 1978), and to exhibit improved job performance in some situations (Larson and Fukami 1984; Mathieu and Zajac 1990). Although the role of organizational commitment in training transfer has received little research attention, it is reasonable to expect that organizational commitment may influence training transfer through its effect on motivation to learn in training and to transfer that learning once back on the job. In one of the few studies to examine this factor Seyler and colleagues found that motivation to transfer was largely a function of both organizational commitment and transfer-related environmental factors (Seyler et al. 1998).

Motivation. Training-related motivation includes the direction, intensity, and persistence of effort that individuals apply to learning-associated, performance-improvement activities before, during, and after training (Tannenbaum and Yukl 1992). Trainees who enter training with higher levels of motivation have been shown to complete training at a higher rate, learn more, and perform at a higher level than trainees with lower levels of pre-training motivation (Baldwin, Majguka, and Loher 1991; Martocchio and Webster 1992; Mathieu et al. 1992; Quinones 1995; Tannenbaum et al. 1991).

More recently, research and thinking has been directed at understanding the underlying factors involved in training-related motivation. For example, Naquin and Holton (2002) proposed and tested a motivation to improve work through learning (MIWTL) construct that posits training-related motivation is a function of motivation to learn, motivation to transfer, attitudes toward training, and performance-outcome expectations. A test of their model showed that four dispositional traits were antecedents to MIWTL. Extraversion and positive affectivity directly influenced MIWTL, and the effects of conscientiousness and agreeableness were mediated by work commitment (a construct containing elements of affective commitment, job involvement, and hard work). Colquitt et al. (2000) conducted a meta-analytic review and synthesis of motivation research and developed perhaps the most conceptually precise theory of motivation to date. They see motivation as a multifaceted construct that is a function of both individual and situational factors. Efforts such as these have expanded our understanding of training-related motivation and the underlying processes that contribute to it. From a transfer perspective, they further underscore the need to consider variables previously ignored in transfer research such as personality characteristics, affective dispositions (anxiety, temperament, self-discipline), goal orientation, and even age.

Instructional Design and Learning Transfer

Content-Valid Training.   A key aspect of training effectiveness is formulating a training program that directly addresses job-performance requirements. Such training is more likely to foster transfer because of its direct correspondence with performance needs. Content-valid training is also likely to motivate trainees to learn, initiate, and maintain transfer efforts because it is perceived to facilitate workplace goals such as increased productivity, reduced errors, or better problem-solving skills (Clark et al. 1993; Holton et al. 1997). A number of authors have suggested that the issue of job relevance concerning the knowledge, skill, and abilities (KSAs) taught in training is critical in determining transfer. Noe (1986), for example, suggests the content validity of training moderates the relationship between learning and behavior change and is therefore an integral part of motivation to transfer. Adult educators (Knowles 1990; Merriam and Caffarella 1991) stress the importance of the relevance and applicability of learning. Expectancy theory (Vroom 1964) suggests trainees who perceive training content to accurately reflect job requirements and to be useful in reaching desired job goals will be more motivated to learn and transfer that learning. Finally, Salomon and Perkins (1989) reviewed a number of studies in which learning transfer did not occur. Their findings indicate that the relevance of instructional content is an important and necessary component of transfer that needs to be complemented by other conditions supporting training transfer.

From a transfer perspective, at least three important implications emerge from this thinking and research. First, it establishes the need for pre-training analysis to identify the specific KSAs that control the performance components of interest (Campbell 1988). Unfortunately research indicates that systematic needs analysis in many cases does not precede the design or delivery of training (Saari et al. 1988). Second, most organizations and training researchers appear to dangerously assume the content of training is valid and relevant to job demands (Baldwin and Magjuka 1991). Only a handful of studies (for example, Bates et al. 2000; Clark et al. 1993; Hicks and Klimoski 1987; Tannenbaum et al. 1991) have attempted to measure or verify the extent to which training content is relevant to job demands. Finally, content validity has at least two dimensions—one that addresses functional validity of training (the "actual" correspondence between technical performance requirements and training content) and one that addresses the perceived validity (the extent to which trainees believe training meets job demands). Research has generally failed to distinguish these dimensions and consequently little is known about their respective roles in the initiation or maintenance of transfer.

Identical Elements and Other Design Strategies. The earliest work on training transfer focused on the use of appropriate instructional-design models to aid transfer. Thorndike and Woodworth's (1901) theory of identical elements, for example, predicted that transfer occurs when two tasks contain identical stimulus and response elements: The greater the number of shared (identical) elements between the learning and transfer task the greater the amount of transfer. This approach to transfer is based on the premise that the structure of the training task determines what is learned and transferred and rests on the assumption that it is possible to isolate a set of defining stimulus parameters for any learning transfer situation. Research, however, has shown this to be a highly complex issue and has provided little guidance about which stimulus and response elements in the training setting are key. It is clear, for example, that fidelity is a multivariate factor that differs in form and meaning from task to task (Baudhuin 1987) and that some stimulus attributes of the training environment are more important (Cormier 1987). Furthermore, little is known about what factors determine trainee perceptions of learning and transfer-task fidelity (Noe and Ford 1992).

A wide range of other instructional-design approaches has been explored as methods for improving training effectiveness. General-principles theory, for example, suggests the key to transfer is identifying and teaching underlying principles so that trainees can apply these principles to performing specific workplace tasks or solving specific problems (Goldstein 1986). Conditions of practice approaches focus on a number of issues, including the distribution of practice (such as practice coupled with periods of no practice) (Dempster 1988) behavioral versus symbolic practice (Bandura, Jeffery, and Bachica 1974; Decker 1983); whole versus part learning (Campbell 1988); and overlearning (Driskell, Willis, and Cooper 1992). Although promising, questions remain about the generalizability of these approaches to learning transfer. For example, research exploring these alternatives has been criticized for its tendency to focus on simple motor or verbal skills (not the more complex problem-solving and reasoning skills typical of organizational-training interventions), predominant use of student samples, deficient criterion measures, and to overlook the situation-specific nature of job performance (Adams 1987; Baldwin and Ford 1988; Simon and Roscoe 1984).

At the same time, it has been noted that one of the shortcomings of transfer research has been the tendency to view learning as conceptually distinct from, and antecedent to, transfer. The predominant transfer perspective sees learning as important, but, in terms of transfer success, potentially less determinant than trainee characteristics or work environment factors. Cognitive and instructional psychologists, on the other hand, see learning and transfer as ends of a continuum and assume that "the psychological processes underlying transfer (generalization and maintenance) and learning are largely inseparable" (Ford and Kraiger 1995, 31). For them, the critical elements of transfer relate to the cognitive processes developed during training (such as encoding, memory structures, retrieval cues) that are needed to generalize and maintain learning on the job. Ford and Kraiger (1995) argued that there is much to gain by incorporating a cognitive approach into the predominantly behaviorist focus of current transfer research and suggest several new directions for instructional design that may enhance learning transfer:

- The use of instructional techniques (such as examples, hypothesis testing, increasing task variability and complexity) to facilitate the development and application of condition-action rules. Condition-action rules are concerned with when and why to use trained skills (for example, if situation A occurs then learned skills can be used in such-and-such a way).
- Building mental models in training that facilitate transfer. The focus here should be on selecting training tasks, exercises, and problems that lead to the development of deeper and more complex cognitive representations. Such mental models enhance a trainee's capacity to see the similarities between what was learned and what the transfer task requires (such as to engage in "transfer appropriate processing").

- The development of metacognitive abilities. Metacognitive abilities are concerned with the ability of individuals to monitor, self-regulate, and evaluate learning and problem-solving (such as transfer) activities. This can include instruction designed to teach trainees how to minimize transfer errors through the development of more effective scanning and response-selection strategies. It can also include efforts to build self-management and self-regulation skills using the techniques such as relapse prevention.

Behavioral Modeling. As a training design strategy, *behavioral modeling* focuses on the use of live or video-taped model(s) to demonstrate behaviors required for job performance (Gist, Schwoerer, and Rosen 1989). Behavioral modeling training is based on Bandura's (1977) social learning theory and pays particular attention to the role of social observation and imitation of modeled behaviors. Four processes control the modeling-training process: (1) attention; (2) retention; (3) motor reproduction; and (4) motivation. The assumption is that as a result of a trainee observing a model performing the task to be learned, remembering what the model did, and reproducing that behavior in training, the trainee will gain the motivation and ability to transfer training to the job. Failure to transfer behaviors may result from deficiencies in any of these processes (Baldwin 1992).

Although a number of studies have shown behavior modeling to be effective in producing learning outcomes (Burke and Day 1986; Decker 1982; Gist et al. 1989; Latham and Saari 1979), again it is less clear the influence modeling can have on learning transfer. There are, for instance, a number of poorly understood process variations in behavior modeling training that could profoundly affect transfer outcomes. These include the type of retention aids used (such as rule-oriented or summary-written instructions) (Robertson, Bell, and Sadri 1991), the type of modeling presentation (for example, live versus video) (Russell, Wexley, and Hunter 1984), the perceived credibility of modeler (Ilgen, Fisher, and Taylor 1979), group size (Decker 1983; Baldwin and Magjuka 1997), and the content of modeling display (such as the combination of positive and negative events) (Baldwin 1992).

Transfer-Design Strategies

Transfer design refers to the degree to which transfer mechanisms are made a part of the design of training itself (Holton et al. 2000). Limited research suggests that the incorporation of certain transfer-design elements along with or subsequent to the presentation of instructional content may enhance transfer. The rationale for these transfer design strategies is that even when relevant learning occurs in training, the skills needed to make the transfer to job behavior may be absent. For example, trainees may successfully learn training content but not how to overcome obstacles in the workplace that prevents learning transfer.

Self-Management. Behavioral *self-management* is a process in which trainees are taught strategies they can use to deliberately regulate "stimulus cues, covert responses, and response consequences to achieve personally identified behavioral outcomes" (Luthans and Davis 1979, 43). This approach focuses on increasing functional behavior and decreasing dysfunctional behavior by helping trainees identify and deal with key interpersonal and job-related stimuli and feelings about those stimuli which transfer, and by building training-related thoughts and behavioral consequences that support transfer (Tziner et al. 1991; Wexley and Baldwin 1986). Studies examining the influence of self-management on transfer have shown it to influence the transfer of negotiation skills (Gist, Bavetta, and Stevens 1990) and job attendance strategies (Frayne and Latham 1987; Latham and Frayne 1989).

Relapse Prevention. *Relapse prevention*, a variant of behavioral self-management, has been forwarded as a potentially valuable transfer strategy (Marx 1982). Relapse prevention fosters training transfer by helping trainees understand and cope with the process of *relapse*, or reversion to pre-training behaviors. It involves teaching strategies to increase awareness of obstacles to transfer, reduce dysfunctional emotions, or create meaningful rewards when none exist (Marx 2000). A handful of studies have examined the role of relapse prevention in organizational training transfer and have found it to be effective (Burke and Baldwin 1999; Marx and Karren 1988; 1990; Tziner et al. 1990).

Taken as a whole, this research provides some evidence that providing trainees with relatively simple transfer strategies through self-management or relapse prevention training can positively influence transfer of training. One added advantage of these strategies is that they can be easily included as part of the training design without changing the basic instructional content. However, research relating these transfer design strategies directly to performance is limited, and that which has been done has generally failed to measure or account for other individual or organizational variables that might influence the effectiveness of these strategies. For example, Burke and Baldwin (1999) showed that transfer outcomes were a result of the interaction of relapse prevention strategies and the organizational transfer climate such that "there is less need for RP tools as the transfer climate becomes more supportive" (235).

Goal Setting.   *Goal setting*, the process of setting specific, often demanding goals in relation to some performance objective, has been demonstrated to be an effective motivational strategy leading to behavioral change in a wide variety of settings (Locke, Shaw, Saari, and Latham 1981). However, only a few studies have investigated goal setting as a transfer strategy. In a study of a management development program for hospital administrators, Wexley and Nemeroff (1975) found that a treatment group that was assigned performance goals and encouraged to monitor their progress toward those goals with checklists were significantly better at applying learned KSAs than a control group. Reber and Wallin (1984) compared improvements in safety-related behavior as a result of safety training in a farm machinery-manufacturing firm. The fifty-six-week-long multiple-baseline investigation showed that significantly more subjects in the training-with-goal-setting group performed their jobs 100 percent safely and had fewer on-the-job injuries than did trainees in the training-only group. Other research indicates that the effectiveness of goal setting can be influenced by the nature and complexity of the target task (Wood, Mento, and Locke 1987), the kinds of goals set (such as distal versus proximal) (Locke and Latham 1990), the source of the goals, level of goal accountability, and the manner in which the goals set (Locke, Latham, and Erez 1988).

In short, a number of factors have the potential to influence the effectiveness of goal setting as a transfer strategy that we know little about. Although goal setting remains a promising transfer strategy more research is needed to provide guidance about how it can be most effectively used. At this time, perhaps the strongest conclusion that can be drawn is that simply setting difficult, hard to reach goals may not be sufficient given different transfer outcomes, tasks, and contexts (Baldwin and Magjuka 1997).

Extending the Transfer Paradigm: The Work Environment and Beyond

Although most empirical work with regard to training effectiveness has focused on training design and individual characteristics, in the last decade or so there has been an increasing number of efforts to systematically expand the transfer paradigm. A good deal of research has shown that a range of work environment factors can influence learning transfer. For example, a number of studies have established the importance of supervisory support in facilitating training transfer (Baldwin and Magjuka 1991; Bates et al. 2000). Efforts to identify and define what kinds of supervisory support are most important have led to the development of a managerial competency model for supporting learning transfer (Bates 2002). Research has also shown that trainees have differential opportunities for skill application on the job (Ford et al. 1992). This has spurred speculation that the extent to which trainees "are provided with or obtain experiences relevant to the tasks for which they were trained" can have a substantial influence on transfer (512). This is consistent with research indicating that a variety of work environment factors (job-related information, tools and equipment, materials and supplies, budgetary support, required services and assistance from others, task preparation, time availability, and ergonomic factors) can interfere with an individual's capacity to convert learning into effective job performance (O'Connors et al. 1984; Peters et al. 1988).

More recently attention has focused on how work environment factors affect training transfer through a transfer of training climate. Transfer climate is seen as a mediating factor in the relationship between the organizational context and an individual's attitudes, motivation, and work behavior. Thus even when learning occurs in training, the transfer climate may either support or inhibit the application of learned behaviors on the job.

Rouiller and Goldstein (1993) were among the first to develop a model of transfer that specifically included a transfer climate construct. Transfer climate was defined as "those situations and consequences that either inhibit or help to facilitate the transfer of what has been learned in training into the job situation" (379). This study offered a conceptual framework based on Luthans and Kreitner's (1985) organizational behavior modification model for operationalizing the transfer climate construct. The framework consisted of two general types of workplace cues comprising eight distinct dimensions of transfer climate (*see* figure 10.1). A test of the model demonstrated that transfer climate perceptions added significantly to the explained variance in transfer performance.

Tracy, Tannenbaum, and Kavanaugh (1995) attempted to replicate and extend this work using items drawn from Rouiller and Goldstein's instrument along with an additional variable presumed to affect transfer, continuous learning culture. A series of LISREL analyses revealed that both the climate and culture constructs explained a significant amount of variance in transfer performance. Exploratory factor analysis of the transfer climate scales, however, did not fully confirm Rouiller and Goldstein's proposed structure of transfer climate.

Recent work by Holton, Bates, and colleagues (Holton et al. 1997; 2000) has been somewhat critical of the use of transfer climate from both a modeling and measurement perspective. They suggested that the transfer climate construct was too narrow a construct to fully understand the transfer process. In addition to a lack of consensus about the nomological network of factors affecting transfer in the workplace, they saw current conceptualizations of transfer climate as simply one subset of factors that can influence transfer. Although transfer climate is important, research in this area has

Situational cues: Cues that serve to remind trainees of their training or provide them with an opportunity to use their training on the job.
<u>Goal cues</u> serve to remind trainees to use their training when they return to their jobs; for example, existing managers set goals for new managers that encourage them to apply their training on the job. ardid<u>Social cues</u> arise from group membership and include the behavior and influence processes exhibited by supervisors, peers, and/or subordinates; for example, new managers who use their training supervise differently from the existing managers. <u>Task cues</u> refer to the design and nature of the job itself; for example, equipment is available in this unit that allows new managers to use the skills they gained in training. <u>Self-control</u> *cues* concern various self-control processes that permit trainees to use what has been learned; for example, I was allowed to practice handling real and job-relevant problems.
Consequences: As employees return to their jobs and begin applying their learned behavior, they encounter consequences that will affect their further use of what they have learned. A number of different types of consequences exist.
<u>Positive feedback</u>. In this instance, the trainees are given positive information about their use of the trained behavior; for example, new managers who successfully use their training will receive a salary increase. <u>Negative feedback</u>. Here, trainees are informed of the negative consequences of not using their learned behavior; for example, area managers are made aware of new managers who are not following operating procedures. <u>Punishment</u>. Trainees are punished for using trained behaviors; for example, more experienced workers ridicule the use of techniques learned in training. <u>No feedback</u>. No information is given to the trainees about the use or importance of the learned behavior; for example, existing managers are too busy to note whether trainees use learned behavior.

FIGURE 10.1   Transfer Climate Constructs (Rouiller and Goldstein, 1993)

tended to ignore other potential influences including training design, personal characteristics, and motivational factors. These authors took a more comprehensive approach to the modeling and measurement of transfer by proposing a *transfer systems* concept. Transfer systems represent all those factors in the person, training and organizational environment that influence learning transfer. Transfer system is thus a broader construct than transfer climate but includes all factors traditionally referred to as transfer climate (Holton et al. 2000). This approach assumes that transfer can only be understood and predicted by examining a more complete system of influences.

Based on a review of transfer studies done since 1988, these authors also concluded that, in general, transfer researchers have not used acceptable scale development procedures (Holton et al. 2000). This represents a significant problem for transfer research because without minimally validated scales the chance for incorrectly specified models, misinterpretation of findings, and measurement error is significantly increased. They suggested that although previous transfer research might not necessarily be flawed, it had reached a stage where researchers need to move to a more rigorously developed and comprehensive set of measures.

Subsequent work produced a theory-based instrument (the Learning Transfer System Inventory) grounded in previous research that contains sixteen scales believed to be critical to transfer. The instrument has shown evidence of construct validity (Holton et al. 2000), convergent and divergent validity (Bookter 1999) and some scales have shown evidence of criterion-related validity in predicting motivation to transfer, perceptions of training utility, use of new procedural tasks on the job (Bates et al. 2000; Seyler et al. 1998). Factors measured by the model are shown in the conceptual model of transfer (*see* figure 10.2).

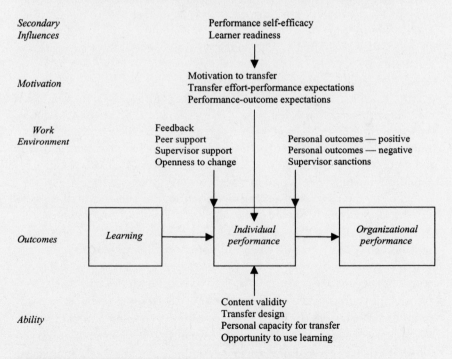

FIGURE 10.2 Learning Transfer System Inventory: Conceptual Model of Instrument Constructs. Source: Holton, Bates, and Ruona 2000.

The LTSI and its learning transfer systems perspective represents a critical evolution both in transfer research and practice. From a research perspective, the transfer systems view embedded in the LTSI offers an approach to learning transfer that operates at multiple levels of analysis (organization, job/process, and individual) and is capable of measuring and linking the distinctive character of these elements to workplace behavior (for example, learning transfer). It provides an organized framework in which systematic research can be conducted, and is attended by a promising set of measures that can facilitate valid cross-study comparisons and consequently add to a more complete understanding of the transfer process. In terms of practice, the LTSI represents an accessible tool organizations can use to diagnose, understand, and improve their learning transfer systems (see Holton 2000).

Conclusion

A good deal of progress has been made in the last 10 years or so in the study of learning transfer. There have been a number of new conceptual developments with the evolution of such constructs as opportunity to use learning, motivation to improve work through learning, and readiness to learn that have provided additional insights in the processes supporting learning transfer. A number of new models have synthesized previous research and provided both a theory base and conceptual mechanisms for discussing transfer-related factors and processes and for guiding future research. Cognitive elements of instructional design have received increasing attention and have added to our understanding about how to design effective training. The transfer phenomenon is being increasingly recognized as a complex of multiple processes (such as Yelon and Ford 1999) that operate along the continuum from learning on one end to transfer on the other.

Although the progress is promising, taken together the research done to date has provided only limited knowledge about *which* factors have the greatest impact on the transfer of training and about *how* these factors affect transfer behavior under different conditions and different kinds of training. Whereas recent reviews (Ford and Weissbein 1997) have indicated that research has begun to take a broader and more eclectic approach to the study of transfer, the current state of affairs does not allow a great number of well-grounded conclusions. In many cases, researchers continue to treat transfer as a unitary phenomenon without differentiating alternative mechanisms by which it might (or might not) occur, and fail to account for key intervening variables in the transfer process. There is still much to be learned about critical design issues, the role of personality, job attitudes, and other individual characteristics (such as goal orientation); the central criterion issues of generalization and maintenance of learning on the job (Baldwin and Ford 1988), specification of which transfer factors are most important for different kinds of training, levels of skill requirements, task complexity, level of trainee ability (both cognitive and psychomotor), and the impact of these factors on different kinds of transfer (such as near, far, vertical).

Transfer of training is a vitally important issue to organizations, HRD practitioners, and researchers. If the HRD profession in general and training interventions in particular are going to be able to contribute effectively to individual development and organizational performance then generating a deeper understanding of the transfer process is needed. Most importantly, until the critical dimensions of the transfer equation have been adequately defined, made validly and reliably measurable, evaluated together in context, and interpreted in a theoretical framework, research will offer only marginal assistance in understanding and overcoming the transfer problem.

11

A Framework for Reframing HRD Evaluation, Practice, and Research

Hallie Preskill
Darlene Russ-Eft

Critical Issues and Current Challenges Related to HRD Evaluation

With increasing frequency, learning and performance professionals are being asked to evaluate the effectiveness and impact of their efforts (Bassi, Benson, and Cheney 1996; Bassi and Lewis 1999; Brown and Seidner 1998; Chelimsky 2001; Phillips 1998; Van Buren and Erskine 2002). As Phillips (1998, 1) notes, "Although organizations have focused much attention on evaluation in the past 40 years, only recently have organizations taken a systematic and comprehensive approach to evaluating training and development, human resource development, and performance improvement initiatives." The urgency to evaluate has emerged from both internal and external customers and clients who are asking for evidence of programs' effectiveness and contributions. The demands for systematic and useful evaluation results are occurring not only in for-profit organizations, but in foundations, nonprofit, and local, state, and federal agencies as well. In spite of this interest in evaluation, we believe that evaluation is currently underconceptualized and underpracticed in organizations, and thus represents at least five critical issues for HRD professionals.

The first critical issue relates to the increasing need for those in HRD, particularly in training and development positions, to show the effectiveness and importance of their efforts (Dionne 1996). In turbulent and unpredictable economic times, organizations often impose considerable cost cutting measures. To effectively lobby for continued support and resources in times like these, it is vital that HRD professionals provide credible evidence that their programs and services are essential to the organization's health and future prosperity. Systematic and rigorously conducted evaluations can be a means for not only justifying HRD initiatives, but also for demonstrating the ways in which HRD practitioners model ongoing learning by using the findings of evaluation to improve their work (akin to continuous process improvement).

The second critical issue relates to the frequency in which training and development professionals are called on to solve a problem. Many times, the problem is presented as a training or performance issue and trainers agreeably design, develop, and implement a training or performance program. Unfortunately, however, trainers often find that the problem still exists after the intervention. Without evaluating the training program's design and implementation, or the trainees' ability to transfer their learning to the job, HRD practitioners are vulnerable to criticisms that may be unfounded. For indeed, a great deal of research exists that suggests management support is vital in employees' transferring their learning (as per Brinkerhoff and Montesino 1995; Rouiller and Goldstein 1993). So, without solid evaluation data that describe the process and outcomes of training, HRD practitioners will continue to be held accountable for results that might be out of their control.

The third critical issue revolves around the fact that, despite the increasing demand and need for evaluation, few HRD practitioners actually conduct systematic evaluations of HRD interventions (Desimone, Werner, and Harris 2002). And those that do engage in some form of evaluation activity focus predominantly on measuring trainees' reactions, and rarely on determining the program's effectiveness and impact. These results provide limited information for decision-making (Van Buren and Erskine 2002).

The fourth critical issue concerns the fact that HRD is still not included or reflected in many organizations' strategic planning processes; HRD managers are rarely at the table for determining HRD's role in helping the organization meet its goals. Indeed, Walton (1999, 7) suggests that HRD practitioners tend to be seen as "far too operationally oriented and restricted in their thinking about their job role to be trusted with strategic decision-making processes." He believes that this might be due to some of the writings published by the Harvard Business School that have dominated much of the management literature (see Beer and Spector 1985).

Where HRD is located within organizations is also considered problematic with regard to including these professionals in strategic planning discussions. As Watkins (2000, 57) explains, "HRD departments that are located either under personnel or within functional units are not well positioned to help an organization recreate itself with a focus on learning. HRD too often is powerless to effect significant change in the organization." By providing data and results that clearly show the effectiveness and impact of HRD on the organization's strategic goals and objectives, HRD may increase its perceived value in the organization.

The fifth critical issue relates to good old common business sense. According to *Training's* 2001 Industry Report (Galvin 2001, 42), "U.S. organizations will spend nearly $57 billion on formal training activities this year." This represents a 5 percent increase over what was spent in 2000. If organizations are spending this kind of money on formal learning (not to mention informal learning), doesn't it make sense to know what effect these dollars are having on individuals, teams, the organization, and possibly, the communities in which they operate? Again, well-planned, systematic, and use-focused evaluation can address this issue.

Though recent attention to evaluation represents an extremely important development, there remain two primary challenges to addressing the above critical issues. In this chapter we will discuss the impact of these two challenges on HRD evaluation practice, and then propose a framework for designing, developing, and implementing HRD evaluations. We close the chapter by describing how using the proposed evaluation framework may benefit both HRD practitioners and researchers.

Challenge #1: HRD Practitioners' Education and Experience with Evaluation

We believe that HRD professionals are often unprepared to assume their role in facilitating adult learning and development and organizational culture and change. Ideally, HRD practitioners would have some undergraduate education in the field and a graduate degree in adult learning, instructional design, training design and delivery, multimedia instructional technologies, organization development, career development, and so on. However, this is most often not the case. Many trainers have been promoted from within because they are effective technicians, they have good presentation skills, or management is cycling people through various departments for cross-training purposes. In some cases, employees wake up on a Monday morning, go to work, and find that they are now trainers because there is a need in the organization and no one else to do it. Individuals who find themselves in these situations may put their best foot forward, and may be bright, energetic, technically competent, and motivated, but even under the best circumstances, they lack the theory, knowledge, and skills required to be an effective HRD practitioner. Though we were unable to locate any studies of trainers' educational or training background in evaluation theory and practice, based on our 45 years of combined experience in teaching graduate education courses and providing training workshops on evaluation to HRD professionals, we have observed that HRD professionals:

- Know what they know about evaluation from either taking brief workshops on the topic, or through their experiences with evaluation on the job;
- Are unaware that evaluation constitutes a profession with its own history, theories, and standards; and,
- Are unaware that professional evaluation organizations exist all across the world (such as the American Evaluation Association, Canadian Evaluation Society, Australasian Evaluation Association, European Evaluation Society).

We believe that this lack of education and comprehensive training has inhibited evaluation's value and growth within many organizations. It has also contributed to an overreliance on Kirkpatrick's four levels of evaluation which has further straightjacketed evaluation of HRD programs within organizations.

Challenge #2: The Monopoly of Kirkpatrick's Four Levels

The second dilemma HRD practitioners face, which is largely related to the lack of knowledge and skills in evaluation described in Challenge #1, is that the models on which they've relied to conduct evaluation are far too simplistic and vague to guide them in the kinds of evaluation work that is required (Russ-Eft and Preskill 2001). For example, Donald Kirkpatrick's four-level evaluation model (1959a,b; 1960a,b; 1994), developed more than forty years ago, continues to offer little more than a taxonomy of evaluation categories. Ask almost any trainer and they know that Level 1 means measuring a participant's reactions to the learning event; Level 2 is associated with measuring how much participants learned; Level 3 relates to determining the extent to which participants' on-the-job behavior has changed as a result of the training; and Level 4, the holy grail of all training evaluation, concerns measuring the results of the learning intervention on the organization, otherwise referred to as cost-benefit analysis or measuring the return-on-investment. Familiarity with Kirkpatrick's four levels is so ubiquitous that a conversation between two HRD practitioners might sound like the following: "So, are you going to do Level 1 evaluation on that training program?" "Yes, but we're thinking about doing Level 3 too—we'd like to do Level 4, but you know, that could be quite difficult." One problem with this brief exchange is that there is no mention of what key questions the evaluation needs to address, why the evaluation is being conducted, what decisions need to be made based on the evaluation's findings, or how the results will be used. All of these issues represent essential steps in designing and conducting a valid and useful evaluation.

The influence of Kirkpatrick's four-level taxonomy can be also observed in the training evaluation literature. For example, the American Society for Training and Development published four booklets on evaluation, each representing one of the levels. But such prominence is not limited to practitioner-oriented publications. Most articles on training that appear in the professional refereed journals, such as the *Human Resource Development Quarterly*, *Human Resource Development International*, *Human Resource Development Review*, *Journal of Applied Psychology*, or *Personnel Psychology*, either use or refer to Kirkpatrick's taxonomy (Alliger et. al 1997; Baldwin 1992; Morgan and Casper 2000; Russ-Eft and Preskill 2001). In addition, most articles on training evaluation that appear in training practitioner magazines, such as *Training* and *Training and Development*, rely heavily on Kirkpatrick's four levels.

Although others have attempted to expand on Kirkpatrick's framework over the last four decades (Brinkerhoff 1989; Hamblin 1974; Holton 1996; Phillips 1995), none has provided a comprehensive, systems-based, practitioner-oriented evaluation framework or model. If HRD professionals are to demonstrate the effects of their efforts, then they must have the necessary knowledge and tools to competently evaluate their programs, products, processes, services, and systems. In essence, they must become internal evaluators. One way to help HRD practitioners assume this role is to provide them with a more comprehensive framework for understanding, and engaging in, evaluation practices that produces effective evaluations of HRD programs.

Reframing HRD Evaluation Theory and Practice

The evaluation framework we offer is the result of our combined experiences in: (a) conducting numerous evaluations of HRD programs; (b) conducting research on various aspects of evaluation theory and practice; (c) providing graduate level courses and practitioner workshops to HRD professionals on evaluation; and (d) our belief that evaluation can be a catalyst for ongoing organizational development and change. We first outline the questions that guided the framework's development, and then describe its theoretical underpinnings. This discussion is followed with an explanation of the model's components, and concludes with a list of the framework's potential benefits to both practitioners and researchers.

Theoretical Framework

The evaluation framework we propose is based on the philosophies, theories, and practices in the fields of: (1) evaluation, (2) organizational learning, and (3) systems thinking. While several definitions of evaluation have been offered in the evaluation literature (Patton 1997; Rossi and Freeman 1985; Scriven 1967, 1991), the framework presented in this chapter is based on the following understanding of evaluation:

> Evaluative inquiry is an ongoing process for investigating and understanding critical organization issues. It is an approach to learning that is fully integrated with an organization's work practices, and as such, it engenders (a) organization members' interest and ability in exploring critical issues using evaluation logic, (b) organization members' involvement in evaluative processes, and (c) the personal and professional growth of individuals within the organization (Preskill and Torres 1999, 1–2).

Implied in this definition is the notion that evaluation is a *systematic process*. It should not be conducted as an afterthought; rather, it is a *planned and purposeful activity*. Second, evaluation involves collecting data regarding questions or issues about society in general, and organizations and programs in particular. Third, evaluation is seen as a *process for enhancing knowledge and decision-making*, whether the decisions are related to improving or refining a program, process, product, system, or organization, or for determining whether or not to continue or expand a program. In addition, evaluation involves some aspect of *judgment about the evaluand's merit, worth, or value*. Finally, the notion of *evaluation use* is embedded in all evaluation activity.

In the last decade, many organizations have embraced the concept and practices of *organizational learning* in an effort to respond to constantly changing global economic, technological, and social conditions. Fiol and Lyles (1985, 811) define organizational learning as changes in the organization's cognition or behavior. This learning represents itself in "the development of insights, knowledge, associations between past actions, the effectiveness of those actions, and future action." Thus, we believe that evaluation can be the mechanism for inquiring into a problematic situation on the organization's behalf (Argyris and Schon 1996), and for helping organization members grow and learn from such inquiry.

Our framework has also been strongly influenced by the concepts of *systems thinking* (Katz and Kahn 1978; Senge 1990; Wheatley 1992). Adopting a systems perspective means that we look at an organization as a set of interrelated parts and interconnected systems that are dependent on one another and influenced by each other. As Senge (1990, 68–69) explains, "It is a framework for seeing interrelationships rather than things, for seeing patterns of change rather than static 'snapshots'. . . . it is a discipline for seeing the 'structures' that underlie complex situations, and for discerning high from low leverage change." A systems approach to organizational learning and change acknowledges that an organization is

Interacting with its environment and has to adapt to it and permanently change in order to survive. The organization is conceptualized as an information processing system, a system which performs certain necessary functions such as the generation of information, as well as the diffusion, the storage and the utilization of this information. This systemic approach aims at describing the way an organization can learn as a system (Finger and Brand 1999, 138).

Therefore, information is a core element of organizations that learn (Thompson 1995; Wick and Leon 1993). Emphasizing the role of information in organizations, Wheatley (1992, 105) passionately writes, "The fuel of life is new information-novelty-ordered into new structures. We need to have information coursing through our systems, disturbing the peace, imbuing everything it touches with new life." Because evaluation provides information for decision-making and learning, we believe that evaluation can serve a critical role in organizations, and for HRD programs in particular.

The Evaluation Process

As depicted in figure 11.1, the evaluation framework's general conception denotes a non-linear understanding of evaluation practice, though the evaluation process itself occurs in a somewhat sequential manner. Starting with the center circle, we outline five critical evaluation phases or processes. Every evaluation starts with the *focusing* phase. This is where primary stakeholders (those who have a vested interest in the program's design and/or outcomes) come together to: (a) discuss the background and history of the evaluand (that which is being evaluated); (b) identify other stakeholders who might be interested in using the evaluation's results; and (c) develop the questions the evaluation will seek to answer. This process is fundamental to ensuring that the evaluation addresses various individuals' and groups' concerns and is-

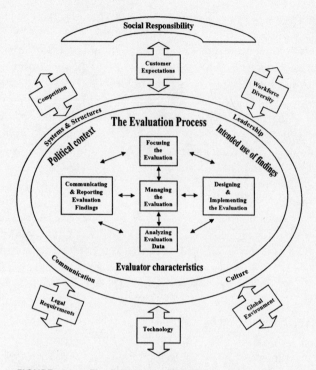

FIGURE 11.1   The Evaluation Process

sues. Throughout our teaching, training, and consulting experiences, we have found that all too often HRD practitioners use the term "evaluation" synonymously with "survey." Without first knowing what questions we wish the evaluation to address, it is difficult to know which methods should be used to collect valid data.

The second phase of the evaluation process is determining the evaluation's *design, methods of data collection,* and *means for implementation.* There should be discussions about which methods (such as surveys, tests, interviews, observation, document reviews) would be best suited to answering the key evaluation questions. In addition, the team should talk about how to ensure the validity of data, how to obtain a high response rate, the timing of data collection, and how to choose a sample population if the entire population cannot be involved.

The next phase in the evaluation involves *analyzing the data,* as well as interpreting and assigning meaning to the data. This process typically involves statistical analysis of quantitative data and/or content or thematic analysis of qualitative data. Involving stakeholders in interpreting the data and developing recommendations often increases their understanding of data as well as their buy-in to the evaluation's results.

The fourth phase of the evaluation process is *communicating and reporting* the evaluation findings. Though it appears as a final phase in the process, it should be noted that it is often important to communicate the evaluation's progress and at times, preliminary findings, to various stakeholders during the evaluation. It is equally important to disseminate the findings via various communication devices such as memos, posters, and newsletters, in addition to the typical final or technical report (Torres, Preskill, and Piontek 1996).

The fifth phase, which often begins prior to the other phases, involves developing one or more management plans that describe in detail the logistics of the evaluation. There may be several different plans including a time line, a roles and responsibilities plan, a communicating and reporting plan, or a plan of options in case obstacles are encountered during the evaluation's implementation. In addition, a budget should outline the various direct and indirect costs for the evaluation (for a more detailed description of each evaluation phase, see Russ-Eft and Preskill 2001).

The Evaluation Context

What we have just described is standard practice for most internal as well as external evaluators and, by itself, does not constitute the uniqueness of this framework. The remaining components are those that have gone unexplained in the HRD evaluation literature. As can be seen in figure 11.1, the *Evaluation Process* sits within an organizational context that includes three components: (1) *Evaluator Characteristics*, (2) *Political Context*, and (3) *Intended Use of Findings*. We have included these additional components because of their potential effect on the evaluation's commissioning, design, implementation, and reporting of findings. Evaluation does not occur in isolation; it is affected by several different personal and organizational factors such as the evaluator's

- credibility
- experience with the program
- previous experience in conducting evaluation
- knowledge of evaluation theory and methods
- position within the organization relative to the program being evaluated
- commitment to evaluation and use of findings
- understanding of the organization's culture and politics
- commitment to ethical behavior—integrity

- group facilitation skills
- verbal and written communication skills
- understanding of program content
- data-analysis skills

HRD professionals who also act as internal evaluators are often concerned about their lack of "objectivity" related to a program they may be working with or for which they are responsible. They wonder how they can possibly evaluate their own work or program since they are obviously "biased." Since this is a valid and important concern, we recommend establishing a task force or workgroup that agrees to collaborate on the evaluation. This approach creates a process of checks and balances throughout the inquiry, and increases the team and organization's learning potential by their involvement in the evaluation. It also allows different individuals to bring their unique strengths to the evaluation's design and implementation.

As evaluation is inherently a political act, it is also important that HRD professionals clearly understand that regardless of the evaluation's depth and scope, it deals with issues of power, position, and resources. In 1973, Carol Weiss, who was one of the first evaluation researchers to publicly recognize the importance of politics and values within the evaluation and policy-making process, identified three ways in which evaluation and politics are related. These include: (1) the policies and programs with which evaluation deals are creatures of political decisions; (2) because evaluation is undertaken in order to feed into decision-making, its reports enter the political arena; and (3) evaluation itself has a political stance. By its very nature, evaluation makes implicit political statements about such issues as the problematic nature of some programs and the unchallengeability of others, the legitimacy of program goals and program strategies, the utility of strategies of incremental reform, and even the appropriate role of the social scientist in policy and program formation (Weiss 1987, 47–48). Thus, the proposition, "evaluation is always disruptive of the prevailing political balance" (Guba and Lincoln 1981, 299), reminds us that even in programs that seem "nonpolitical," there are political implications from the mere act of evaluation, not to mention the findings. As a group begins to engage in the evaluation process, they should consider the ways in which the evaluation could be political and identify ways in which the politics can be managed.

The third component is *Intended Use of Findings*. For more than twenty-five years, evaluation researchers have explored the topic of evaluation use or utilization. Michael Q. Patton, who has written most extensively on this topic, suggests that evaluation without intention to use the findings should not be conducted at all (1997). We concur. We like to think that *use* is to evaluation what *transfer* of learning is to training. In other words, for every evaluation that is conducted, there should be a plan for the intentional use of findings; otherwise, investing the resources in an evaluation may be questionable. Use of findings can take several forms, however. Most common is what is referred to as "instrumental use." With this kind of use, there is a direct application of the evaluation findings. For example, if a particular case study exercise in a training workshop consistently receives low ratings, the trainer may decide to eliminate the case and replace it with a different experiential activity. This represents a direct or instrumental use of evaluation findings.

The second type of use is called "conceptual" or "knowledge" use. This type of use cannot be seen directly, as the information from the evaluation becomes integrated with what the "user" already knows or believes about that which is being evaluated (referred to as an "evaluand"). The evaluation information serves to inform the individual, and contributes to a higher level of understanding or cognition about the program being evaluated. The individual might make a decision later that in part was based on the evaluation findings. However, she might be hard pressed to say it was based solely on the evaluation's results.

Finally, evaluation findings might be used in a "symbolic," "political," or "persuasive" way. For example, many programs are required to participate in an accreditation- or certification-related evaluation, which includes a self-evaluation component. Members of the organization might not be particularly interested in the evaluation and thus do it, symbolically. They may not use the findings to improve their programs, but they can show that "they did it." Another common example is when we use the findings of an evaluation to lobby for additional program resources. This political act is often a justifiable use of evaluation results. Weiss (1998, 316) suggests that,

> Rather than yearning to free evaluation from the pressures of politics, a more fruitful course would be to undertake and report evaluation with full awareness of the political environment. A study will be more useful and more likely to be used if it addresses the issues that are in contention and produces evidence directly relevant to political disputes.

In many evaluations the results may be used in all three ways: (1) instrumentally for improving the program, (2) conceptually to inform others about the program's effects, or (3) symbolically, to increase the credibility of the HRD function. It is important that the evaluation team discuss these potential uses before the evaluation's design is finalized and data are collected.

The Organization's Infrastructure

Even if the evaluation process is well defined and articulated, and even if the evaluation team has considered the evaluator's characteristics, the political context, and the intended uses of the evaluation's findings, evaluation still must be implemented within an even larger organizational context. The outer circle (figure 11.1) describes the necessary organizational infrastructure for supporting evaluation practice (Preskill and Torres 1999). Though rarely discussed in other HRD evaluation models, we believe that for evaluation to contribute to learning and decision-making in organizations, there must be at least some presence of four elements—leadership, culture, communications, and systems and structures.

The first is the organization's *leadership*. The more leaders support a learning environment, the more likely organization members will support systematic and ongoing evaluation. If organizational leaders suggest that they know it all, or that learning from our experiences is unnecessary, then evaluation will be more difficult to implement. On the other hand, if leaders model learning, create a spirit of inquiry, and use data to act, then evaluation practice may be more successful.

The second element, the organization's *culture,* is fundamental to creating learning from evaluation practice. If the culture is one that supports the asking of questions, open and honest communication, teamwork, risk-taking, valuing mistakes, and employees trusting each other, evaluation may be welcomed and successful. However, if organization members are afraid to give their opinions, don't believe managers will act on the evaluation's results, or fear that the findings will be used to punish individuals or groups, then the evaluation process and outcomes will be less able to contribute to organizational decision-making and action.

The third element, organization *communications,* is closely related to the *intended use of evaluation findings.* The more systems and channels an organization has to communicate and report the progress and findings of an evaluation, the more likely the evaluation will have an impact on individuals, teams, and the organization overall. However, if there are few means to share what is learned from the evaluation (for example, knowledge-management systems, action-planning sessions, publication of the results), or organization members are restricted from sharing their learning, then evaluation will lose an important opportunity for enhancing the organization's performance.

The fourth element is the organization's *systems and structures.* How employees' jobs are designed, how they are rewarded and recognized for their work, and how learning is expected to occur are all important factors in how often and how well evaluation may be conducted by organization members. The more cross-trained they are, the more they are encouraged to learn from each another, the more their jobs allow for teamwork, and the more employees understand the interrelatedness of their jobs, the more likely evaluation will serve its learning function.

The Organizational Context

The framework does not end with the organizational infrastructure. Rather, it takes into account the fact that organizations, more than ever, are being influenced by a myriad of external forces (Drucker 1997; Judy and D'Amico 1997; Marquardt 1999) (*see* figure 11.1). These include:

- increasing competition for personnel and other resources;
- evolving customer or client expectations;
- an increasingly diverse workforce;
- new requirements for working in a global environment;
- technological advances which are literally altering the way we work and communicate;
- ever-changing legal rules and regulations.

While HRD professionals do not need to conduct a complete scan of these variables when designing and implementing an evaluation, they should at least be aware of where and how the organization is responding to these factors at any given point. It is entirely possible that the evaluation's process and findings could be seriously affected by any one of these variables.

A final component of the framework is that of social responsibility. Including social responsibility emphasizes the systems orientation of the framework by recognizing the relationships between the organization, society, and the global community (Capra 1996). This corresponds with the notion that HRD professionals "take responsibility for the world beyond our organization, and recognize that with each interaction we have and each action we take, we are co-constructing a new organization" (Hatcher and Brooks 2000, 9). Therefore, issues of social responsibility can influence each evaluation; and in turn, each evaluation has the potential of affecting the larger society. Given the possibilities of these interactions, HRD professionals should reflect upon the potential influences their work has on society, and consider the ways in which the evaluation might reflect the organization's social responsibility.

Benefits of Using the Evaluation Framework

Many writers on management today believe that the future success of organizations will be dependent on their ability to build core competencies within a context of collaboration. Technology, and quick and easy access to information will help create weblike structures of work relationships, which will facilitate their working on complex organizational issues (Hargrove 1998; Helgeson 1993; Limerick and Cunnington 1993; Stewart 1997). With this in mind, we believe that evaluation can be a means for: (a) collectively identifying information needs; (b) gathering data on critical questions; and (c) providing information that when used, becomes part of the organization's knowledge base for decision-making, learning, and action. As organizations have been forced to respond to an increasingly competitive environment that is volatile and unpredictable, and as they are likely to continue being pressured to do things better, faster, and cheaper, they are looking at evaluation as a means to help them determine how best to proceed. To that end, we believe that using the evaluation framework presented in this chapter may benefit both HRD practitioners and researchers.

Benefits for the HRD Practitioner

For the HRD practitioner, the proposed framework offers a type of road map for undertaking an evaluation. Instead of deciding to gather only participant reactions, as has been the common form of training program evaluation, HRD practitioners can work with program stakeholders (for example, designers, trainers, internal consultants, management, clients) using the framework to determine the political context and intended uses of findings. Doing so will help to identify what questions should be answered by the evaluation. As a result, HRD professionals will be following a more comprehensive and systematic evaluation process. Such a process should increase the probability that the evaluation findings are valid and can be used for decision-making. In so doing, organization members may experience an increased understanding of how evaluation can contribute to organizational success. This newfound belief in the value and possibilities of evaluation could foster evaluation's integration with other HRD processes, systems, and programs.

Benefits for the HRD Researcher

For the HRD researcher, the proposed framework offers new research opportunities. For example, researchers could examine the specific effects of evaluator characteristics, the political context, and the intended use on decisions regarding the evaluation design of a learning and performance initiative. Furthermore, researchers need to determine the effects of these factors on the actual use of evaluation findings. Other questions might concern the effects of the evaluation process on organizational decision-making. For example, do certain evaluation designs and methods tend to emerge from particular evaluator characteristics, political contexts, or intended uses? Do organizations or functions within organizations that routinely evaluate programs and processes yield higher levels of learning and performance than those organizations or functions that do not evaluate? To what extent does the quality of the evaluation contribute to higher levels of learning and performance? Addressing these and other questions would not only add to the field's knowledge base about evaluation within organizational contexts, but it would likely provide HRD practitioners with specific guidance for improving their evaluation practice.

Conclusion: Our Hopes

In the knowledge era, where we now find ourselves, it is critical that organization members learn from their experiences, that they see themselves as part of a larger system, and that they use quality information for making timely decisions. We hope that the proposed evaluation framework will provide HRD practitioners and researchers with a tool that can help them collect and use valid information that contributes to individual, group, and organizational development and learning, which ultimately leads to increased organizational satisfaction and effectiveness.

Socially Conscious HRD

Laura L. Bierema
Michelle D'Abundo

We are in the midst of a changing world characterized by globalization, political unrest, technological advancement, corporate dominance, population explosion, and environmental destruction. Organizations, particularly corporations, have vast power and resources, and influence over the changing world. Although corporations have the resources and influence to "do good" in the world, they do not often use them to enhance public welfare. Instead, corporate interests prevail over human ones as corporations cater to investors, court customers, pursue suppliers of materials and natural resources, and seek global dominance. Of the world's 100 largest economies, 51 are corporations (Korten 1998). The corporate model with its values of competition and survival of the fittest has become the prototype for all governmental and recently educational institutions (Barlow and Robertson 1996). This value system is being exported across the world as business seeks global dominance and superlative performance from employees and suppliers. The world is undeniably affected by corporate values, and the field and practice of HRD is no exception.

The influence of the corporate model of enhancing performance to satisfy stockholders is evident in HRD's objectives to harness intellectual capital, align training with strategy, and attain optimal performance of employees. Although these are acceptable goals for both HRD professionals and organizations, the human has gotten lost in the global rush to dominate commerce and maximize performance. Corporations have been accused of exploiting employees, the environment, communities, and even nations. HRD has been critiqued for becoming management's handmaiden, and ignoring the interests of employees and wider community issues. Consequently, it is important to emphasize that HRD is about *development*, not profit. HRD professionals need to carefully consider how their work impacts human growth, learning and development, not just that of the corporate wallet, and reflect on what it means to be socially conscious in their practice and research.

The prospect of acting with social consciousness in organizations is challenging and creates a paradox as explained by David Korten (1995, 212):

> With financial markets demanding maximum short-term gains and corporate raiders standing by to trash any company that isn't externalizing every possible cost, efforts to fix the problem by raising the social consciousness of managers misdefine the problem. The problem is a predatory system that makes it difficult for them to survive. This creates a terrible dilemma for managers with a true social vision of the corporation's role in society. They must either compromise their vision or run a great risk of being expelled by the system.

How can HRD encourage the restructuring of organizational practice that includes emphasis on social consciousness? Korten argues, "The solution does *not* lie in appeals to the conscience of corporate executives, who are themselves captives of a global economic system that had delinked financial interests and community interests" (Korten 1996a, 5). He argues that we must look beyond corporate capitalism and state socialism as solutions and entertain a third option of restructuring the system of finance and ownership to link business interests with community interests.

People need to work, and HRD has a responsibility to create a socially conscious work environment that benefits the whole social system, not just the organization. Merely focusing on performance- and productivity-based HRD effectively removes the human from the process and is more costly to the organization in the long run. There are long term costs associated with failure to provide the resources and infrastructure to support whole-person development such as turnover, mistakes, and employees leaving to work for the competition. There are also social costs of such neglect that will impact lives, communities, and the environment.

Assumptions of the Chapter

We are not the first authors to challenge the field of HRD to incorporate social consciousness into practice. For example, Burke (1997) presents the challenge as, "If organization development practitioners want to sleep better at night, they need to live the basic values of their profession, challenge actions they know are immoral, and play a more expansive role in improving organizational life" (Burke 1997, 7). We argue that HRD possesses the skills, strategies, and philosophy to live up to Burke's challenge. HRD has a unique opportunity to educate organizations about social responsibility and use HRD strategies to integrate social consciousness into organization activities that have the potential to effect significant social change. The purpose of this chapter is to define social consciousness in organizations, offer a definition and explanation of socially conscious HRD, and propose a model of socially conscious HRD.

This chapter was written according to the following assumptions. First, we write from our experience as white, middle-class, U.S. citizens who have worked in a wide range of organizations. We believe that employers are accountable to employees and stakeholders. We view stakeholders as those affected by organizations such as employees, communities, and the environment. We also believe that there are unwritten rules or contracts between employees and employers that bind employers to treat employees and environments with dignity. We feel that current performance measurement standards are too narrow and detract attention away from issues of social responsibility that organizations should be addressing. We also argue that organizations have an ethical responsibility to live up to their formal and implied agreements. We do not regard management as a morally neutral process. In every sector (for profit, nonprofit, and so forth) employment relationships have public dimensions; thus, HRD practices have public dimensions. Accordingly, HRD has a responsibility to management, employees, and the broader community.

Social Consciousness Defined

The many models of organizational social responsibility are traceable back to the 1950s (Acar, Aupperle, and Lowy 2001). However, since that time, there has been much debate about each perspective with little consensus about the model of organizational social consciousness that is "correct." Just as the concept of social consciousness varies, so too does the term when used to describe social consciousness, as it also refers to corporate social responsibility, corporate social performance, social responsibility, organizational social responsibility, and ethics. These terms will be used interchangeably in this chapter. This section defines social consciousness historically, and compares and contrasts definitions.

Corporate social responsibility (CSR) is defined as:

The obligation of the firm to use its resources in ways to benefit society, through committed participation as a member of society, taking into account society at large, and improving welfare of society at large independently of direct gains of the company (Stahl and Grigsby 2001, 287).

Business Impact (2000, 1.02, cited in Moir 2001) describes CSR as based on the following principles: to treat employees fairly and equitably; to operate ethically and with integrity; to respect basic human rights; to sustain the environment for future generations; to be a caring neighbor in their communities.

Corporate social responsibility (CSR) has come to refer to Carroll's (1999) four categories of economic, legal, ethical, and discretionary responsibilities. *Economic responsibility* refers to the traditional function of business as a provider of products and services and a producer of profits. Profit generation is its most important responsibility. *Legal responsibility* is compliance with governmental rules and regulations. *Ethical responsibilities* include societal defined expectations that are not dictated by formal law. An example of ethical behavior would be recalling defective products or spending money to ensure quality control. *Discretionary responsibilities* are voluntary and philanthropic and are often expected by society. An example is Ted Turner's philanthropic gestures of monetary support to nonprofit organizations.

The next term is corporate social performance (CSP), which originally stemmed from an economic framework based on the belief that social responsibility yields financial gain. However, corporate social performance has evolved into a more moralistic quest with attention to increasing beneficial outcomes for society (Wood 1991). In some cases corporate social performance has moved away from the purely economic perspective; however, the conceptual separation of economical or ethical orientations of practice still exists (Wood 1991) and may result in conflicting views of corporate social performance.

Acar, Aupperle, and Lowy (2001) describe how historically the concept of social responsibility has been conceptualized and researched only in the business context. They make an important contribution in originating the term "organization social responsibility" (OSR) as a broader, more encompassing process than "corporate social performance" (CSP). Acar, Aupperle, and Lowy (2001) argue that organizations are dissimilar in their degree of concern for social responsibility based on organization type. They identify five types of organizations: privately held for-profit, publicly traded for-profit, regulated for-profit, revenue generating not-for-profit, and non-revenue generating not-for-profit. They explored how a continuum of organizational types, from for-profit to non-profit, value their economic versus social orientation. Although they considered social responsibility based on organization type, they note that non-profits are also faced with the dilemma of balancing economic and social concerns. Not surprisingly they found that not-for-profits registered higher CSR scores than for-profits at a high level of statistical significance. They conclude that business still places a greater emphasis on economic concerns and that total social responsibility increases with the move toward not-for-profit.

Stakeholders Versus Stockholders

One of the debates characterizing definitions of social consciousness in organizations is over accountability. Some argue that organizations are answerable to stockholders only. The stockholder orientation is toward economics and performance, with approval of social responsibility only when it is profitable. Acar, Aupperle, and Lowy explain that many empirical studies attempt to demonstrate the financial gain from social responsibility. They also lament that much of the empirical CSP research has created a dialectic between the stockholder and the stakeholder. They describe the "stockholder" viewpoint as:

> A corporation is the private property of its stockholders and exists to create wealth and provide goods and services to the market. While obligated to comply with legal constraints, its primary goal is profitability; only secondarily is it to be concerned with goals, policies and strategies aimed at serving the needs of external publics (2001, 29).

Others argue for a broader organizational responsibility to affected stakeholders. Freeman (1984, 46) describes stakeholders as "any group or individual who can affect or is affected by the achievement of the organization's objectives." Clarkson (1995) defines primary stakeholders as those on whom a corporation depends for its survival such as investors, employees, customers, and suppliers. Secondary stakeholders are those who are influenced or affected by the organization but not engaged in transactions that are essential to the organization's survival. Moir (2001) notes that a split in stakeholder theory is whether it is a coherent theory or a set of theories. There is also debate about which stakeholders deserve the most accountability.

Using Ackoff's (1974) "vested interests" perspective and Freeman's (1984) notion of corporate impact, Acar, Aupperle, and Lowy (2001, 29) define "stakeholder" as "a corporation [that] exists by permission of society and, as such, is the servant of external stakeholder groups." They note that most organizations fall along a continuum between stockholder and stakeholder orientation, making defining social responsibility fairly ambiguous.

Simpson and Kohers offer that attempts to explore the relationship between corporate social performance and financial performance have shown that a complicated relationship exists between these two dynamics. The authors raise important questions about exploring this link, such as "What resources should managers direct to socially responsible activities? How should stockholders react to resource allocations for social purposes? How can public policy best promote socially responsible behavior?" (2002, 97). By addressing these questions, both the interests of stakeholders and stockholders would be represented.

Models of Organization Social Responsibility

The most common models of social responsibility exhibited by organizations (Moir 2001; Stahl and Grigsby 1997) are neoclassical, enlightened self-interest, and moral obligation. The neoclassical view of the firm purports "that the only social responsibilities to be adopted by business are the provision of employment and payment of taxes" (Moir 2001, 17). This perspective was first expressed by Milton Friedman: "Few trends would so thoroughly undermine the very foundations of our free society as the acceptance by corporate officials of a social responsibility other than to make as much money for their shareholders as they possibly can" (1962, 133). This approach to social responsibility can be seen as minimal legal compliance because managers and organizations pursue social responsibility to the minimum degree to which they are required by the government or to maintain market integrity. Departures from this view broaden to consider the political aspects and non-economic influences on managerial behavior and are grounded in a moral and ethical view that organizations are responsible for using their resources to address social problems.

Enlightened self-interest, the next level according to Stahl and Grigsby (1997), adopts a socially responsible stance because it helps to retain employees and enhances the organization's reputation and moral obligation. Organizations that adopt this stance view socially responsible behavior as being profitable in the long run and use it as a strategic weapon against competitors. Enlightened self-interest is more pragmatic than philanthropic.

Organizations that go above and beyond compliance with the law—and view their social consciousness as a duty to improve society—fall into the moral-obligation or proactive-change orientation. These organizations use their assets to improve social welfare regardless of directly benefiting the organization. See figure 12.1 for a summary of Stahl and Grigsby's (1997) levels of corporate responsibility.

Minimum Legal Compliance	Enlightened Self-Interest	Proactive Change
Managers comply with the minimum legal requirements.	Managers use social responsibility programs as a strategic weapon to communicate to the market that they are better than their competitors and view social responsibility as yielding long-term profitability.	Managers use assets to improve society independent of a direct benefit to the firm. They take stances that extend beyond the requirements of the law.

FIGURE 12.1   Levels of Corporate Responsibility

Auditing Social Responsibility

Corporate social responsibility is assessed in many ways. Brand (1989), working from a total quality-management perspective, asks three questions that are relevant to assessing levels of social responsibility. First, does the organization's mission statement consider social impact and responsibility? Next, does the organization solicit input from the public in the formulation of its mission? Finally, does the organization demand ethical codes of behavior? He argues that socially conscious organizations address these concerns as they formulate and implement strategic plans.

Kok, VanderWiele, McKenna, and Brown (2001) propose a corporate social responsibility audit following the methodology of international quality award and excellence models. They suggest that although business ethics and social responsibility have been topics of concern, the quality movement has not incorporated these themes into their award criteria. They also underscore that these issues are becoming increasingly important in how businesses evaluate themselves when they are concerned with excellence in all respects. Garvin (1988) explains how the scope of quality has evolved from an initial focus on products and services to increasingly complex and systemic foci, in ascending order, to process, systems and environmental impact.

Socially conscious organizations conduct social audits. Social audits are deliberate reflections on and evaluations of the degree of organizational social responsibility. Humble (1975) advocates using social audits because they allow a review of existing organizational practices in light of internal and external social responsibility. They are important to strategic and operations planning, and can help organizations define strengths and weaknesses in strategy and in practice. Social audits help to formulate improvement plans and measure progress in social responsibility, and are most effective when they obtain the participation of those who are able to contribute to developing social responsibility (Kok et al. 2001).

Kok et al. (2001) define ethical awareness as requiring organization members to be morally autonomous and the organization climate to be ethical and/or have a strong code of conduct. They describe moral autonomy as "the capacity individuals possess to own their own moral values and apply them" (291). They outline four levels of social responsibility policy that can be identified during an audit and then compare them with levels of corporate social responsibility and ethical behavior:

The first level is *ad hoc policy,* where no policy exists. Social issues are ignored by management except when neglecting them becomes problematic or attention is forced by legal action. There is no ethical behavior at this level.

The second level is *standard policy,* where the organization complies with the law on social issues. Social issues are only integrated into organizational policy when they are compelled by law. Standard policy fits into the minimum-legal-compliance model of corporate social responsibility and into the transaction model of ethical behavior. Transactional ethics involve adopting the lowest level of policy, and focusing on self-preservation and pursuit of individual goals. Cooperation with others occurs when there is mutual benefit, but society at large is not a concern (Brand 1989; Kok et al. 2001).

Planned policy is the third level, where the law is followed by the company that also pays attention to other needs of society. There is neither an in-depth understanding nor development of the organization's own social responsibility with participation of all stakeholders. Only parties with social claims related directly to the business can participate in discussion. Enlightened self-interest is the model of corporate social responsibility, and the category of ethical behavior is recognition ethics. Recognition ethics aim to balance rights and obligations and assure general welfare, ever cognizant of social duty beyond making a profit. The organization will consider society at large, but it is not focused on improving social welfare (Brand 1989; Kok et al. 2001).

The fourth and last level, *evaluated and reviewed policy,* is when there is broad and continuous reflection on the actions and impacts of the organization on society at large. All stakeholders are involved in decision-making on social responsibility issues. Priorities are articulated, integrated into policy, and reviewed. The organization commits resources to addressing social problems regardless of a direct relationship to business performance. There is a structured approach to developing an ethical climate. Proactive change is the model of corporate social responsibility and change ethics is the level of ethical awareness. Change ethics are concerned with social welfare and are established with it in mind with the goal of fostering change for the social good. Improving the social good forms the core of change ethics. Levels of social responsibility audits are summarized in figure 12.2.

	Ad Hoc Policy	Standard Policy	Planned Policy	Evaluated Reviewed Policy
Definition	No policy exists.	The organization complies with the law on social issues.	The law is followed by the company that also pays attention to other needs of society.	There is broad and continuous reflection on the actions and impacts of the organization on society at large.
Models of CSR		Minimum legal compliance	Enlightened self-interest	Proactive Change
Ethical Behavior		Transaction ethics	Recognition ethics	Change ethics

FIGURE 12.2   Levels of Social Responsibility Audits

Figure 12.3 outlines Kok et al.'s (2001) audit instrument. It highlights policy approaches depending on the level of organizational social consciousness, from ad hoc to evaluated and reviewed-policy levels. The instrument recognizes three broad levels of social consciousness that are measurable: the external environment, the internal environment, and the level of ethical awareness in both environments. The external environment incorporates social responsibility in its community, consumer, supplier, and shareholder relations, and a commitment to preserving the environment for future generations.

Aspects of the internal environment incorporate the physical environment: working conditions, organization diversity, organization structure, manage-

Ad Hoc Policy	Standard Policy	Planned Policy	Evaluated and Reviewed Policy
✓ Costs	✓ Costs	✓ Costs	✓ Following law
✓ Governmental pressure	✓ Following law	✓ Following law	✓ Take in account needs of society, independent of influence on business results
	✓ No structural ethics approach	✓ Take into account needs of society as influencing business results	✓ Structured approach: review and integrate social responsibility aspects
		✓ Some structure in ethics approach	✓ Clear norms and values
			✓ Attention to development of an ethical climate
			✓ Development of ethics codes
			✓ Attention to organizational deployment

FIGURE 12.3   Kok et al.'s Corporate Social Responsibility Audit Instrument (2001)

ment style, communication and transparency, industrial relations, and education and training (Kok et al. 2001).

Socially Conscious HRD

So far, this chapter has offered definitions and models of organizational social consciousness. We contend that it is not only the HRD professionals' responsibility to conduct themselves with a high level of social consciousness, but also to seek to educate the organization so that it becomes more socially conscious. We advocate the "proactive change" stance and a spirit of evaluation and review of policy as it relates to socially responsible business. This section offers a definition and model of socially conscious HRD. We define socially conscious HRD as:

> Socially conscious human resource development serves an educative and supportive role to help organizations uphold implied contracts, promote ethical management and leadership, advocate for stakeholders, broaden definitions and measures of organization performance, challenge and revise socially "unconscious" policies and practices, analyze and negotiate power relations, and promote the use of organization resources to create social benefit and improve social welfare.

We view HRD's role as developmental with respect to social consciousness for HRD is about growth and learning, and consciousness development is a learning process. We support that focusing on individual development has long-term benefits for the individual, organization, and society (Bierema 1996; Dirkx, 1996).

The following sections address each major aspect of the definition of socially conscious HRD. We will address the issue of downsizing in each element of the definition to illustrate how socially conscious HRD would attend each aspect in a downsizing situation. Downsizing is one reality of organization life that is often accomplished with social unconsciousness. VanBuren (2000) observes that few employment or managerial practices have caused as much uproar as corporate downsizing. Neither workers nor employers seem as frightened of environmental destruction, discrimination, insider trading, or human rights violations abroad as they are about downsizing. VanBuren (2000) argues that this is because downsizing threatens people most directly, affecting their livelihood more significantly perhaps than the other issues.

Downsizing tracked for more than ten years found that fewer than 37 percent of companies realized any productivity improvements and less than half experienced any increases in net worth. Yet, businesses continue to downsize and reengineer with fervor (Fagiano 1996; Miller 1998). In fact, U.S. *Fortune 500* industrials reduced total employment by 4.4 million jobs between 1980 and 1993 while simultaneously increasing sales 1.4 times, assets 2.3 times, and CEO compensation 6.1 times. Consequently, HRD has a responsibility to critically examine the practice, process, and effects of downsizing.

Uphold Implied Contracts and Expectations

VanBuren (2000, 206–7) offers that "the vast majority of agreements that are made between people are unwritten rather than written. . . . many societal (and for that matter, personal) expectations of employers are neither codified into law nor included in a formalized contract . . . ," and provides evidence that social contracts have been used to analyze societal relationships since the 1600s. Rosseau (1995, 9) suggests that employers avoid explicit written contracts and defines the psychological contract as "individual beliefs, shaped by the organization, regarding terms of an exchange agreement between individuals and their organization." Rosseau argues that psychological contracts are valid because humans behave in accord with what they assume to be implied agreements. When organizations breach such unwritten agreements they are not at risk of legal liability, but rather the loss of employee loyalty.

Rather than being a spectator to the erosion of these unspoken agreements between organizations and their employees, HRD has a moral obligation to advocate for employees on the basis of these expectations. HRD is positioned to make these implied contracts explicit in a manner that binds employers to the commonly held expectations of their employees and other stakeholders in the system.

VanBuren (2000) offers propositions for a framework for downsizing that have broader relevance to how organizations should govern themselves in the formulation of socially conscious HRD policy and practice and uphold implied contracts. His ideas are summarized as:

1. Implied contracts exist that bind the actions of employers.
2. Employment is not a purely private matter (employees deserve due process).
3. Reasonable social and psychological contracts are morally binding upon employers.
4. Employers have discretion to pursue goals other than strict maximization of profit; to the degree that reasonable psychological and social contracts exist, they may be morally compelled to do so.

5. Because employment has a public as well as a private dimension, the decision to dismiss employees is justifiable to the degree that it is necessary for organizational survival.

VanBuren's (2000) points offer a starting point for HRD in articulating social consciousness beyond downsizing and have applicability to other HRD functions.

Promote Ethical Management and Leadership

Kok et al. (2001) suggest that problems managers face are that definitions of "ethical" vary from person to person and organization to organization. The authors further note that the ongoing dilemma for managers is the fact that they control neither the ethics of their organization nor the employees. They offer an alternative perspective called the virtues model that views ethics as primarily an individual issue requiring managers to manage ethically, given the reality that one cannot always control organizational ethics. Enron is a good example. Although the corporation behaved highly unethically, there were ethical managers who attempted to warn about, and eventually exposed, the wrongdoing.

HRD has expertise in educating individuals and fostering organization change. This knowledge must be applied to teaching the organization about ethical management and leadership, and helping the organization implement such practices. Kok et al. (2001) propose the use of "pressure groups" to help managers take more social responsibility into account in their thinking and action. Pressure groups bring issues to the attention of management and highlight the consequences of unethical behavior. "Pressure groups" could be internal or external. The rise of pressure or "affinity" groups in organizations offers one strategy for promoting social consciousness. These groups are often based on gender, race, or sexual orientation, and they function to educate and lobby management to create policies that make the workplace hospitable for more than just white male employees. External pressure groups could be nonprofits, political groups, or educational institutions that apply pressure to the organization and "vote with their wallet." In the event of a downsizing, a pressure group of downsized employees could be formed to give this group a voice in policy development and function as an employee liaison with management.

Advocate for Stakeholders

Socially conscious HRD requires that organization practices be implemented democratically. Further, when engaging in policy development and oversight,

HRD should ensure that a diverse range of stakeholders, including customers, employees, suppliers, and citizens, are involved. HRD can play a role in involving these parties by making the decision-makers more aware of these groups as strategies are being formulated and implemented. Emphasis needs to move away from management interests to more ethical, responsible practices. This can be accomplished by giving stakeholders other than management, such as employees and communities, more opportunities to represent their interests.

In organizations, examples of advocacy appear in different forms. For example, employee interests are sometimes represented by unions. Formal and informal networks are popular among minorities and women as a way of representing interests of employees or management in corporate communities. However, during a major organizational event such as downsizing, employees and other stakeholders are completely left out of the decision-making process. During a downsizing, socially conscious HRD would be concerned with assisting and advocating for employees losing jobs, focusing on easing the transition with affected families, and involving the community to address issues related to the downsizing. If advocacy exists before downsizing, it is realistic to expect advocacy to occur during downsizing. Socially conscious HRD is practiced not only in times of profit, but in times of major upheaval.

Broaden Definitions and Measures of Organization Performance

Some organizations have broadened the meaning of corporate social responsibility. Wagner (2001) reports on the 2001 *Business Ethics* recognition of corporations that are good corporate citizens. She quotes Marjorie Kelly, editor of *Business Ethics,* as explaining that the term "corporate citizenship" has broader meaning in today's environment due to increasing awareness that business has more responsibility than just profitability. The five-year-old rating system is based on the following criteria: environment, minorities, non-U.S. stakeholders, stakeholders, stockowners, customers, employees, and the community. The magazine also does a "scandal scan" and disqualifies companies that are engaged in lawsuits or other allegations of misconduct, such as excluding Microsoft due to its antitrust conviction.

Socially conscious HRD requires that the traditional standards of performance measurement be challenged and more socially conscious performance measures be devised. If performance improvement is the organization's ultimate goal, then learning serves not as an end to human growth, but rather as a means to corporate growth. The goal and rhetoric of performance improvement has become HRD's dominant discourse. Striving for performance is an acceptable goal, but HRD must continually question its assumptions and beneficiaries. It is imperative for workplace educators to critically assess their HRD assumptions and practices. To counter the influence of performance assumptions in HRD research researchers must approach the knowledge-creation process more critically through challenging traditional research designs, and ask questions that move beyond the boundaries of performance. This involves seeking and adapting new methods of evaluation and research. For example, Participatory Action Research is an innovative approach to research where, "people have to recover not only control over their means of production but, more profoundly, the *control over the means of knowledge production*" (Finger and Austin 2001, 92).

Challenge and Revise Socially "Unconscious" Policies and Practices

Socially conscious HRD involves challenging policies and practices that disenfranchise other individuals or organizations. A socially "unconscious" practice is one that involves little or no consideration of the ramifications of actions, and involves minimum compliance with legal requirements. Earlier, the importance of upholding implied contracts was introduced; this aspect of socially conscious HRD illustrates one way in which HRD can challenge unconscious practice. This can become particularly important in a downsizing. VanBuren (2000) makes the argument that although downsizing is not governed by statutory or common law—like equal employment opportunity, environmental damage, fair lending, or bribery—implied unwritten contracts (both psychological and social) exist. The recommendations in this chapter build on VanBuren's (2000) proposition and advocate socially responsibly behavior beyond profitability to include: respecting the environment (beyond just following regulations), paying a fair wage, contributing to the well-being of the community, and producing a socially useful product. Organizational life is characterized by unspoken expectations; it is highly questionable whether progress has been made for workers as corporate life is unstable and more and more is being demanded of employees.

Not only is downsizing often unintentional in HRD, but so is the process of knowledge creation. The field has not strenuously researched topics relating to women, international workers, minority groups, or settings other than corporations (Bierema and Cseh, in press). HRD researchers would benefit by stepping back and assessing how, or if, HRD research contributes to social and political change, versus reinforcing the status quo. HRD practitioners need to evaluate how practices, research, and policies affect all workers—not just management or the employees of the organization, but the wider community.

Analyze and Negotiate Power Relations

Socially conscious HRD professionals have a moral obligation to analyze and negotiate power relations in a manner that facilitates socially conscious thought and action in organizations. HRD cannot be neutral with the complexity of social, political, and environmental factors involved in the practice. Rather, HRD is a highly political practice where power, political institutions, social issues, and the interests of multiple parties interface. HRD has been criticized for theory and practice that have been historically aligned with corporate interests, oftentimes at the expense of workers with less clout and power. The field has been critiqued as not recognizing the conflict of interests, priorities, and values between employee and employer (Schied, Carter and Howell 2001). Korten (1996a, 1) observed in a speech to the Academy of Human Resource Development Conference that there is a "serious disconnect between your own values and the realities of life in many of the corporations in which you work."

There is a growing body of literature that provides a critical view of power, politics, and practice that can be applied to HRD practice. Cervero and Wilson (2001) believe power, interests, and values need to be negotiated among stakeholders. Based on critiques that HRD ignores power issues, the field may benefit by addressing power issues in practice. HRD practitioners must recognize the multiple interests of all stakeholders in any practice with attention to conflicting agendas.

Another perspective of power relations is represented by Forester (1989, 5) in his writing on planning and the importance of the practitioner's ability to "anticipate obstacles and respond practically, effectively, in ways that nurture rather than neglect—but hardly guarantee—a substantively democratic process." The idea of the democratic process of practice is salient to the theory of integrating social justice into practice. In this perspective, the interaction of power, values, and ethics are recognized as important forces in practice. With attention to conflicting interests, Forester emphasizes the need for practitioners to act responsibly through disclosing information to all people involved and affected by issues and policy. Institutional constraints and resources are also discussed as potential sources of problems, but can be addressed by being aware of the context of practice.

An example of analyzing and negotiating power relations in HRD may be addressing of issues of diversity in the workplace. Although issues of diversity are not always as obvious as other issues such as downsizing, organizations with high social consciousness may adapt proactive approaches to diversity in the workplace. By implementing an anticipatory and democratic approach to diversity—with recognition to interests, values, and beliefs of employees as well as to other stakeholders—organizational development may be improved.

Promote Social Benefit and Improvement of Social Welfare

The last aspect of our definition underscores the importance of the organization's use of research and power to foster benefit to society. Korten (1998) defines three principles for the third millennium, which are grounded in the creation of a just, sustainable democratic society and include the principles of sustainable equity and civic engagement. Korten (1998) identifies the world's most pressing needs as food security, adequate shelter, clothing, health care, and education. Nearly every country in the world has the resources to meet these needs, yet they still go unmet. Organizational social consciousness elevates awareness beyond the walls of the organization to the community and world at large.

Russo (2001, 12) argues that "Business has a responsibility to invest in the soul of the community and contribute to its wellbeing. There should be a perception that the company is promoting equality and fairness in its relationships with people, demonstrating leadership in the wise long-term allocation of resources, and contributing to the community's philanthropic needs." He advises that the issue be addressed through a "good citizen" strategy that goes back to basic issues of revising organization purpose, communicating with stakeholders, and promoting and rewarding civic mindedness among all employees.

To truly achieve social benefit and improve social welfare, HRD needs to broaden the population it represents. This population has primarily been corporations and should expand to include nonprofit organizations, professional associations, government, and small business. Finally, HRD needs to critically assess whether it is working to reinforce the status quo, or bring about meaningful, lasting change.

A Model of Socially Conscious HRD

A useful mantra for socially responsible HRD practice is captured in Stahl and Grigsby's (1997) definition of ethics as "doing the right thing right the first time." Building on the work of Kok et al. (2001) and Stahl and Grigsby (1997), we propose a model of socially conscious HRD in figure 12.4 that incorporates the elements of our definition and builds on earlier models of corporate responsibility, levels of social responsibility, and ethical orientation. Within this model, socially conscious practice is determined by attention to issues of legal-

	Socially Unconscious HRD	Socially Compliant HRD	Enlightened Self-Interest HRD	Socially Conscious HRD
Legality	Compliance with law	Compliance with law	Compliance with law	Compliance with law
Contracts	Implied contracts not upheld	Implied contracts may be upheld when expedient	Implied contracts upheld	Implied contracts upheld and enhanced
Ethical Management	No promotion of ethical management or leadership	Little promotion of ethical management or leadership	Promotion of ethical management or leadership	Promotion of ethical management or leadership
Performance	Narrow definitions of performance	Narrow definitions of performance	Broader definitions of performance	Revised, broad measures of performance
Policy	No challenging or revision of socially unconscious policies	Little challenging or revision of socially unconscious policies	•Some challenging and revision of socially unconscious policies •Social issues integrated into organization policy •No HRD driven policy development •Pressure groups	•Active challenging and revision of socially unconscious policies •Social issues integrated into organization policy •HRD driven policy •Pressure groups •Evaluated and reviewed policy
Power	No analysis or negotiation of power relations	Little analysis or negotiation of power relations	Some analysis or negotiation of power relations	Ongoing analysis or negotiation of power relations
Social Orientation	No use of organization resources to promote social good	Little use of organization resources to promote social good	Strategic use of organization resources to promote social good	•Liberal use of organization resources to promote social good •Organization social orientation

FIGURE 12.4   Levels of Socially Conscious HRD

ity, contracts, ethical management, definitions of performance, policy, power, social orientation, organization or community orientation, and ethical behavior. The aforementioned categories are used in figure 12.4 to organize HRD practice into four categories, including socially unconscious, socially compliant, enlightened self-interest, and socially conscious practice.

Socially "Unconscious" HRD

Socially "unconscious" HRD is characterized by minimum legal compliance. This might mean that the organization follows the bare minimum rules regarding employment and environmental sensitivity. This minimal compliance orientation causes implied contracts to be ignored. There is no promotion of ethical management or leadership, and such behaviors are not rewarded. The organization defines performance narrowly as outcomes that benefit the organization. The lack of social consciousness results in an uncritical acceptance of socially "unconscious" policies that may lead to discrimination, worker exploitation, or environmental damage. Power relations are not analyzed and the resources of the organization are channeled back into the organization, rather than devoted to promoting public welfare. Ethics are transactional.

Socially Compliant HRD

Socially compliant HRD observes minimum legal requirements and may uphold implied contracts when it is expedient or beneficial to the organization to do so. There is little promotion of ethical management or leadership, and performance continues to be narrowly defined. Although individuals may challenge socially "unconscious" policies, no organizational awareness of or commitment to revising them exists. Little analysis or negotiation of power relations occurs, and affected employees and communities have little voice in the policy development of the organization. Organizational resources are seldom used to promote social good, and the organization is oriented toward stockholders. There is recognition that social consciousness can be beneficial in that it keeps the organization out of legal trouble, and it promotes goodwill in the market. To that end, the organization conducts some internal education on issues related to social consciousness (such as diversity training), and seeks socially responsible practices and policies when they are clearly profitable. Internal "pressure groups" are occasionally used and the organization engages in transaction and recognition ethics.

Enlightened Self-Interest HRD

Socially conscious HRD based on enlightened self-interest is committed to social responsibility, because such behaviors and policies are viewed as providing long-term profitability and promoting a positive market image for the organization. To that end, implied contracts are upheld, and ethical management and leadership are promoted and rewarded. These organizations adopt broader definitions of performance and engage in some challenging, and revision of, socially "unconscious" policies. There is some analysis or negotiation of power relations and strategic use of organization resources to promote social good. Although the enlightened self-interest position is focused on stockholders, stakeholders also get attention, because it will result in profitability. The organization conducts internal education on issues related to social consciousness and supports a range of "pressure groups." The organization operates with recognition and change ethics.

Socially Conscious HRD

Organizations and practitioners that are socially conscious not only comply with the law, but also adopt socially conscious behaviors and policies because they are the "right thing to do." Implied contracts are upheld and enhanced, and ethical management and leadership behaviors are encouraged and rewarded. These organizations apply broad measures of performance, and actively challenge and revise socially "unconscious" policies. There is an ongoing analysis and negotiation of power relations and a liberal use of organization resources to promote social good. The organization not only educates internally about socially conscious behaviors, but plays an external educative role in the community. Social issues are integrated into organization policy, and HRD drives socially conscious policy development. The organization values socially conscious HRD because it promotes social goodwill and adopts a strong stakeholder orientation and change ethics. Policy is reviewed and revised on an ongoing basis, and the organization is engaged in critical reflection about its policies and practices. "Pressure groups" are strongly supported and involved in policy development.

Conclusion

Socially conscious HRD demands several competencies. First, new standards of accountability must be developed and implemented for research and practice. HRD professionals must have clearly articulated ethical principles and be continually engaged in reflective practice to assess the accountability of HRD and organizational practices and policies with respect to social consciousness. Though we prescribe ethical practices for individual HRD practitioners, we believe that ethical management and leadership is fundamental in HRD and that all HRD professionals have a responsibility to reflect and act on ethical principles that are reflective of personal values and the ethical standards set forth by the Academy of Human Resource Development (1999).

The goal of socially conscious HRD raises many questions and dilemmas. How does a socially conscious manager remain true to her ideals and employer? Is it reasonable for implied contracts (psychological and/or social) to be binding? What is the intersection of the individual psychological contract and society's social contract? Does management's responsibility end with following the law (living up to formalized agreements, but the obligation ends there) or extend beyond compliance? If corporations are members of their communities, what are their responsibilities beyond making profit (VanBuren 2000)? Is HRD responsible for socially responsible behavior and for helping the organization become more socially responsible? Should social responsibility be pursued even when it is not profitable? It is our hope that these questions are addressed in future research and practice.

HRD continues to evolve as a discipline drawing from both education and business perspectives of theory, research, and practice. HRD has the opportunity to humanize business by drawing from each perspective with attention to social issues in practice. The multifaceted underpinning of HRD prepares practitioners to integrate issues of business, awareness of power, negotiation of conflicting interests, and the presence of social consciousness into practice. HRD has the potential and opportunity to create, implement, and assess socially conscious theory, research, and practice, if it so chooses.

References

Chapter One: A Return to Leadership

Avolio, B. (2001, March–April). Winning with the full range of leadership. *Military Review*, 55–57.

Baldoni, J. (2002, April). Effective leadership communications: It's more than talk. *Harvard Management Communication Letter*.

Barth, S. (2001, December). 3-D chess: Boosting team productivity through emotional intelligence. *Harvard Management Update*.

Blanchard, K. (2001, November 6). Timeless truths. *Sixth Annual Worldwide Lessons in Leadership Series*, 210–216.

Bogner, A. (1998, January–February). Tales from twelve o'clock high: Leadership lessons for the 21st century. *Military Review*, 94–99.

Bowers, D., & Franklin, J. (2000). Survey guided development: Using human resource management in organizational change. In W. French, C. Bell, and R. Zawacki (Eds.), *Organizational development and transformation* (pp. 215–224). New York: Irwin Mc-Graw-Hill.

Brearley, M. (2000, November 4). Teams: Lessons from the world of sport. *British Medical Journal*. Located at http://findarticles.com/cf_0/m0999/7269_321/675.

Buckingham, M., & Clifton, D. (2001). *Now, discover your strengths*. New York: Simon and Schuster.

Buffett, W. (2002). *2001 Berkshire Hathaway annual report*. Omaha, NE: Berkshire Hathaway, Inc.

Burke, W. (1992). *Organizational development*. New York: Addison-Wesley.

Christman, D. (2002). 21st century leadership: The broadened attributes of a soldier. In C. Kolenda (Ed.), *Leadership: The warrior's art* (pp. 251–258). Carlisle, PA: The Army War College Foundation Press.

Collins, J. (2001). *Good to great*. New York: HarperCollins.

Department of the Army Pamphlet 350-58. (1994). *Leader development for America's army*. Washington, DC: Headquarters, Department of the Army.

Drucker, P. (1992). *Managing for the future*. New York: Truman Talley Books.

Dubrin, A. (2000). *Essentials of management*. New York: Southwestern College Publishing.

Farrell, K. (2001). Culture of confidence: The tactical excellence of the German army of World War Two. In C. Kolenda (Ed.), *Leadership: The warrior's art* (pp. 177–204). Carlisle, PA: The Army War College Foundation Press.

Field Manual 3–90. (2001). *Tactics*. Washington, DC: Headquarters, Department of the Army.

Field Manual 22–100. (1999). *Army leadership*. Washington, DC: Headquarters, Department of the Army.

Field Manual 22–103. (1987). *Leadership and command at senior levels*. Washington, DC: Headquarters, Department of the Army.

French, W., Bell, C., & Zawacki, R. (2000). *Organizational development and transformation*. New York: Irwin McGraw-Hill.

Gallup, Inc. Web site. Located at http://www.gallup.com/solutions/path_detail.asp.

Gilley, J. W., & Maycunich, A. (2000). *Organizational learning, performance, and change*. Cambridge, MA: Perseus Publishing.

Goleman, D. (2000). Leadership that gets results. *Harvard Business Review, 78*(2), 78–90.

Goleman, D. (1998). What makes a leader? *Harvard Business Review, 76*(6), 92–102.

Greenwald, G., & Madigan, C. (2001). *Lessons from the heart of American business: A roadmap for managers in the 21ˢᵗ century.* New York: Warner Books.

Increase visibility to show you care. (2002). *Executive Leadership, 17*(2).

Keegan, J. (1987). *The mask of command.* New York: Penguin Books.

Kolenda, C. (2001). Alexander the Great: A study in vision, character, and perception. In C. Kolenda (Ed.), *Leadership: The warrior's art* (pp. 99–120). Carlisle, PA: Army War College Foundation Press.

Kolenda, C. (Ed.). (2001). *Leadership: The warrior's art.* Carlisle, PA: Army War College Foundation Press.

Kotter, J. (2001). What leaders really do. *Harvard Business Review, 68*(3), 103–111.

Leadership is back. (2002). *Executive Leadership, 17,* 1.

Lute, D. (2001). Looking up: Leadership from a follower's perspective. In C. Kolenda (Ed.), *Leadership: The warrior's art* (pp. 277–286). Carlisle, PA: Army War College Foundation Press.

Maccoby, M. (2000, January–February). Narcissistic leaders: The incredible pros, the inevitable cons. *Harvard Business Review,* 68–77.

Madden, R. (2001). Living on the edge: Building unit cohesion and the will to win. In C. Kolenda (Ed.), *Leadership: The warrior's art* (pp. 50–80). Carlisle, PA: Army War College Foundation Press.

Malone, D. (1983). *Small unit leadership.* Novato, CA: Presidio Press.

Meigs, M. (2001, Summer). Generalship: Qualities, instincts, and character. *Parameters, 31*(2), 4–17.

Overman, S. (2002). Develop leaders to boost your bottom line. *Executive Leadership, 17*(2).

Peters, T. (2001a, November 6). Leading in totally screwed-up times. In *Sixth annual worldwide lessons in leadership series* (p. 1). Lexington, KY: Wycom.

_____. (2001b). No bull: Peters proclaims new age for leaders. *Executive Leadership, 16*(7).

Roberts, W. (1987). *Leadership secrets of Attila the Hun.* New York: Warner Books.

Simonsen, P. (1997). *Promoting a development culture in your organization.* Palo Alto, CA: Davies-Black Publishing.

Useem, M. (2001). The leadership lessons of Mount Everest. *Harvard Business Review, 79*(9), 51–58.

Yeakey, G. (2002, January–February). Situational leadership. *Military Review,* 72–82.

Chapter Two: Strategic HRD and Its Transformation

Argyris, C., & Schon, D. (1996). *Organizational learning II: A theory of action perspective.* Reading, MA: Addison-Wesley.

Argote, L., & Ingram, P. (2000). Knowledge transfer: A basis for competitive advantage in firms. *Organizational Behavior and Human Decision Processes, 82*(1), 150–169.

Barnhart, R. K. (Ed.). (1995). *The Barnhart concise dictionary of etymology: The origins of American English words.* New York: HarperCollins.

Baron, J. N., & Kreps, D. M. (1999). *Strategic human resources: Frameworks for general managers.* New York: John Wiley & Sons.

Bass, B. M. (1985). Leadership: Good, better, best. *Organizational Dynamics, 13*(1), 26–40.

Becker, B. E., Huselid, M. A., Pickus, P. S., & Spratt, M. F. (1997). HR as a source of shareholder value: Research and recommendations. *Human Resource Management, 36*(1), 39–47.

Beer, M., Eisenstat, R. A., & Spector, B. (1990). *The critical path to corporate renewal.* Boston: Harvard Business School Press.

Bierema, L. L. (2000). Human resource development for humans: Moving beyond performance paradigms on workplace development. In S. B. Merriam (Ed.), *2000 handbook of adult and continuing education.* San Francisco: Jossey-Bass.

Block, P. (1999). *Flawless consulting: A guide to getting your expertise used* (2nd ed.). San Diego: Pfeiffer.

Brethower, D. M. (1999). General systems theory and behavioral psychology. In H. D. Stolovitch & E. J. Keeps (Eds.), *Handbook of human performance technology: Improving individual and organizational performance worldwide* (pp. 67–81). San Francisco: Jossey-Bass.

Brinkerhoff, R. O., & Apking, A. (2002). *High impact learning.* Cambridge, MA: Perseus Publishing.

Brinkerhoff, R. O., & Gill, S. J. (1994). *The learning alliance.* San Francisco: Jossey-Bass.

Broad, M., & Newstrom, J. (1992). *Transfer of training. Action-packed strategies to ensure high payoff from training investment.* Reading, MA: Addison-Wesley.

Brockbank, W. (1999). If HR were really strategically proactive: Present and future directions in HR's contribution to competitive advantage. *Human Resource Management, 38*(4), 337–352.

Burke, W. W. (1992). *Organizational development: A process of learning and changing.* Reading, MA: Addison-Wesley.

Clifton, D. O., & Nelson, P. (1992). *Soar with your strengths.* New York: Delacorte.

Conner, D. (1992). *Managing at the speed of change.* New York: Villard Books.

Dare, D. (1996). Education and human resource development: A strategic collaboration. *Journal of Industrial Teacher Education, 33*(3), 91–95.

Dean, P. J. (1999a). Designing better organizations with human performance technology and organization development. In H. D. Stolovitch & E. J. Keeps (Eds.), *Hand-*

book of human performance technology: Improving individual and organizational performance worldwide (pp. 321–334). San Francisco: Jossey-Bass.

_____. (1999b). *Performance engineering at work.* Washington, DC: International Board of Standards for Training, Performance and Instruction, IBSTPI Publications and International Society for Performance Improvement.

Drucker, P. F. (1994, November). The age of social transformation. *The Atlantic Monthly,* 53–80.

Eichinger, B., & Ulrich, D. (1995). *Human resource challenges.* New York: Human Resource Planning Society.

French, W. L., Bell, C. H., Jr., & Zawacki, A. (1999). *Organizational development and transformation: Managing effective change* (5th ed.) New York: McGraw-Hill.

Fuller, J., & Farrington, J. (1999). *From training to performance improvement: Navigating the transition.* San Francisco: Jossey-Bass.

Gilbert, T. F. (1978). *Human competence: Engineering worthy performance.* New York: McGraw-Hill.

Gill, S. (1995). Shifting gears for high performance. *Training and Development Journal,* 49(5), 24–31.

Gilley, J. W., & Coffern, A. J. (1994). *Internal consulting for HRD professionals: Tools, techniques, and strategies for improving organizational performance.* New York: McGraw-Hill.

Gilley, J. W., & Maycunich, A. (1998). *Strategically integrated HRD: Partnering to maximize organizational performance.* Cambridge, MA: Perseus Publishing.

Gilley, J. W., Maycunich, A., & Quatro, S. A. (2002). Comparing the roles, responsibilities, and activities of transactional and transformational HRD professionals. *Performance Improvement Quarterly.*

Gilley, J. W., Quatro, S. A., Hoekstra, E., Whittle., D. D., & Maycunich, A. (2001). *The manager as change agent: A practical guide to developing high-performance people and organizations.* Cambridge, MA: Perseus Publishing.

Greer, C. R., Youngblood, S. A., & Gray, D. A. (1999). Human resource management outsourcing: The make or buy decision. *Academy of Management Executives, 13*(3), 85–96.

Harless, J. H. (1970, 1974). *An ounce of analysis is worth a pound of objectives.* Newman, GA: Harless Performance Guild.

Honderich, T. (Ed.) (1995). *The Oxford companion to philosophy.* New York: Oxford University Press.

Horwitz, F. M. (1999). The emergence of strategic training and development: The current state of play. *Journal of European Industrial Training, 23*(4/5), 180–190.

Jacobs, R. W. (1987). *Human performance technology: A systems-based field for the training and development profession.* Columbus: ERIC Clearinghouse on Adult, Career, and Vocational Education, National Center for Research in Vocational Education, Ohio State University.

Jick, T. D. (1992). *Managing change: Cases and concepts.* Chicago: Richard Irwin.

Kaplan, R. S., & Norton, D. P. (1996). *The balanced scorecard: Translating strategy into action.* Boston: Harvard Business School Press.

Kemper, J. E., & Kemper, J. J. (1996, Spring). Welcome to the future: A practical step-by-step guide to strategic planning. *CUPA Journal,* 21–24.

Kotter, J. P. (1996). *Leading change.* Boston: Harvard Business School Press.

Lengel, R. H., & Daft, R. L. (1988). The selection of communication media as an executive skill. *Academy of Management Executive, 2*(8), 225–232.

Lewin, K. (1951). *Field theory in social science.* New York: HarperCollins.

Lupine, J. A., & Van Dyne, L. (2001, January). Peer responses to low performers: An attribution model of helping in the context of groups. *Academy of Management Review,* 67–82.

Mager, R. F. (1975). *Preparing instructional objectives* (2nd ed.). Belmont, CA: Fearon.

McCracken, M., & Wallace, M. (1999). Toward a redefinition of strategic HRD. *Journal of European Industrial Training, 24*(5), 281–290.

_____. (2000). Exploring strategic maturity in HRD: Rhetoric, aspiration, or reality? *Journal of European Industrial Training, 24*(8), 425–467.

Mezirow, J. (1991). *Transformative dimensions of adult learning.* San Francisco: Jossey-Bass.

Marquardt, M. J. (1999). *Action learning in action: Transforming problems and people for world-class organizational learning.* Palo Alto, CA: Davies-Black Publishing.

Nadler, D. A. (1998). *Champion for change: How CEO's and their companies are mastering the skills of radical change.* San Francisco: Jossey-Bass.

Parasuraman, A., Zeithaml, V. A., & Berry, L. L. (1985). A conceptual model of service quality and its implications for future research. *Journal of Marketing, 49*(4), 41-50.

Patterson, J. (1997). *Coming clean about organizational change.* Arlington, VA: American Association of School Administrators.

Pfeffer, J. (1995). *Competitive advantage through people: Unleashing the power of the work force.* Boston: Harvard Business School.

Pinderit, S. K. (2000). Rethinking resistance and recognizing ambivalence: A multidimensional view of attitudes toward an organizational change. *Academy of Management Executive, 14*(10), 783–789.

Provo, J. M., Ruona, W. E. A., Lynham, S. A., & Miller, R. F. (1998). Scenario building: An integral methodology for learning, decision-making, and human resource development. *Human Resource Development International, 1*(3), 327–340.

Quatro, S. A., Hoekstra, E., & Gilley, J. W. (2002). A holistic model for change agent excellence: Core roles and competencies for successful change agency. In R. Sims (Ed.), *Changing the way we manage change: The consultants speak.* New York: Quorum Books.

Redding, J. (1994). *Strategic readiness: The making of the learning organization.* San Francisco: Jossey-Bass.

Robinson, D. G., & Robinson, J. C. (1989). *Training for impact: How to link training to business needs and measure the results.* San Francisco: Jossey-Bass.

Robinson, D. G., & Robinson, J. C. (1996). *Performance consulting: Moving beyond training.* San Francisco: Berrett-Koehler.

_____. (1999). *Moving from training to performance: A practical guide.* San Francisco: Berrett-Koehler.

Rosenberg, M. J. (1996). Human performance technology: Foundation for human performance improvement. In W. Rothwell (Ed.), *The ASTD models for human performance improvement: Roles, competencies, and outputs* (pp. 5–9). Alexandria, VA: American Society for Training and Development.

Rossett, A. (1999). *First things fast: A handbook for performance analysis.* San Francisco: Pfeiffer.

Ruona, W. E. A., & Lynham, S. A. (1999). Unpublished doctoral examination preparation notes, University of Minnesota, St. Paul.

Rummler, G. A., & Brache, A. P. (1995). *Improving performance: How to manage the white spaces on the organizational chart.* San Francisco: Jossey-Bass.

Senge, P. M. (1990). *The fifth discipline: The art and practice of the learning organization.* New York: Doubleday.

Silber, K. (1992). Intervening at different levels in organizations. In H. D. Stolovitch & E. J. Keeps (Eds.), *Handbook of human performance technology: A comprehensive guide for analyzing and solving performance problems in organizations* (pp. 50-65). San Francisco: Jossey-Bass.

Snyder, D. P. (1995–1996, Winter). Roller-coaster 2000: The strategic outlook for employment in trans-millenial America. *CUPA Journal, 1*–12.

Soukhanov, A. H. (Ed.). (1996). *The American Heritage dictionary of the English language* (3rd ed.). New York: Houghton Mifflin.

Stolovitch, H. D., & Keeps, E. J. (1999). *Handbook of human performance technology: Improving individual and organizational performance worldwide.* San Francisco: Jossey-Bass.

Swanson, R. A. (1994). *Analysis for improving performance. Tools for diagnosing organization and documenting workplace expertise.* San Francisco: Berrett-Koehler.

Swanson, R. A., & Holton, E. F. (2001). *Foundations of human resource development.* San Francisco: Berret-Koehler.

Swanson, R. A., & Torraco, R. J. (1995). The strategic roles of human resource development. *Human Resource Planning, 18*(4), 10–21.

Swanson, R. A., Lynham, S. A., Ruona, W. E. A., & Provo, J. M. (1998). Human resource development's role in supporting and shaping strategic organizational planning. In E. F. Holton III (Ed.), *The annual proceedings of the Academy of Human Resource Development* (pp. 589–594). Baton Rouge, LA: AHRD.

Schwartz, P. (1991). *The art of the long view: Planning for the future in an uncertain world.* New York: Doubleday.

Tichy, N. M. (1983). *Managing strategic change: Technical, political and cultural dynamics.* New York: John Wiley & Sons.

Ulrich, D. (1997). *Human resource champions: The next agenda for adding value and delivering results.* Boston: Harvard Business School Press.

———. (1998). A new mandate for human resources. *Harvard Business Review, 76*(1), 124–134.

Watkins, K. E., & Marsick, V. J. (1993). *Sculpting the learning organization: Lessons in the art and science of systematic change.* San Francisco: Jossey-Bass.

Walton, J. (1999). *Strategic human resource development.* Essex, England: Prentice Hall.

Welch, J. F., & Byrne, J. A. (2001). *Jack: Straight from the gut.* New York: Warner Business Books.

Chapter Three: Managing the Human Aspect of Organizational Change

American Productivity and Quality Center (APQC). (1997). *Organizational Change: Managing the Human Side.* Located at http://www.apqc.org/free/whitepapers/disp-WhitePaper.cfw?ProductID=670.

Bridges, W. (1993). *Managing transitions: Making the most of change.* Reading, MA: Addison-Wesley.

Collins, J. (2001). *Good to great*. New York: HarperCollins.

Connor, J., & Ulrich, D. (1996). Human resource roles: Creating value, not rhetoric. *Human Resource Planning, 19*(3), 38.

Drucker, P. (1999). *Management challenges for the 21st Century*. New York: Harper-Collins.

Gilley, J. W., Quatro, S. A., Hoekstra, E., & Maycunich, A. (2001). *The Manager as change agent*. Cambridge, MA: Perseus Publishing.

Goleman, D. (2002). *Primal leadership: Realizing the power of emotional intelligence*. Boston: Harvard Business School Publishing.

Kotter, J. P. (2000, March–April). Leading change: Why transformation efforts fail. *Harvard Business Review,* 59.

Linkow, P. (1999) What gifted strategic thinkers do. *Training and Development, 53,* 34–37.

Senge, P., Kleiner, A., Roberts, C., Ross, R., Roth, G., & Smith, B. (1999). *The dance of change*. New York: Doubleday.

White, J. B. (1996, November 26). Next big thing: Re-engineering gurus take steps to remodel their stalling vehicles. *The Wall Street Journal,* 1.

Chapter Four: Globalization and HRD

Arnold, M., & Day, R. (1998). *The next bottom line: Making sustainable development tangible*. Washington, DC: World Resources Institute.

Bates, R. (2002). Human resource development objectives. In M. Marquardt (Ed.), *UNESCO encyclopedia on life support systems*. Paris: UNESCO.

Bhagwati, J. (2002) *Free trade today*. Princeton, NJ: Princeton University Press.

Dalton, M., Ernst, C., Deal, J., & Leslie, J. (2002). *Success for the new global manager*. San Francisco: Jossey-Bass.

Drucker, P. (2001). *The essential Drucker*. New York: HarperBooks.

Friedman, T. (2000). *The Lexus and the olive tree: Understanding globalization*. New York: Anchor Books.

Hofstede, G. (2001). *Culture's consequences: Comparing values, behaviors, institutions, and organizations across nations*. San Francisco: Sage.

Kaplan, R. (2001). *The coming anarchy: Shattering the dreams of the post Cold War*. New York: Vintage Books.

Kelleher, A., & Klein, L. (1999). *Global perspectives. A handbook for understanding global issues*. Upper Saddle River, NJ: Prentice Hall.

Korten, D. (1999). *The post-corporate world*. San Francisco: Berrett-Koehler.

Marquardt, M. (1998). *The global advantage: How world class organizations improve performance through globalization*. Houston: Gulf Publishing.

Marquardt, M. (Ed.). (2001). *Developing human resources in the global economy*. San Francisco: Berrett-Koehler.

Marquardt, M., & Reynolds, A. (1994). *The global learning organization*. Houston: Gulf Publishing.

Marquardt, M., & Berger, N. (2001) *Global leaders for the 21st century*. Albany: State University of New York Press.

Marquardt, M., & Kearsley, G. (1998). *Technology-based learning*. Boca Raton, FL: St. Lucie Press.

McLean, G. (2001). *Human resource development as a factor in the inevitable move to globalization.* In O. Aliagra (Ed.), *Academy of Human Resource Development 2001 conference proceedings* (pp. 731–738). Tulsa, OK: Academy of Human Resource Development.

Micklethwait, J., & Wooldridge, A. (2000). *A future perfect: The challenge and hidden promise of globalization.* New York: Times Books.

Moore, M. (2000). Trade, poverty and the human face of globalization. Speech at London School of Economics.

Rhinesmith, S. (1993). *A manager's guide to globalization.* Houston: Gulf Publishing.

Stewart, T. (1997). *Intellectual capital.* New York: Doubleday.

Wheatley, M. (1992). *Leadership and the new science.* San Francisco: Berrett-Koehler.

World Bank report on knowledge and development. (1999). Washington, DC: Oxford University Press.

Zuboff, S. (1988). *In the age of the smart machine: The future of work and power.* New York: Basic Books.

Chapter Five: A View to Human Capital Metrics

Brown, B. L. (1997). New learning strategies for generation X. *ERIC Digest, 184,* 1–5. Columbus, OH: ERIC Clearinghouse on Adult Career and Vocational Education.

DeRogatis, J. (2001, September 25). What's up with generation Y? *Salon.Com.*

Geroy, G. D., & Swanson, R.A. (1984). Forecasting the training costs and benefits in industry. *Journal of Epsilon Pi Tau, 10*(2), 15–19.

Gilley, J. W., & Maycunich, A. (2000). *Beyond the learning organization: Creating a culture of continuous growth and development through state-of-the-art human resource practices.* Cambridge, MA: Perseus Books.

Phillips, J. J., Stone, R. D., & Phillips, P. P. (2002). *The human resources scorecard: Measuring the return on investment.* Boston. Butterworth Heinemann.

Swanson, R. A., & Geroy, G. D. (1987, May).

———. (1986). Forecasting training cost and benefits in industry. *Training and Development Journal, 135.*

———. Forecasting the economic benefits of training. In J. W. Pfeiffer & L. D. Goodsteing (Eds.), *The 1986 annual developing human resources* (pp. 213–224). San Diego: University Associates Publishers.

Wang, G. (2002). *People development strategies in the new economy,* West Chester, PA: PerformTek, LLC.

Zemke, R., Raines, C., & Filipczak, B. (2000). *Generations at work: Managing the clash of veterans, boomers, Xers, and nexters in your workplace.* New York: American Management Association.

Chapter Six: Performance Management in the New Millennium

Bates, R. A. (1997). Measuring performance improvement. *Advances in Developing Human Resources, 1,* 47–67.

Bates, R. A. (1998). Measuring performance improvement. In R. J. Torraco (Ed.), *Performance improvement theory and practice* (pp. 47–67). San Francisco: Berrett-Koehler.

Beer, M. (1997). The transformation of the human resource function: Resolving the tension between a traditional administrative and a new strategic role. In D. Ulrich,

M. R. Losey, & G. Lake (Eds.), *Tomorrow's HR management: 48 thought leaders call for change* (pp. 84–95). New York: John Wiley & Sons.

Clifton, D. O., & Nelson, P. (1992). *Soar with your strengths.* New York: Delacorte.

Collins, J. (2001). *Good to great: Why some companies make the leap . . . and others don't.* New York: HarperBusiness.

Drucker, P. (1988, September–October). Management and the world's work. *Harvard Business Review,* 65–76.

Fitz-enz, J. (1995). On the edge of oblivion. *HR Magazine, 41,* 84–90.

Fletcher, J. L. (1993). *Patterns of high performance: Discovering the ways people work best.* San Francisco: Berrett-Koehler.

Garfield, C. (1986). *Peak performers: The new heroes of American business.* New York: Avon Books.

Gilley, J. W., & Boughton, N. W. (1996). *Stop managing, start coaching! How performance coaching can enhance commitment and improve productivity.* New York: McGraw-Hill.

Gilley, J. W., & A. Maycunich. (2000a). *Beyond the learning organization: Creating a culture of continuous growth and development through state-of-the-art human resource practices.* Cambridge, MA: Perseus Publishing.

_____. (2000b). *Organizational learning, performance, and change: An introduction to strategic human resource development.* Cambridge, MA: Perseus Publishing.

Gilley, J. W., Boughton, N. W., & Maycunich, A. (1999). *The performance challenge: Developing management systems to make employees your organization's greatest asset.* Cambridge, MA: Perseus Books.

Harris, J., & Brannick, J. (1999) *Finding and keeping great employees.* New York: American Management Association.

Horowitz, A. S. (1999). *The unofficial guide to hiring and firing people.* New York: Macmillan.

Katzenbach, J. R. (2000). *Peak performance: Aligning the hearts and minds of your employees.* Boston: Harvard Business School Press.

Kochan, T. A. (1997). Rebalancing the role of human resources. In D. Ulrich, M. R. Losey, & G. Lake (Eds.), *Tomorrow's HR management: 48 thought leaders call for change* (pp. 119–129). New York: John Wiley & Sons.

Leibler, S. N., & Parkman, A. W. (1999). Human resources selection. In H. D. Stolovitch & E. J. Keeps (Eds.), *Handbook of human performance technology: Improving individual and organizational performance worldwide* (2nd ed.) (pp. 351–372). San Francisco: Jossey-Bass/Pfeiffer.

Peters, T. (1994) *The pursuit of WOW.* New York: Vintage Original.

Pfeffer, J. (1995). *Competitive advantage through people: Unleashing the power of the work force.* Boston: Harvard Business School Press.

Price Waterhouse Change Integration Team. (1996). *The paradox principles: How high-performance companies manage chaos, complexity, and contradiction to achieve superior results.* Chicago: Irwin Professional Publishing.

Rummler, G. A., & Brache, A. P. (1990). *Improving performance: How to manage the white spaces on the organization chart.* San Francisco: Jossey-Bass.

Swanson, R. A. (1999). The foundations of performance improvement. *Advances in Developing Human Resources, 1,* 1–25.

Tosti, D., & Jackson, S. F. (1999). Feedback. In H. D. Stolovitch & E. J. Keeps (Eds.), *Handbook of human performance technology: Improving individual and organizational performance worldwide* (2nd ed.) (pp. 395–410). San Francisco: Jossey-Bass/Pfeiffer.

Ulrich, D. (1997). *Human resource champions: The next agenda for adding value and delivering results.* Boston: Harvard Business School Press.

Ulrich, D., & Lake, D. (1990). *Organizational capability: Competing from the inside out.* New York: John Wiley & Sons.

Werbel, J. D., & Johnson, D. J. (2001) The use of person-group fit for employment selection: A missing link in person-environment fit. *Human Resource Management, 40*(3), 227–240.

Chapter Seven: Performance Coaching

Block, P. (1999). *Flawless consulting: A guide to getting your expertise used* (2nd ed.). San Diego: Pfeiffer.

Bolton, R. (1986). *People skills: How to assert yourself, listen to others, and resolve conflicts.* New York: Simon & Schuster.

Gilley, J. W. (1998). *Improving HRD practice.* Malabar, FL: Krieger.

Gilley, J. W., & Boughton, N. W. (1996). *Stop managing, start coaching: How performance coaching can enhance commitment and improve productivity.* New York: McGraw-Hill.

Gilley, J. W., Boughton, N. W., & Maycunich, A. (1999). *The performance challenge: Developing management systems to make employees your greatest asset.* Cambridge, MA: Perseus Publishing.

Hudson, F. M. (1999). *The handbook of coaching: A comprehensive resource guide for managers, executives, consultants, and human resource professionals.* San Francisco: Jossey-Bass.

Oncken & Wass (1974). Management time: Who's got the monkey. *Harvard Business Review, 52*(6).

Peterson, D. B., & Hicks, M. D. (1995). *Leader as coach: Strategies for coaching and developing others.* Minneapolis, MN: Personnel Decisions International.

Rummler, G. A., & Brache, A. P. (1995). *Improving performance: How to manage the white spaces on the organizational chart.* San Francisco: Jossey-Bass.

Stone, F. M.(1999). *Coaching, counseling, and mentoring: How to choose and use the right technique to boost employee performance.* New York: AMACOM.

Whitmore, J. (1997). *Coaching for performance: The new edition of the practical guide.* London: Nicholas Brealey.

Chapter Eight: Performance-Focused HRD

Dean, P. (Ed.). (1999). *Performance engineering at work.* Washington, DC: International Society of Performance Improvement.

Fuller, J. (1998). Making the transition to a focus on performance. In D. G. Robinson & J. C. Robinson (Eds.), *Moving from training to performance: A practical guidebook.* San Francisco: American Society of Training and Development and Berrett-Koehler.

Gilbert, T. (1996). *Human competence: Engineering worthy performance.* (Tribute ed.) Washington, DC: International Society for Performance Improvement.

Phillips, J. (1998). *Handbook of training evaluation and measurement methods.* (3d ed.). Washington, DC: Gulf Publishing and American Society of Training and Development.

Phillips, J. (Ed.). (2000). *In action: Performance consulting and analysis.* Alexandria, VA: American Society of Training and Development.

Robinson, D. G., & Robinson, J. C. (1995). *Performance consulting: Moving beyond training.* San Francisco: Berrett-Koehler.

_____. (1998). *Moving from training to performance: A practical guidebook.* San Francisco: American Society of Training and Development and Berrett-Koehler.

Robinson, J. (2000). *The evolving performance consultant job: A four-year study.* Pittsburgh: Partners in Change.

Robinson, J. C., & Robinson, D. G. (1999). Performance consultant: The job. In H. D. Stolovich & E. J. Keeps (Eds.), *Handbook of human performance technology* (pp. 713–729). San Francisco: International Society of Performance Improvement and Jossey-Bass.

Rothwell, W. (Ed.). (1996). *ASTD models for human performance improvement.* Washington, DC: American Society of Training and Development.

Rummler, G. A. (1998). The three levels of alignment. In D. G. Robinson & J. C. Robinson (Eds.), *Moving from training to performance: A practical guidebook* (pp. 13–35). San Francisco: American Society of Training and Development and Berrett-Koehler.

Rummler, G. A., & Brache, A. (1995). *Improving performance: How to manage the white spaces on the organization chart* (2nd ed.). San Francisco: Jossey-Bass.

Stolovich, H. D., & Keeps, E. J. (Eds.). (1999). *Handbook of human performance technology.* San Francisco: International Society of Performance Improvement and Jossey-Bass.

Training Industry Report 2000. (2000, October). *Training: Special industry report.* Minneapolis: Lakewood.

Van Adelsberg, D., & Trolly, E. A. (1999). *Running training like a business: Delivering unmistakable value.* San Francisco: Berrett-Koehler.

Wykes, L. M. (1998). Performance analysts at Steelcase. In D. G. Robinson & J. C. Robinson (Eds.), *Moving from training to performance: A practical guidebook* (pp. 78–93). San Francisco: American Society of Training and Development and Berrett-Koehler.

_____. (2001). Holistic training and development: Beyond classroom solutions. In Lisa A. Burke (Ed.), *High impact training solutions: Top issues troubling trainers* (pp. 117–150). Westport, CT: Quorum Books.

Wykes, L. M., March-Swets, J., & Rynbrandt, L. (2000). Performance analysis: Field operations management. In J. Phillips (Ed.), *In action: Performance consulting and analysis* (pp. 135–153). Alexandria, VA: American Society of Training and Development.

Chapter Nine: Organizational Learning

Antonacopoulou, E. (1999). Developing learning managers within learning organizations: The case of three major retail banks. In M. Easterby-Smith, J. Burgoyne, & L. Araujo (Eds.), *Organizational learning and the learning organization: Developments in theory and practice* (pp. 217–242). London: Sage.

Bierema, L. L. (2001). Philosophy of organizational learning. In J. W. Gilley, P. Dean, & L. L. Bierema (Eds.), *Philosophy and practice of organizational learning, performance, and change* (pp. 13–40). Cambridge, MA: Perseus Books.

Bierema, L. L., Bing, J. W., & Carter, T. J. (2002). The global pendulum. *Training and Development, 56*(5), 70–78.

Bigge, M. L., & Shermis, S. S. (1992). *Learning theories for teachers* (5th ed.). New York: HarperCollins.

Bradach, J. (1997). Flexibility: The new social contract between individuals and firms? Harvard Business School Working Paper.

Callahan, J. L. (2000). Emotion management and organizational functions: A case study of patterns in a not-for-profit organization. *Human Resource Development Quarterly, 11*(3), 245–268.

Callahan, J. L., & McCollum, E. E. (2002). Conceptualizations of emotion research in organizational contexts. *Advances in Developing Human Resources, 4*(1), 4–21.

Cangelosi, V. E., & Dill, W. R. (1965). Organizational learning: Observations toward a theory. *Administrative Science Quarterly, 10*(2), 175–203.

Crossan, M., & Guatto, T. (1996). Organizational learning research profile. *Journal of Organizational Change Management, 9*(1), 107–112.

Dodgson, M. (1993). Organizational learning: A review of some literatures. *Organization Studies, 14*(3), 375–394.

Easterby-Smith, M., & Araujo, L. (1999). Organizational learning: Current debates and opportunities. In M. Easterby-Smith, J. Burgoyne, & L. Araujo (Eds.), *Organizational learning and the learning organization: Developments in theory and practice* (pp. 1–21). London: Sage.

Easterby-Smith, M., Burgoyne, J., & Araujo, L. (Eds.). (1999). *Organizational learning and the learning organization: Developments in theory and practice.* London: Sage.

Finger, M., & Brand, S. B. (1999). The concept of the "learning organization" applied to the transformation of the public sector: Conceptual contributions for theory development. In M. Easterby-Smith, J. Burgoyne, & L. Araujo (Eds.), *Organizational learning and the learning organization: Developments in theory and practice* (pp. 130–156). London: Sage.

Fiol, C. M., & Lyles, M. (1985). Organizational learning. *Academy of Management Review, 10*(4), 803–813.

Frank, K. A, & Fahrbach, K. (1999). Organization culture as a complex system: Balance and information in models of influence and selection. *Organization Science, 10*(3), 253–277.

Gilley, J. W., & Maycunich, A. (2000). *Organizational learning, performance, and change: An introduction to strategic human resource development.* Cambridge, MA: Perseus Publishing.

Harvey, J. B. (1988). *The Abilene paradox and other meditations on management.* New York: Lexington Books.

Hedberg, B. (1981). How organizations learn and unlearn. In P. C. Nystrom & W. H. Starbuck (Eds.), *Handbook of organizational design* (pp. 1–26). Oxford: Oxford University Press.

Huber, G. P. (1991). Organizational learning: The contributing processes and the literatures. *Organization Science, 2*(1), 88–115.

Huysman, M. (1999). Balancing biases: A critical review of the literature on organizational learning. In M. Easterby-Smith, L. Araujo, & J. Burgoyne (Eds.), *Organizational learning and the learning organization: Developments in theory and practice* (pp. 59–74). London: Sage.

Jones, J. (1981). The organizational universe. In J. Jones & J. Pfeiffer (Eds.), *The 1981 handbook for group facilitators.* San Diego: University Associates.

Kuchinke, K. P. (2002a). Institutional and curricular characteristics of leading graduate HRD programs in the US. *Human Resource Development Quarterly, 13*(2), 127–144.

Kuchinke, K. P. (2002b). *Passions for excellence: HRD graduate programs at US universities.* Paper presented at the Academy of Human Resource Development, Honolulu, HI.

Merriam, S. B., & Caffarella, R. S. (1991). *Learning in adulthood: A comprehensive guide.* San Francisco: Jossey-Bass.

Nadler, L. J. (1985). HRD in perspective. In W. R. Tracey (Ed.), *Human resources management & development handbook.* New York: AMACOM.

Parsons, T. (1951). *The social system.* Glencoe, IL: The Free Press.

Parsons, T., & Shils, E. A. (Eds.). (1951). *Towards a general theory of action.* Cambridge, MA: Harvard University Press.

Prange, C. (1999). Organizational learning: Desperately seeking theory? In M. Easterby-Smith, J. Burgoyne, & L. Araujo (Eds.), *Organizational learning and the learning organization: Developments in theory and practice* (pp. 23–43). London: Sage.

Ruona, W. E. A. (2000). Core beliefs in human resource development: A journey for the profession and its professionals. *Advances in Human Resource Development, 7,* 1–27.

_____. (2001). The foundational impact of the Training Within Industry project on the human resource development profession. *Advances in Human Resource Development, 3*(2), 119–126.

Sashkin, M. (1996). Organizational culture assessment questionnaire (unpublished manuscript). Washington, DC: The George Washington University.

Sashkin, M., & Rosenbach, W. E. (1993). A new vision of leadership. In W. E. Rosenbach & R. L. Taylor (Eds.), *Contemporary issues in leadership.* Boulder, CO: Westview Press.

Schwandt, D. R. (1994). Organizational learning as a dynamic sociological construct: Theory and research. Paper presented at the 10th Systems Dynamics Society Meeting, Edinburgh, Scotland.

_____. (1995). Learning as an organization: A journey into chaos. In S. Chawla & J. Renesch (Eds.), *Learning organizations: Developing cultures for tomorrow's workplace* (pp. 365–379). Portland, OR: Productivity Press.

Schwandt, D. R., & Marquardt, M. J. (2000). *Organizational learning: From world-class theories to global best practices.* Boca Raton, FL: St. Lucie Press.

Senge, P. M. (1991). *The fifth discipline: The art and practice of the learning organization.* New York: Doubleday.

Shrivastava, P. A. (1983). A typology of organizational learning systems. *Journal of Management Studies, 20*(1), 7–28.

Swanson, R. A. (1995). Human resource development: Performance is the key. Paper presented at the Academy of Human Resource Development, St. Louis, MO.

Swanson, R. A., & Holton, E. F. (2001). *Foundations of human resource development.* San Francisco: Berrett-Koehler.

Tsang, E. W. K. (1997). Organizational learning and the learning organization: A dichotomy between descriptive and prescriptive research. *Human Relations, 50*(1), 73–89.

Urdang, L. (Ed.). (1988). *Random House college dictionary* (revised ed.). New York: Random House.

Watkins, K. E., & Marsick, V. J. (1993). *Sculpting the learning organization.* San Francisco: Jossey-Bass.

_____. (1995). The case for learning. Paper presented at the Academy of Human Resource Development, St. Louis, MO.

Weinberger, L. (1998). Commonly held theories of human resource development. *Human Resource Development International, 1*(1), 75–93.

Chapter Ten: Training Transfer

Adams, J. A. (1987). Historical review and appraisal of research on the learning, retention, and transfer of human motor skills. *Psychological Bulletin, 101*(1), 41–74.

Andrisani, P. J., & Nestel, G. (1976). Internal-external control as a contributor to and outcome of work experience. *Journal of Applied Psychology, 61*(2), 156–165.

Baldwin, T. T. (1992). Effects of alternative modeling strategies on outcomes of interpersonal skills training. *Journal of Applied Psychology, 77*(2), 147–154.

Baldwin, T. T., & Ford, J. K. (1988). Transfer of training: A review and directions for future research. *Personnel Psychology, 41*(1), 63–105.

Baldwin, T. T., & Magjuka, R. J. (1991). Organizational training and signals of importance: Effects of pre-training perceptions on intentions to transfer. *Human Resource Development Quarterly, 2*(1), 25–36.

_____. (1997). Organizational context and training effectiveness. In J. K. Ford, S. W. J. Kozlowski, K. Kraiger, E. Salas, & M. S. Teachout (Eds.), *Improving training effectiveness in work organizations* (pp. 99–128). Mahwah, NJ: Erlbaum.

Baldwin, T. T., Magjuka, R. J., & Loher, B. T. (1991). The perils of participation: Effects of choice of training on trainee motivation and learning. *Personnel Psychology, 44*, 51–65.

Bandura, A. (1977). *Social learning theory.* Englewood Cliffs, NJ: Prentice-Hall.

_____. (1991). Social cognitive theory of self-regulation. *Organizational Behavior and Human Decision Processes, 50*, 248–287.

Bandura, A., Jeffery, R. W., & Bachicha, D. L. (1974). Analysis of memory codes and cumulative rehearsal in observational learning. *Journal of Research in Personality, 7*, 295–305.

Barrick, M. R., & Mount, M. K. (1991). The big five personality dimensions and job performance: A meta-analysis. *Personnel Psychology, 44*, 1–26.

Barrick, M. R., & Mount, M. K. (1995). The big five personality dimensions: Implications for research and practice in human resource management. *Research in Personnel and Human Resources Management, 13*, 153–200.

Barrick, M. R., Stewart, G. L., Neubert, M. J., & Mount, M. K. (1998). Relating member ability and personality to work-team processes and team effectiveness. *Journal of Applied Psychology, 83*, 377–391.

Bar-Tal, D., & Bar-Zohar, Y. (1977). The relationship between perception of locus of control and academic achievement. *Contemporary Educational Psychology, 2*, 181–199.

Bates, R. A. (2000). Developing managerial competency as learning transfer agents. *Advances in Developing Human Resources, 8*, 49–62.

Bates, R. A., & Holton, E. F., III. (2000). The relationship between basic workplace literacy skills and learning transfer system perceptions. In P. Kuchinke (Ed.), *2000 proceedings of the Academy of Human Resource Development annual meeting* (pp. 462–469).

Bates, R. A., Holton, E. F., III, Seyler, D. A., & Carvalho, M. A. (2000). The role of interpersonal factors in the application of computer-based training in an industrial setting. *Human Resource Development International, 3*(1), 19–43.

Baudhuin, E. S. (1987). The design of industrial and flight simulators. In S. M. Cormier & J. D. Hagman (Eds.), *Transfer of learning* (pp. 217–237). San Diego: Academic Press.

Baumgartel, H., Reynolds, M. J., & Pathan, R. Z. (1984). How personality and organizational climate variables moderate the effectiveness of management development programs: A review and some recent research findings. *Management and Labour Studies, 9*(1), 1–16.

Bookter, A. (1999). *Convergent and divergent validity study of the Learning Transfer Questionnaire.* Unpublished doctoral dissertation, Louisiana State University.

Broad, M. L., & Newstrom, J. W. (1992). *Transfer of training.* Reading, MA: Addison-Wesley.

Burke, L. A., & Baldwin, T. T. (1999). Workforce training transfer: A study of the effect of relapse prevention training and transfer climate. *Human Resource Management, 38*(3), 227–242.

Burke, M. J., & Day, R. R. (1986). A cumulative study of the effectiveness of managerial training. *Journal of Applied Psychology, 71,* 232–245.

Butterfield, E. C., & Nelson, G. D. (1989). Theory and practice of teaching for transfer. *Educational Technology Research and Development, 37,* 5–38.

Campbell, D. T. (1988). Training design for performance improvement. In J. P. Campbell & R. J. Campbell (Eds.), *Productivity in organizations* (pp. 417–430). San Francisco: Jossey-Bass.

Clark, C. S., Dobbins, G. H., & Ladd, R. T. (1993). Exploratory field study of training motivation: Influence of involvement, credibility, and transfer climate. *Group and Organization Management, 18*(3), 292–307.

Cohen, D. J. (1990). What motivates trainees. *Training and Development Journal, 11,* 91–93.

Colquitt, J. A., LePine, J. A., & Noe, R. A. (2000). Toward an integrative theory of training motivation: A meta-analytic path analysis of 20 years of research. *Journal of Applied Psychology, 85*(5), 678–707.

Colquitt, J. A., & Simmering, M. J. (1998). Conscientiousness, goal orientation, and motivation to learn during the learning process: A longitudinal study. *Journal of Applied Psychology, 83*(4), 654–665.

Cormier, S. M. (1987). The structural processes underlying transfer of training. In S. M. Cormier & J. D. Hagman (Eds.), *Transfer of learning* (pp. 152–181). San Diego: Academic Press.

Cormier, S. M., & Hagman, J. D. (1987). *Transfer of learning: Contemporary research applications.* San Diego: Academic Press.

Day, D. V., & Silverman, S. B. (1989). Personality and job performance: Evidence of incremental validity. *Personnel Psychology, 42,* 25–36.

Decker, P. J. (1982). The enhancement of behavior modeling training of supervisory skills by the inclusion of retention processes. *Personnel Psychology, 35,* 323–332.

_____. (1983). The effects of rehearsal group size and video feedback in behavior modeling training. *Personnel Psychology, 36,* 763–773.

Dempster, F. N. (1988). The spacing effect: A case study in the failure to apply the results of psychological research. *American Psychologist, 43,* 627–634.

Driskell, J. E., Willis, R. P., & Cooper, C. (1992). Effect of overlearning on retention. *Journal of Applied Psychology, 77,* 615–692.

Dweck, C. S. (1986). Motivational processes affecting learning. *American Psychologist, 41*, 1040–1048.

Dweck, C. S., & Leggett, E. L. (1988). A social-cognitive approach to motivation and personality. *Psychological Review, 95*, 256–273.

Eden, D., & Kinnar, J. (1991). Modeling Galatea: Boosting self-efficacy to increase volunteering. *Journal of Applied Psychology, 76*(6), 770–780.

Eden, D., & Ravid, G. (1982). Pygmalion versus self-expectancy: Effects of instructor and self-expectancy on trainee performance. *Organizational Behavior and Human Performance, 30*, 351–364.

Eden, D., & Shani, A. (1982). Pygmalion goes to boot camp: Expectancy, leadership, and trainee performance. *Journal of Applied Psychology, 67*, 194–199.

Fisher, S. L., & Ford, J. K. (1998). Differential effects of learner efforts and goal orientation on two learning outcomes. *Personnel Psychology, 51*, 397–420.

Ford, J. K. (1994). Defining transfer: The meaning is in the answers. *Adult Learning, 5*(4), 23–30.

Ford, J. K., & Kraiger, K. (1995). The application of cognitive constructs and principles to the instructional systems model of training: Implications for needs assessment, design, and transfer. In C. L. Cooper & I. T. Robertson (Eds.), *International review of industrial and organizational psychology* (vol. 10, pp. 1–48). New York: John Wiley & Sons.

Ford, J. K., & Weissbein, D. A. (1997). Transfer of training: An updated review and analysis. *Performance Improvement Quarterly, 10*(2), 22–41.

Ford, J. K., Quinones, M., Sego, D., & Dorra, J. (1992). Factors affecting the opportunity to use trained skills on the job. *Personnel Psychology, 45*, 511–527.

Frayne, C. A., & Latham, G. P. (1987). Application of social learning theory to employee self-management of attendance. *Journal of Applied Psychology, 72*(3), 387–392.

Gagne, R. M. (1985). *The conditions of learning and theory of instruction* (4th ed.). New York: Holt, Rinehart & Winston.

Garavaglia, P. L. (1993). How to ensure transfer of training. *Training and Development,* 63–68.

Gist, M. E. (1987). Self-efficacy: Implications for organizational behavior and human resource management. *Academy of Management Review, 12*(3), 472–485.

Gist, M. E., Bavetta, A. G., & Stevens, C. K. (1990). Transfer training method: Its influence on skill generalization, skill repetition, and performance level. *Personnel Psychology, 43*, 501–523.

Gist, M. E., Schwoerer, C., & Rosen, G. (1989). Effects of alternative training methods on self-efficacy and performance in computer software training. *Journal of Applied Psychology, 74*(6), 884–891.

Goldstein, I. L. (1986). *Training in organizations: Program development, needs assessment, and evaluation.* Pacific Grove, CA: Brooks/Cole.

Haccoun, R. R. (1996). *Enhancing transfer of training: The results of four field experiments.* Paper presented at the International Congress of Psychology, Montreal, Canada.

Hicks, W. D., & Klimoski, R. J. (1987). Entry into training programs and its effects on training outcomes: A field experiment. *Academy of Management Journal, 30*(3), 542–552.

Hill, T., Smith, N. D., & Mann, M. F. (1987). Role of efficacy expectations in predicting the decision to use advanced technologies: The case of computers. *Academy of Management Journal, 39*(3), 542–552.

Hollenbeck, J. R., & Brief, A. P. (1987). The effects of individual differences and goal origin on goal setting and performance. *Organizational Behavior and Human Decision Processes, 40,* 392–414.

Holton, E. F., III. (2000). What's really wrong: Diagnosis for learning transfer system change. *Advances in Developing Human Resources, 8,* 7–22.

Holton, E. F., III, Bates, R. A., & Ruona, W. E. A. (2000). Development of a generalized Learning Transfer Systems Inventory. *Human Resource Development Quarterly, 11*(4), 333–360.

Holton, E. F., III, Bates, R. A., Seyler, K. L., & Carvalho, M. A. (1997). Toward construct validation of a transfer climate instrument. *Human Resource Development Quarterly, 8*(2), 95–113.

Hunter, J. E. (1986). Cognitive ability, cognitive aptitudes, job knowledge, and job performance. *Journal of Vocational Behavior, 29,* 340–362.

Hunter, J. E., & Hunter, R. F. (1984). Validity and utility of alternative predictors of job performance. *Psychological Bulletin, 96,* 72–98.

Ilgen, D. R., Fisher, C. D., & Taylor, M. S. (1979). Consequences of individual feedback on behavior in organizations. *Journal of Applied Psychology, 64*(4), 349–371.

Joyce, W. F., Slocum, J. W., & Von Glinow, M. A. (1982). Person-situation interaction: Competing models of fit. *Journal of Occupational Behavior,* 265–280.

Kaemar, K. M., Wright, P. M., & McMahan, G. C. (1997). The effects of individual differences on technological training. *Journal of Management Issues, 9,* 104–120.

Katz, D., & Kahn, R. L. (1978). *The social psychology of organizations* (2nd ed.). New York: John Wiley & Sons.

Knowles, M. (1990). *The adult learner: A neglected species* (4th ed.). Houston: Gulf Publishing.

Kozlowski, S. W. J., Brown, K., Weissbein, D., Cannon-Bowers, J., & Salas, E. (2000). A multilevel approach to training effectiveness: Enhancing horizontal and vertical transfer. In K. Klein & S. W. J. Kozlowski (Eds.), *Multilevel theory, research, and methods in organizations.* San Francisco: Jossey-Bass.

Kren, L. (1992). The moderating effects of locus of control on performance incentives and participation. *Human Relations, 45*(9), 991–1012.

Laker, D. R. (1990). Dual dimensionality of training transfer. *Human Resource Development Quarterly, 1*(3), 209–223.

Larson, E. W., & Fukami, C. V. (1984). Relationships between worker behavior and commitment to the organization and union. *Academy of Management Proceedings, 34,* 222–226.

Latham, G. P., & Frayne, C. A. (1989). Self-management training for increasing job attendance: A follow-up and replication. *Journal of Applied Psychology, 64*(3), 239–246.

Latham, G. P., & Saari, L. M. (1979). Application of social learning theory to training supervisors through behavioral modeling. *Journal of Applied Psychology, 64*(3), 239–246.

Locke, E. A., & Latham, G. P. (1990). *A theory of goal setting and task performance.* Englewood Cliffs, NJ: Prentice-Hall.

Locke, E. A., Latham, G. P., & Erez, M. (1988). The determinants of goal commitment. *Academy of Management Review, 13,* 23–39.

Locke, E. A., Shaw, K. N., Saari, L. M., & Latham, G. P. (1981). Goal setting and task performance: 1969–1980. *Psychological Bulletin, 90*(1), 125–152.

Lodahl, T. M., & Kejner, M. (1965). The definition and measurement of job involvement. *Journal of Applied Psychology, 49,* 24–33.

Luthans, F., & Davis, T. (1979). Behavioral self-management: The missing link in managerial effectiveness. *Organizational Dynamics, 8*(1), 42–60.

Luthans, F., & Kreitner, R. (1985). *Organizational behavior modification and beyond.* Glenview, IL: Scott Foresman.

Martocchio, J. J. (1992). Microcomputer usage as an opportunity: The influence of context in employee training. *Personnel Psychology, 45,* 529–551.

Martocchio, J. J., & Webster, J. (1992). Effects of feedback and cognitive playfulness on performance in microcomputer software training. *Personnel Psychology, 45,* 553–578.

Marx, R. D. (1982). Relapse prevention for managerial training: A model for maintenance of behavior change. *Academy of Management Review, 7*(3), 433–441.

Marx, R. D., & Karren, J. R. (1988). The effects of relapse prevention training and interactive feedback on positive transfer of training. Paper presented at the annual Academy of Management meeting, Anaheim, CA.

Marx, R. D., & Karren, J. R. (1990). The effects of relapse prevention and post-training follow-up on time management behavior. Paper presented at the annual Academy of Management meeting, San Francisco, CA.

Mathieu, J. E., & Zajac, D. M. (1990). A review and meta-analysis of the antecedents, correlated, and consequences of organizational commitment. *Psychological Bulletin, 108*(2), 171–194.

Mathieu, J. E., Martineau, J. W., & Tannenbaum, S. I. (1993). Individual and situational influences on the development of self-efficacy: Implications for training effectiveness. *Personnel Psychology, 46,* 125–147.

Mathieu, J. E., Tannenbaum, S. I., & Salas, E. (1992). Influences of individual and situational characteristics on measures of training effectiveness. *Academy of Management Journal, 35,* 828–847.

McFarlane, R., Shore, L., & Wayne, S. J. (1993). Commitment and employee behavior: Comparison of affective commitment and continuance commitment with perceived organizational support. *Journal of Applied Psychology, 78*(5), 774–780.

Merriam, S. B. & Caffarella, R. S. (1991). *Learning in adulthood.* San Francisco: Jossey-Bass.

Naquin, S. S., & Holton, E. F., III. (2002). The effects of personality, affectivity, and work commitment on motivation to improve work through learning. *Human Resource Development Quarterly, 13(3).*

Noe, R. A. (1986). Trainees' attributes and attitudes: Neglected influences on training effectiveness. *Academy of Management Review, 11*(4), 736–749.

Noe, R. A., & Ford, J. K. (1992). Emerging issues and new directions for training research. *Research in Personnel and Human Resource Management, 10,* 345–384.

Noe, R. A., & Schmitt, N. (1986). The influence of trainee attitudes on training effectiveness: Test of a model. *Personnel Psychology, 39,* 497–523.

O'Connor, E. J., Peters, L. H., Pooyan, A., Weekley, J., Frank, B., & Erenkrantz, B. (1984). Situational constraint effects on performance, affective reactions, and turnover: A field replication and extension. *Journal of Applied Psychology, 69*(4), 663–672.

Peters, L. H., O'Connor, E. J., Eulberg, J. R., & Watson, T. W. (1988). An examination of situational constraints in Air Force work settings. *Human Performance, 1*(2), 133–144.

Phillips, J. M., & Gully, S. M. (1997). Role of goal orientation, ability, need for achievement, and locus of control in the self-efficacy and goal-setting process. *Journal of Applied Psychology, 82*, 792–802.

Quinones, M. A. (1995). Pretraining context effects: Training assignment as feedback. *Journal of Applied Psychology, 80*, 226–238.

Reber, R. A., & Wallin, J. A. (1984). The effects of training, goal setting, and knowledge of results on safe behavior: A component analysis. *Academy of Management Journal, 27*(3), 544–560.

Ree, M. J., Carretta, T. R., & Teachout, M. S. (1995). The role of ability and prior job knowledge in complex training performance. *Journal of Applied Psychology, 80*, 721–730.

Robertson, I. T., Bell, R., & Sadri, G. (1991). Behavior modeling training: Variations in retention processes. *Personnel Review, 20*(4), 25–28.

Rouiller, J. Z., & Goldstein, I. L. (1993). The relationship between organizational transfer climate and positive transfer of training. *Human Resource Development Quarterly, 4*(4), 377–390.

Russell, J. S., Wexley, K. N., & Hunter, J. E. (1984). Questioning the effectiveness of behavior modeling training in an industrial setting. *Personnel Psychology, 37*, 465–481.

Saari, L. M., Johnson, T. R., McLaughlin, S. D., & Zimmerle, D. M. (1988). A survey of management training and education practices in U.S. companies. *Personnel Psychology, 41*, 731–743.

Salas, E., & Cannon-Bowers, J. A. (2001). The science of training: A decade of progress. *Annual Review of Psychology*, 471–496.

Salomon, G., & Perkins, D. N. (1989). Rocky roads to transfer: Rethinking mechanisms of a neglected phenomenon. *Educational Psychologist, 24*, 113–142.

Schmidt, R. A., & Young, D. E. (1987). Transfer of movement control in motor skill learning. In S. M. Cormier & J. D. Hagman (Eds.), *Transfer of Learning* (pp. 48–79). San Diego: Academic Press.

Schneider, B. (1983). Interactional psychology and organizational behavior. In L. L. Cummings & B. M. Staw (Eds.), *Research in organizational behavior* (Vol. 5, pp. 1–31). Greenwich, CT: JAI.

Seyler, D. L., Holton, E. F., III, Bates, R. A., Burnett, M. F., & Carvalho, M. A. (1998). Factors affecting the motivation to use training. *International Journal of Training and Development, 2*, 2–16.

Simon, C. W., & Roscoe, S. N. (1984). Application of a multi factor approach to transfer of training research. *Human Factors, 26*, 591–612.

Smith-Jentsch, K. A., Jentsch, F. G., Payne, S. C., & Salas, E. (1996). Can pretraining experiences explain individual differences in learning? *Journal of Applied Psychology, 81*(1), 110–116.

Spector, P. E. (1982). Behavior in organizations as a function of employees' locus of control. *Psychological Bulletin, 91*(3), 482–497.

Steers, R. M. (1977). Antecedents and outcomes of organizational commitment. *Administrative Science Quarterly, 22*, 46–56.

Storms, P. L., & Spector, P. E. (1987). Relationships of organizational frustration with reported behavioral reactions: The moderating effects of locus of control. *Journal of Occupational Psychology, 60*, 227–234.

Tannenbaum, S. I., & Yukl, G. (1992). Training and development in work organizations. *Annual Review of Psychology, 43,* 399–441.

Tannenbaum, S. I., Mathieu, J. E., Salas, E., & Cannon-Bowers, J. A. (1992). Meeting trainees' expectations: The influence of training fulfillment on the development of commitment, self-efficacy, and motivation. *Journal of Applied Psychology, 76,* 759–769.

Thorndike, E. L., & Woodsworth, R. S. (1901). (I) The influence of improvement in one mental function upon the efficiency of other functions. (II) The estimation of magnitudes. (III) Functions involving attention, observation, and discrimination. *Psychological Review, 8,* 247–261, 384–395, 553–564.

Tracy, J. B., Tannenbaum, S. I., & Kavanaugh, M. J. (1995). Applying trained skills on the job: The importance of the work environment. *Journal of Applied Psychology, 80,* 239–252.

Tziner, A., Haccoun, R. R., & Kadish, A. (1991). Personal and situational characteristics influencing the effectiveness of transfer of training improvement strategies. *Journal of Applied Psychology, 80,* 239–252.

Vroom, V. H. (1964). *Work and motivation.* New York: John Wiley & Sons.

Warr, P., & Bunce, D. (1995). Trainee characteristics and the outcomes of open learning. *Personnel Psychology, 48,* 347–375.

Wexley, K. N., & Latham, G. P. (1991). *Developing and training human resources in organizations* (2nd ed.). New York: HarperCollins.

Wexley, K. N., & Nemeroff, W. (1975). Effectiveness of positive reinforcement and goal setting as methods of management development. *Journal of Applied Psychology, 64,* 239–246.

Wood, R. E., Mento, A. J., & Locke, E. A. (1987). Task complexity as a moderator of goal effects: A meta-analysis. *Journal of Applied Psychology, 72,* 416–425.

Yelon, S. L., & Ford, J. K. (1999). Pursuing a multidimensional view of transfer. *Performance Improvement Quarterly, 12*(3), 58–78.

Chapter Eleven: A Framework for Reframing HRD Evaluation, Practice, and Research

Alliger, G. M., Tannenbaum, S. I., Bennett, W., Traver, H., & Shotland, A. (1997). A meta-analysis of the relations among training criteria. *Personnel Psychology, 50,* 341–359.

Argyris, C., & Schon, D. A. (1996). *Organizational learning II.* Reading, MA: Addison-Wesley.

Baldwin, T. T. (1992). Effects of alternative modeling strategies on outcomes of interpersonal skills training. *Journal of Applied Psychology, 77*: 147–154.

Bassi, L. J., & Lewis, E. M. (1999). *Linking training and performance: Benchmarking results.* Alexandria, VA: American Society for Training and Development.

Bassi, L. J., Benson, G., & Cheney, S. (1996). The top ten trends. *Training & Development, 50*(11), 28–42.

Beer, M., & Spector, B. (1985). Corporate transformations in human resource management. In R. E. Walton & P. B. Lawrence (Eds.), *HRM trends and challenges.* Cambridge, MA: Harvard Business School Press.

Brinkerhoff, R. O. (1989). *Achieving results from training.* San Francisco: Jossey-Bass.

Brinkerhoff, R. O., & Montesino, M. U. (1995). Partnerships for training transfer: Lessons from a corporate study. *Human Resource Development Quarterly*, 6(3), 263–274.

Brown, S. M., & Seidner, C. J. (1998). *Evaluating corporate training: Models and issues.* Boston: Kluwer.

Capra, F. (1996). *The web of life: A new scientific understanding of living systems.* New York: Anchor Books.

Chelimsky, E. (2001). What evaluation could do to support foundations: A framework with nine component parts. *American Journal of Evaluation, 22*(1), 13–28.

Desimone, R. L., Werner, J. M., & Harris, D. M. (2002). *Human resource development* (3rd ed.) Fort Worth, TX: Harcourt College Publishers.

Dionne, P. (1996). The evaluation of training activities: A complex issue involving different stakes. *Human Resource Development Quarterly, 7,* 279–286.

Drucker, P. F. (1997). The future that has already happened. *Harvard Business Review, 75*(5), 19–23.

Finger, M., & Brand, S. B. (1999). The concept of the "learning organization" applied to the transformation of the public sector. In M. Easterby-Smith, J. Burgoyne, & L. Araujo (Eds.), *Organizational learning and the learning organization.* London: Sage.

Fiol, C. M., & Lyles, M. A. (1985). Organizational learning. *Academy of Management Review, 10,* 803–813.

Galvin, T. (2001). 2001 industry report. *Training, 38*(10), 40–75.

Guba, E. G., & Lincoln, Y. S. (1981). *Effective evaluation.* San Francisco: Jossey-Bass.

Hamblin, A. C. (1974). *Evaluation and control of training.* London: McGraw-Hill.

Hargrove, R. (1998). *Mastering the art of creative collaboration.* New York: McGraw-Hill.

Hatcher, T., & Brooks, A. K. (2000). Social responsibility of human resource development: How our definitions and worldviews impact our leadership role. In K. P. Kuchinke (Ed.), *Academy of Human Resource Development 2000 conference proceedings* (Vol. 1, pp. 7–13). Baton Rouge, LA: Academy of Human Resource Development.

Helgeson, S. (1993). *The web of inclusion.* New York: Currency/Doubleday.

Holton, E. F., III. (1996). The flawed four-level evaluation model. *Human Resource Development Quarterly, 7*(1), 5–21.

Judy, R. W., & D'Amico, C. (1997). *Workforce 2020: Work and workers in the 21st century.* Indianapolis, IN: Hudson Institute.

Katz, D., & Kahn, R. L. (1978). *The social psychology of organizations.* (2nd ed.). New York: John Wiley & Sons.

Kirkpatrick, D. L. (1959a, November). Techniques for evaluating programs. *Journal of the American Society of Training Directors (Training and Development Journal), 13*(11), 3–9.

_____. (1959b, December). Techniques for evaluating programs—Part 2: Learning. *Journal of the American Society of Training Directors (Training and Development Journal), 13*(12), 21–26.

_____. (1960a, January). Techniques for evaluating programs—Part 3: Behavior. *Journal of the American Society of Training Directors (Training and Development Journal), 14*(1), 13–18.

_____. (1960b, January). Techniques for evaluating programs—Part 4: Results. *Journal of the American Society of Training Directors (Training and Development Journal), 14*(1), 28–32.

_____. (1994). *Evaluating training programs: The four levels.* San Francisco: Berrett-Koehler.

Limerick, D., & Cunnington, B. (1993). *Managing the new organization.* San Francisco: Jossey-Bass.

Marquardt, M. J. *Action learning in action.* Palo Alto, CA: Davies-Black Publishing.

Michalski, G. V., & Cousins, J. B. (2001). Multiple perspectives on training evaluation: Probing stakeholder perceptions in a global network development firm. *American Journal of Evaluation, 22*(1), 37–54.

Morgan, R. B., & Casper, W. J. (2000). Examining the factor structure of participants' reactions to training: A multidimensional approach. *Human Resource Development Quarterly, 11*(3), 301–317.

Patton, M. Q. (1997). *Utilization-focused evaluation: The new century text.* Thousand Oaks, CA: Sage.

Phillips, J. J. (1995). Return on investment—beyond the four levels. In E. Holton (Ed.), *Academy of Human Resource Development conference proceedings.* Baton Rouge, LA: Academy of Human Resource Development.

Phillips, J. J. (1998). Systematic evaluation: Trends and practices. In J. J. Phillips (Series Ed.), *Implementing evaluation systems and processes in action.* Alexandria, VA: American Society for Training and Development.

Preskill, H., & Torres, R. T. (1999). *Evaluative inquiry for learning in organizations.* Thousand Oaks, CA: Sage.

Rossi, P. H., & Freeman, H. E. (1985). *Evaluation: A systematic approach.* Thousand Oaks, CA: Sage.

Rouiller, J. Z., & Goldstein, I. L. (1993). The relationship between organizational transfer climate and positive transfer of training. *Human Resource Development Quarterly, 4*(4), 377–390.

Russ-Eft, D., & Preskill, H. (2001). *Evaluation in organizations: A systematic approach for enhancing learning, performance, and change.* Boston: Perseus Books.

Scriven, M. (1967). The methodology of evaluation. In R. E. Stake (Ed.), *Curriculum evaluation* (pp. 39–83). (American Educational Research Association Monograph Series on Evaluation, No. 1). Chicago: Rand McNally.

_____. (1991). *Evaluation thesaurus* (4th ed.). Thousand Oaks, CA: Sage.

Senge, P. M. (1990). *The fifth discipline.* New York: Doubleday.

Stewart, T. A. (1997). *Intellectual capital.* New York: Doubleday/Currency.

Thompson, J. W. (1995). The renaissance of learning in business. In S. Chawla & J. Renesch (Eds.), *Learning organizations: Developing cultures for tomorrow's workplace* (pp. 85–99). Portland, OR: Productivity Press.

Torres, R. T., Preskill, H., & Piontek, M. (1996). *Evaluation strategies for communication and reporting: Enhancing learning in organizations.* Thousand Oaks, CA: Sage.

Van Buren, M. E., & Erskine, W. (2002). *State of the industry: ASTD's annual review of trends in employer-provided training in the United States.* Alexandria, VA: American Society for Training and Development.

Walton, J. (1999). *Strategic human resource development.* London: Financial Times Prentice Hall.

Watkins, K. (2000). Aims, roles, and structures for human resource development. In R. A. Swanson (Series Ed.) & W. Ruona & G. Roth (Issue Eds.), *Philosophical Founda-*

tions of Human Resource Development Practice: Vol. 2 (7) Advances in developing human resources. San Francisco: Berrett-Koehler.

Weiss, C. H. (1973). The politics of impact measurement. *Policy Studies Journal, 1*(3), 179–183.

_____. (1998). *Evaluation* (2nd ed.). Upper Saddle River, NJ: Prentice Hall.

Wheatley, M. J. (1992). *Leadership and the new science.* San Francisco: Berrett-Koehler.

Wick, C. W., & Leon, L. S. (1993). *The learning edge.* New York: McGraw-Hill.

Chapter Twelve: Socially Conscious HRD

Academy of Human Resource Development. (1999). *Standards for Ethics and Integrity.*

Acar, W., Aupperle, K. E., & Lowy. (2001). An empirical exploration of measures of social responsibility across the spectrum of organizational types. *The International Journal of Organizational Analysis, 9*(1), 26–57.

Ackoff, R. L. (1974). *Redesigning the future.* New York: John Wiley & Sons.

Barlow, M., & Robertson, H. (1996). Homogenization of education. In J. Mander & E. Goldsmith (Eds.), *The case against the global economy and for a turn toward the local.* San Francisco: Sierra Club Books.

Bierema, L. L. (1996). Development of the individual leads to more productive workplaces. *New Directions for Adult and Continuing Development, 72,* 21–28.

Brand, K. B. (1989). *Business ethics in the Netherlands.* Het, Netherlands: Spectrum.

Business Impact. (2000). Winning with integrity: A guide to social responsibility. *Business in the Community.*

Carroll, A. B. (1999). Corporate social responsibility: Evolution of a definitional construct. *Business & Society, 38,* 268–295.

Cervero, R. M., & Wilson, A. L. (2001). *Power in practice: Adult education and the struggle for knowledge and power in society.* San Francisco: Jossey-Bass.

Clarkson, M. B. E. (1995). A stakeholder framework for analyzing and evaluating corporate social performance. *Academy of Management Review, 24,* 92–117.

Dirkx, J. (1996). Human resource development as adult education: Fostering the educative workplace. *New Directions for Adult and Continuing Development, 72,* 41–47.

Fagiano, D. (1996, June). The legacy of downsizing. *Management Review,* 5.

Finger, M., & Asun, J. M. (2001). *Adult education at the crossroads: Learning our way out.* New York: Zed Books.

Forester, J. (1989). *Planning in the face of power.* Berkeley: University of California Press.

Freeman, R. E. (1984). *Strategic management: A stakeholder approach.* Boston: Pitman.

Friedman, M. (1962). *Capitalism and freedom.* Chicago: University of Chicago Press.

Garvin, D. A. (1988). *Managing quality, the strategic and competitive edge.* New York: The Free Press.

Hinkley, R. C. (2002). How corporate law inhibits social responsibility. *Humanist, 62*(2), 26–28.

Humble, J. (1975). *The responsible multinational enterprise.* London: Foundation for Business Responsibilities.

Kok, P., Van der wiele, T., McKenna, R., and Brown, A. (2001). A corporate social responsibility audit within a quality management framework. *Journal of Business Ethics, 31,* 285–297.

Korten, D. C. (1995). *When corporations rule the world.* San Francisco: Berrett-Koehler.

_____. (1996, March). *When corporations rule the world.* Paper presented at the meeting of the Academy of Human Resource Development Conference, Minneapolis, MN.

_____. (1998). *Globalizing civil society: Reclaiming our right to power.* New York: Seven Stories Press.

Kuchinke, K. P. (1999). Adult development towards what end? A philosophical analysis of the concept as reflected in the research, theory, and practice of human resource development. *Adult Education Quarterly, 49*(4), 148–162.

Miller, R. A. (1998). Lifesizing in an era of downsizing: An ethical quandary. *Journal of Business Ethics, 17,* 1693–1700.

Moir, L. (2001). What do we mean by corporate social responsibility? *Corporate Governance, 1*(2), 16–21.

Ray, M., & Rinzler, A. (Eds.). (1993). *The new paradigm in business: Emerging strategies for leadership and organizational change.* New York: G. P. Putnam's Sons.

Rosseau, D. M. (1995). *Psychological contracts in organizations: Understanding written and unwritten agreements.* Thousand Oaks, CA: Sage.

Russo, A. R. (2001). Observations on corporate citizenship. *The CPA Journal, 71*(9), 12.

Simpson, W. G., & Kohers, T. (2002). The link between corporate social and financial performance: Evidence from the banking industry. *Journal of Business Ethics, 35,* 97–109.

Stahl, M. J., & Grigsby, D. W. (1997). *Strategic management; total quality and global competition.* Oxford: Blackwell.

Stone, C. D. (1975). *Where the law ends: The social control of corporate behavior.* Prospect Heights, IL: Waveland Press.

Suchman, M. C. (1995). Managing legitimacy: Strategic and institutional approaches. *Academy of Management Review, 20,* 571–610.

Swanson, D. L. (1995). Addressing a theoretical problem by reorienting the corporate social performance model. *Academy of Management Review, 20,* 43–64.

Training. (1997, October). 1997 industry report. *Training,* 33–75.

VanBuren, J. J. (2000). The bindingness of social and psychological contracts: Toward a theory of social responsibility in downsizing. *Journal of Business Ethics, 25,* 205–219.

Wagner, C. (2001, July–August). Evaluating good corporate citizenship. *The Futurist,* 16.

Wartick, S. L., & Wood, D. J. (1998). *International business and society.* Malden: Blackwell Publishers.

Wood, D. J. (1991). Corporate social performance revisited. *Academy of Management Review, 16,* 691–718.

About the Contributors

REID BATES is Assistant Professor in the Human Resource and Leadership Development Program in the School of Human Resource Education at Louisiana State University. Dr. Bates teaches undergraduate and graduate courses in human resource development. His research interests include employee development, learning transfer, and the role of values and culture in human resource development. He has nearly twenty years of experience working with private and public sector organizations in the United States, Africa, and the Republic of the Marshall Islands to design and implement a range of projects related to human resource development.

LAURA L. BIEREMA is Assistant Professor, Department of Adult Education, University of Georgia. Dr. Bierema's primary assignment is with the graduate program in Human Resource and Organization Development. Prior to joining academia, Dr. Bierema held a variety of human resource management positions in the automotive industry. Dr. Bierema holds both bachelor's and master's degrees from Michigan State University and a doctoral degree in adult education from the University of Georgia. Her articles have appeared in both research and professional publications including *Human Resource Development Quarterly, Adult Education Quarterly, Performance Improvement Quarterly, Performance Improvement, NASSP Bulletin, Innovative Higher Education, Adult Learning,* and *Human Resource Development Review.* She is the editor of *Women's Career Development Across the Lifespan: Insights and Strategies for Women, Organizations, and Adult Educators,* and coauthor of *The Philosophy and Practice of Organization Learning, Performance and Change.* Dr. Bierema is a Cyril O. Houle Scholar in Adult and Continuing Education, and a Lilly Teaching Fellow. She is also the 1998 recipient of the Richard A. Swanson Excellence in Research Award, and the Academy of Human Resource Development's "Cutting Edge" Award for one of the ten best papers presented at the 1997 conference.

NATHANIEL W. BOUGHTON is President of The Performance Consulting Group, which specializes in aligning strategy to organizational performance. His books include *The Performance Challenge* and *Stop Managing, Start Coaching.*

JAMIE L. CALLAHAN is Assistant Professor in the Educational Human Resource Development Program at Texas A&M University. She is actively involved in the Academy of Human Resource Development and the Academy of Management. Her primary research interests focus on emotion management and its relationship to organizational learning, leadership, and culture. Dr. Callahan's work has appeared in journals such as *Human Resource Development Quarterly, Human Resource Development International, Management Learning,* and *Organization Studies;* she recently edited a special issue on emotion for the journal *Advances in Human Resources.* A former United States Air Force officer specializing in human resources and organization development consulting, she continues to actively consult with public, private, and nonprofit institutions.

MICHELLE D'ABUNDO is a Ph.D. candidate and research assistant in adult education at the University of Georgia. She holds a Master's of Science in Health from the University of North Florida and a B.A. in sociology from the American University. Her research has focused on organizational wellness and women's health and social issues in workplace, community, and college settings.

SHARON K. DRAKE is an HRD/Education Consultant with a focus on management and adult education. Dr. Drake is the former director of Training and Development at Iowa State University and a member of the graduate faculty. She holds positions of Lecturer and Adjunct Assistant Professor in Professional Studies and Industrial Education and Technology at Iowa State University. She is the codirector of LINC, a community-college leadership program in Iowa.

GARY D. GEROY is Professor of Human Capital and Economic Development at Colorado State University. Previous professional roles include management in government and private enterprise. He has worked internationally with communities and enterprise on program transfer and human capital and economic development strategies. Dr. Geroy's research embraces human dimensions of economic development, international and cross-culture training, and strategic planning of education for work and economic development. In recent European-based field research, he examined social and economic issues at individual, family, and work-group levels relating to implementation of EU economic strategy and treaties. He has published more than 200 articles and papers, and coauthored three books.

ANN MAYCUNICH GILLEY is Vice-President of Trilogy Performance Group, a performance consulting firm, and a faculty member at Colorado State University where she teaches courses in Strategy, Strategic Management, Consulting, and Communications. She spent approximately fourteen years working in a variety of managerial capacities for financial and insurance institutions. Dr. Gilley has authored and coauthored numerous articles, book chapters, and books, including *The Manager as Change Agent, The Performance Challenge, Beyond the Learning Organization, Principles of Human Resource Development* (2nd ed.), *Strategically Integrated HRD,* and *Organizational Learning, Performance, and Change,* which won the Academy of Human Resource Development (AHRD) Book of the Year award for 2000. She serves on the editorial board for the *New Perspectives in Organizational Learning, Performance, and Change* book series from Perseus Publishing.

JERRY W. GILLEY is Professor and Program Chair of Organizational Performance and Change at Colorado State University, and was previously the Director of Organizational and Executive Development at William M. Mercer, Inc. Dr. Gilley has authored or coauthored fourteen books and more than seventy-five articles, book chapters, and monographs. His books include *The Manager as Change Agent* (2001), *Philosophy and Practice of Organizational Learning, Performance, and Change* (2001), and *Organizational Learning, Performance, and Change: An Introduction to Strategic HRD* (2000), which was selected the HRD Book of the Year (2000) by the Academy of HRD. Other books include *Beyond the Learning Organization* (2000), *The Performance Challenge* (1999), *Stop Managing, Start Coaching* (1996), and *Principles of HRD* (2002 and 1989). He is the editor of the New Perspectives in Organizational Learning, Performance, and Change Book Series for Perseus Publishing, has been the director of the HRD Professors Network (ASTD) and has been a Board of Directors Member of the Academy of HRD and International Board of Standards for Training, Performance, and Improvement.

ERIK HOEKSTRA is Vice President of The Harbor Group, the parent company for a variety of firms in the construction, engineering, and factory automation circles. He holds an M.B.A. from Rotterdam School of Management in the Netherlands and is a Ph.D. candidate in Organizational Learning and Human Resource Development at Iowa State University. He is also the coauthor of *The Manager as Change Agent*.

SUSAN A. LYNHAM is Assistant Professor in the Human Resource Development (HRD) program at Texas A&M University. She holds a Ph.D. and a master's of education from the University of Minnesota, an M.A. in Organizational Leadership from the College of St. Catherine, and a B.Econ. from the University of Stellenbosch (South Africa). Her consulting includes work with South African and North American businesses, and work with British and Swiss organization change consultants. She has delivered educational and scholarly speeches and papers in the United States and South Africa, covering a wide range of human resource development (HRD) related topics. Her focus of research and practice is increasingly on leadership and leadership development for performance, and she has a growing list of publications in the areas of strategic human resource development, leadership, leadership development, and theory building in HRD. She currently lives in Bryan, Texas.

MICHAEL J. MARQUARDT is Professor of Human Resource Development and Program Director of Overseas Programs at George Washington University. He has held a number of senior management, training, and marketing positions with organizations such as Grolier, World Center for Development and Training, Association Management Inc., Overseas Education Fund, TradeTec, and the U.S. Office of Personnel Management. Dr. Marquardt has trained more than 45,000 managers in nearly 100 countries since beginning his international experience in Spain in 1969. He has consulted with many of the Fortune 500 companies as well as the governments of Indonesia, Laos, Ethiopia, Zambia, Egypt, Kuwait, Saudi Arabia, Turkey, Russia, Jamaica, Honduras, and Swaziland.

Dr. Marquardt is the author of fourteen books and more than fifty professional articles in the fields of leadership, learning, globalization, and organizational change.

Dr. Marquardt's achievements and leadership have been recognized through numerous awards, including the International Practitioner of the Year Award from the American Society for Training and Development. He presently serves as a Senior Advisor for the United Nations Staff College in the areas of policy, technology, and learning systems.

JENNIFER V. MILLER is CEO of SkillSource, a firm specializing in performance improvement strategies. She has managed the human resource and training functions for Marshall Fields, Foremost Insurance Company, and Herman Miller. Ms. Miller is a former board member of the West Michigan Chapter of the International Society for Performance Improvement and a popular keynote speaker on topics including leadership, change, networking, and sales. She can be reached at jmiller@people-equation.com.

CHRIS PETTY graduated from the United States Military Academy at West Point in 1987 and was commissioned as a Second Lieutenant in the US Army. Major Petty has spent nearly eight years as a commander or deputy commander of various units, including an air assault aviation company, a light utility helicopter company, a state area command headquarters detachment, and a Weapons of Mass Destruction (WMD) civil support team. He has operational experience leading units in a wide array of missions from the National Training Center at Ft. Irwin and state emergencies such as floods, blizzards, and manhunts, to actual WMD response missions. Major Petty is an airborne, ranger, senior aviator, and instructor pilot, and recipient of the Meritorious Service Medal. His education includes a B.S. in Economics and an M.A. in Human Resource Development. He currently works full-time in the Colorado Army National Guard, and can be reached at cpetty16@attbi.com.

HALLIE PRESKILL is Professor of Organizational Learning and Instructional Technologies at the University of New Mexico, Albuquerque. She teaches graduate-level courses in program evaluation (introductory and advanced), organizational learning, consulting, and training design, development, and delivery. Dr. Preskill is coauthor of *Evaluation in Organizations: A Systematic Approach to Enhancing Learning, Performance and Change* (Perseus, 2001), *Evaluative Inquiry for Learning in Organizations* (Sage, 1999), and *Evaluation Strategies for Communication and Reporting* (Sage, 1996), and coeditor of *Human Resource Development Review* (Sage). She has served on the Board of Directors of the American Evaluation Association and the Academy of Human Resource Development, and is the section editor of the *Teaching Evaluation* column in the *American Journal of Evaluation*. For the last twenty-one years she has provided consulting services in the areas of program evaluation, training, and organization development. She has also written numerous articles and book chapters on evaluation methods and processes, and has conducted program evaluations in schools, healthcare, nonprofit, human service, and corporate organizations.

SCOTT A. QUATRO is Assistant Professor of Management in the College of Business and Professional Studies at Grand Canyon University in Phoenix, Arizona. An experienced Human Resource Management and Organizational Development professional, Dr. Quatro has been a senior consultant with a major management-consulting firm and a human resource manager for a Fortune 500 retail company. His consulting and research work focuses on organization and job design, corporate culture, change management, and organizational spirituality. He has authored and coauthored several articles, chapters, and books, including *The Manager as Change Agent* (2001). He serves on the editorial board for the *New Perspectives in Organizational Learning, Performance, and Change* book series from Perseus Publishing. Dr. Quatro received a B.A. in English from Pepperdine University, an M.B.A. from the College of William and Mary, and holds a Ph.D. in Organizational Learning and Human Resource Development from Iowa State University. He lives in Paradise Valley, Arizona with his wife Jamie and their four children.

DARLENE RUSS-EFT is Assistant Professor at Oregon State University. She was formerly a principal with zmresearch, a research group focused on human resource development in organizations. She is the former Director of Research at Achieve-Global, Inc., and the former Director of Research Services at Zenger-Miller. She has presented at national and international conferences and has authored books and articles about human resource development, research, and evaluation. Her most recent book, *Evaluation in Organizations: A Systematic Approach to Enhancing Learning, Performance, and Change* (Perseus), was selected as one of the top business books for 2000–2001 by *Strategy + Business*. Dr. Russ-Eft is the current editor of *Human Resource Development Quarterly*, a refereed journal of AHRD and ASTD. She is Past Chair of the Research Committee of the American Society for Training & Development (ASTD) and a past member of the Board of the American Evaluation Association (AEA). She received the 1996 Times Mirror Editor of the Year Award for her research work and the Year 2000 Outstanding Scholar Award from the Academy of Human Resource Development (AHRD).

DONALD L. VENNEBERG is pursuing his Ph.D. in Human Capital Development at Colorado State University. Mr. Venneberg recently retired from a career in the federal government as a senior executive at the U.S. General Services Administration (GSA). During his career, Mr. Venneberg headed several large organizations associated with the logistics and information technology fields. His most recent position was as the Deputy Chief Information Officer for the U.S. General Services Administration agency.

L. MICHAEL WYKES has had success as a performance analyst, consultant, instructional designer, trainer, and manager. He is currently a principal performance analyst/consultant for a Fortune 500 manufacturing corporation. Mike's education includes master's degrees in Educational Leadership and Human Resource Development. He is a member of ASTD and ISPI, and has presented and facilitated workshops, both nationally and locally, to a variety of organizations. Mike's publications include book reviews and chapter contributions to books such as the ASTD best-selling publication *Moving from Training to Performance: A Practical Guidebook*, ASTD's *In Action: Performance Consulting*, and *High-Impact Training Solutions: Top Issues Troubling Trainers*.

Index